HEMINGWAY ‧ ‧ ‧
The Writer's Art of Self-Defense

by

Jackson J. Benson

UNIVERSITY OF MINNESOTA PRESS
Minneapolis

QUOTATIONS from the following works of Ernest Hemingway are fully protected by United States and International Copyright: *Across the River and Into the Trees, Death in the Afternoon, A Farewell to Arms, For Whom the Bell Tolls, Green Hills of Africa, The Old Man and the Sea, The Short Stories of Ernest Hemingway, The Sun Also Rises,* and *To Have and Have Not.* Used by permission of Charles Scribner's Sons, the Executors of the Ernest Hemingway Estate, and Jonathan Cape Ltd. The quotation from "Desert Places" on page 138 is from *Complete Poems of Robert Frost.* Copyright 1936 by Robert Frost. Copyright © 1964 by Lesley Frost Ballantine. Reprinted by permission of Holt, Rinehart and Winston, Inc., and Laurence Pollinger Ltd. Material from Sean O'Faolain, *The Vanishing Hero* (Boston: Little, Brown, 1957), on page 80, is used by permission of Little, Brown and Company.

Second printing 1969

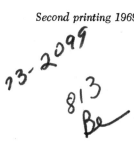

*for Sue Ellen,
Katrina Adele, and Belinda Sue*

ACKNOWLEDGMENTS

✦ ✦ ✦ OF THE MANY people who have given me help in preparing the manuscript for this book, I should like to acknowledge particularly the proofreading and criticism of the early manuscript by Yvonne Mayer, and Charles R. Metzger's criticism and advice concerning those portions of the present manuscript which were included in my dissertation. For proofreading and help with the various other manuscripts which led to the present book, I should like to thank my wife, Sue Ellen Benson.

I should also like to thank several of my colleagues at San Diego State: James Hinkle, for several ideas he has graciously allowed me to use; Kermit Vanderbilt, who gave me needed encouragement and sound advice; and Karl Keller, who carefully proofread the final manuscript and made a number of helpful suggestions. I should also like to acknowledge the financial help provided by the San Diego State College Foundation which made the final preparation of the manuscript possible. Finally, I should like to express my gratitude to the University of Minnesota Press, and particularly to the editor whose acumen and knowledge of Hemingway's work made the publication process so painless.

NOTE ON THE HEMINGWAY TEXTS

◆ ◆ ◆ SINCE I have been at some pains to note the page references for almost all the Hemingway quotations included in the following study, I was concerned in my choice of text with the availability to the reader of the editions I cited most frequently. For this reason, and because I have found nothing to impeach their accuracy, I have chosen to use the widely available Scribner Library editions of the major novels and the College Edition of *The Old Man and the Sea*. However, I have stayed with the first edition of the collected stories since the Modern Library edition used (apparently) the same plates for the text. For the lesser novels and nonfiction volumes, which I refer to much less frequently, I have also used first editions.

On the following list of editions used, all books have been published by Charles Scribner's Sons. Wherever possible, I have noted on the list any editions, by Scribner's or some other publisher, which have similar pagination ("same" on the following list should be interpreted as meaning "same textual pagination"). Occasionally in my text I abbreviate the title of one of Hemingway's works; these abbreviations precede the following titles in parentheses.

(S.A.R.) *The Sun Also Rises* (New York, 1960), The Scribner Library (the same as the "uniform edition" of 1953 and the Student's edition of 1957).

(*F.T.A.*) *A Farewell to Arms* (New York, 1962), The Scribner Library (the same as the "uniform edition" of 1953).

(*D.I.A.*) *Death in the Afternoon* (New York, 1932), First Edition (essentially the same as Halcyon House edition of 1937, the text numbered the same as the Collier edition of 1942, and essentially the same as the Scribner's reprint edition of 1953, reissued in 1961).

(*G.H.A.*) *Green Hills of Africa* (New York, 1935), First Edition (the same as the "uniform edition" of 1953 and The Scribner Library edition of 1962).

(*T.H.H.N.*) *To Have and Have Not* (New York, 1937), First Edition (the same as the Grosset & Dunlap edition of 1939, the Collier edition of 1942, and the "uniform edition" of 1953).

(*1st 49*) *The Fifth Column and the First Forty-Nine Stories* (New York, 1938), First Edition (the same as the Collier edition of 1942 and The Modern Library edition of 1942).

(*F.W.B.T.*) *For Whom the Bell Tolls* (New York, 1960), The Scribner Library (the same as the first edition of 1940, the Collier edition of 1942, Modern Standard Authors edition of 1957, and the "uniform edition" of 1962).

(*A.R.I.T.*) *Across the River and into the Trees* (New York, 1950), First Edition (the same as the "uniform edition" of 1956).

(*O.M.*) *The Old Man and the Sea* (New York, 1960), College Edition (the text itself numbered the same in the School Edition of 1961).

A Moveable Feast (New York, 1964), First Edition.

In my text I refer to the sketches of the Paris edition of *in our time* which should be distinguished from the later *In Our Time*. (The latter includes the earlier sketches as interchapters within a collection of short stories. Both sketches and stories are included in *1st 49* cited above.) Although I do not quote from *The Torrents of Spring*, I should note that the only recent reprinting of this first novel is in Charles Poore's *The Hemingway Reader* (New York, 1953).

For help in preparing the above list of editions I should like to thank the staff of the Humanities Library at the University of California at San Diego for making its special Hemingway collection available to me, and to express my gratitude to Audre Hanneman for her indispensable *Ernest Hemingway: A Comprehensive Bibliography* (Princeton, 1967).

TABLE OF CONTENTS

◆ ◆ ◆ **HEMINGWAY**

He gave emotion always and, finally, as he steadily improved his style, he was an artist.

—HEMINGWAY speaking of the bullfighter Maera

THE TERMS OF THE STRUGGLE

◆ ◆ ◆ ERNEST HEMINGWAY was a fighter. He fought to discipline himself, he fought to bring meaning to language, and he fought to purge himself and his readers of the illusions, the sentiments, and the slogans of a genteel America. Whereas another writer of the same generation, John Dos Passos, sought systematically and rationally to expose the tawdry reality behind the glitter of the cliché, Hemingway characteristically put himself on the firing line. His reaction to the world he found beyond the tasseled Victorian blinds of Oak Park, Illinois, was an emotional reaction; his books are emotional books. When Hemingway wrote, he put his whole soul in hock.

Hemingway was the American in the middle, whose conflict was never resolved, and whose pain was relieved only temporarily by the use of a portable Corona. He was the boy who was taught to be courageous and who found himself caught between family, home, and what he read on one side, and the testimony of being slugged, propositioned, and shot at, on the other. He was the young man who found, contrary to what he had been led to believe, that the wounds of war or love were neither neat nor clean, and that one could very easily get physically and emotionally splattered. Rather than the Light Brigade, war was the broken forelegs of drowning packhorses. Rather than the tantalizing sword between forest lovers, love was the dim memory of a fat prostitute, the gentle blackjacking of a punch-drunk fighter, or the loss of a wife in childbirth.

The trauma that formulated the young Hemingway's views of life and writing was not the sudden, single event of being seriously wounded in war, as Philip Young has suggested, but rather the more gradual accumulated perceptions of the sharp contrasts between Oak Park, and all it stands for, and a world at war with the individual.[1]

The revolt by each generation against the pretense and illusion of a continuing middle-class Victorianism is an old story in this century. But in the case of one rebel, Ernest Hemingway, it was a particularly violent and deeply felt rebellion, one that was to lead him eventually to cut off all ties to family and community and to drive him from his native land for most of his adult life. It was the rebellion of a boy who read, perhaps, too much, of a boy who took things a little too hard, and of a boy who grew up in an emotionally repressed environment with a mother and a father who had almost entirely exchanged traditional parental roles.

Certainly no community at the turn of the century was more genteel than the Chicago suburb of Oak Park, a community called "Saint's Rest" for the number of retired clergy it contained. And surely, despite its idiosyncrasies, no family better fit the genteel family pattern than the Hemingways. Mrs. Hemingway was culture personified, a woman who gave up a career as an opera singer to become a reluctant mother and an absentee housewife. (The household chores were shared by the hired help and Dr. Hemingway, who developed a love for cooking.) Dr. Hemingway had a good many strikes against him—he not only was responsible for depriving the world of Mrs. Hemingway's voice, he couldn't even carry a tune very well. The main feature of the house built by

---

[1] *Ernest Hemingway* (New York, 1952), Ch. III. Young in the new edition of his book notes that if he were to rewrite the book, one of the things he would change would be to "deal at much more length with the writer's parents. . . . Their Victorianism was so preposterous—so, too, their lack of understanding—that as a context for his general rebellion the family now looks bigger than the war." *Ernest Hemingway: A Reconsideration* (University Park, Penn., 1966), pp. 273–74.

the Hemingways after their initial years of marriage was a magnificent music room, where Mrs. Hemingway frequently retired to practice and write music, and where she gave lessons and presented student recitals. Mrs. Hemingway earned money so that she might help pay for the servants who did the chores that her mother had insisted were beneath her.[2]

Although Papa was strict and ruled at times with an iron hand, it was always Mama who set the patterns, and it is from Mama that the spiritual, moral, and cultural energy of the household radiated. The gentility of the Hemingways, like the gentility of the Oak Parks of America, was based largely on female-inspired standards of conduct. Typically, in the youth of Ernest Hemingway, all those aspects of masculinity associated with aggressive male behavior were either held in abeyance or transferred to other, more "appropriate" locations. All the basic aspects of living—birth, sex, and death—are discovered in the Michigan woods by Nick, the young, semiautobiographical protagonist of the Hemingway short stories ("Indian Camp," "Ten Indians," "Fathers and Sons"), and Nick's initiation to the masculine role and male activities—hunting, fishing, drinking, and the problems of courtship—take place in the woods also ("The End of Something," "The Three-Day Blow," "Fathers and Sons").

In a sense, Oak Park symbolized all those things in American culture that make it impossible, especially for the male, to express emotion and to achieve individuality. When Krebs, in "Soldier's Home," returns to his town, he returns to an atmosphere that he feels is emotionally and intellectually suffocating. The point of the story is not that war has ruined him for normal life; it is, paradoxically, that he has found so-called "normal life" abnormal and unendurable. When Ford Madox Ford spoke of the Midwestern youth that "leaped" into the freedom of postwar Paris, he refers, of course, not only to the attractions of Paris but to the severe climate of repression that existed at home.[3]

[2] Marcelline Hemingway Sanford, *At the Hemingways* (Boston, 1961), p. 54.
[3] As quoted in Maxwell Geismar, *Writers in Crisis* (New York, 1947), p. 41.

No matter how brilliant a biography is eventually produced, it will likely never get very far into the things that made all the difference in Hemingway's life. For what is important to know about a writer who felt as deeply as Hemingway did is not so much the things that happened, but his reactions to them. What little we can ever know about how Hemingway felt about his home and family is mostly contained in a small number of the Nick Adams stories: "The Doctor and the Doctor's Wife," "Now I Lay Me," "Ten Indians," and "Fathers and Sons." (It is very revealing of the emotional conflict within Hemingway at this early age to compare his reactions to his parents in these stories with the reactions of Hemingway's sister, Marcelline, who represents in her book rather well the female and conventional points of view.) Since these stories are not labeled autobiography, we cannot be assured of the accuracy of events, but we might be forgiven for assuming that the reactions of Nick are, in a general sense, representative of Hemingway's own reactions—reactions which define the terms for a life-long struggle against the smothering falsity that Hemingway felt was characteristic of his early environment. These stories also set the stage for Hemingway's continuing struggle to achieve a masculine independence in reaction to the antipathy he feels for a domineering mother and the shame he feels for a father he thought was weak. Not until toward the end of his life, as we shall see in *The Old Man and the Sea*, does Hemingway achieve any kind of resolution to the mixed emotions he had for his parents. The fact that these Nick Adams stories were written, for the most part, a good many years after the events described in them had transpired is testimony to the enduring strength of the emotions contained in them.

In these stories, Nick's mother is a woman who smothers sweetly with that peculiar self-righteous intensity which is born of Victorian moral certainty. She addresses her husband with a quiet "dear" and a smile after performing the most heinous operations on his affections and pride, castrations performed in full, humiliating view of her son and with full knowledge that the strict code of her husband's own upbringing will allow no retribution, no open breach of the peace. The short scenes of confrontation in these stories are masterpieces of understated emotional intensity.

One such scene in "Now I Lay Me" is prefaced by a note which describes how Nick's parents have moved into a new house "designed and built by my mother" and how (in beautifully passive terms) the "many things that were not to be moved were burned in the back-yard." One of the "things not to be moved" turns out to be the specimen collection of Dr. Adams, a collection which was one of the few joys of Nick's father (as well as of the real Dr. Hemingway). In rather direct symbolic terms, Nick's recollection focuses on the bursting jars, the flaming alcohol, and the "snakes burning in the fire in the back-yard" (p. 463).

The confrontation between the mother and father which follows this note begins with a recollection of how the new house was always being cleared of unnecessary things, and how, on one occasion when Nick's father was away on a hunting trip, Nick's mother made a "good," thorough cleaning of the basement and burned everything that "should not have been there" (*1st 49*, p. 464). Again, it is Dr. Adams' possessions that have been quietly disposed of in his absence, and as he gets down from the buggy to view the smoking remains of his collection of Indian artifacts, his wife informs him sweetly that she has "been cleaning out the basement, dear" (p. 464). The emotional attachment of the doctor to these things is indicated by the quiet deliberate way in which he does his best to salvage what he can from the smoking ashes, raking the knives, tools, pieces of pottery, and arrowheads from the fire, carefully laying them out on the grass, and finally wrapping them up in a piece of newspaper. The damage to Dr. Adams and to Nick is summed up in the quiet, poignant concluding comment by the doctor: "The best arrow-heads went all to pieces" (p. 464).

During this scene the doctor's shotgun is first cast aside on the lawn, then transferred to Nick, who, in attempting to carry it into the house, finds the gun in its leather case "too heavy to carry" as it bangs against his legs. In another confrontation between Dr. and Mrs. Adams, the doctor loads and unloads his shotgun in irritation and frustration, pumping the yellow shells out of the gun so that they are scattered on the bed.

In this second scene, Dr. Adams has just been humiliated in front of his son by Dick Bolton, a big man who likes to get into fights ("The Doctor and the Doctor's Wife"). Dr. Adams is forced to back down after telling Bolton to shut up or he'll knock his teeth down his throat. When the doctor turns away to walk back to the house, "they could see from his back how angry he was" (p. 199).

Instead of backing her husband up or sympathizing with him, Mrs. Adams scolds her husband and expresses the suspicion that it was Dr. Adams who caused all the trouble. Her tone effectively reduces the doctor's status to that of a little boy. Her further refusal to believe her husband after patronizingly urging him not to "try and keep anything from me" belittles him into a posture not only of a naughty little boy, but a sulky and not even a very trustworthy one. Like a queen bee or despotic invalid, Mrs. Adams sends forth her pronouncements from a darkened room with the blinds drawn against the harsh light of reality (a familiar image in contemporary American fiction), and her stubborn blindness and self-righteousness is given further impetus by Hemingway's device of making her a Christian Scientist. Mrs. Adams' denial of what we have just seen to be true effectively creates in the reader the same irritated frustration which causes Dr. Adams to leave the house to go hunting, slamming the door behind him. As the door slams, Mrs. Adams audibly catches her breath, forcing her husband to the further humiliation of having to apologize for even this minor expression of emotion.

At this point, both Dr. Adams and Nick are ready to go hunting. Although his mother wants him to come into the house to her, Nick tells his father, "I want to go with you" (p. 201). Dr. Adams takes the book that Nick has been reading and, so that Nick need not go back into the house, puts it in his pocket. The expression of emotion here, as well as in other such scenes, is continually repressed by the father to conform to Victorian norms. Nice people do not have scenes; nice people do not raise their voices, quarrel, or openly express hostility, anger, or passion of any sort. And Hemingway's father, the extremely close model for Dr. Adams, was the soul of propriety in such matters. He was, from all accounts, an expert in controlling himself, and his son was later to display this same kind of iron control in his writing processes and in the self-discipline of his prose style.

The only alternative outlets for emotion were Dr. Hemingway's (and Dr. Adams') passions for hunting and fishing, passions that expressed themselves in the opportunities that such sports gave to escape the civilized-feminine environment and to offer a release from tension in the techniques, rules, and rituals required by these sports. The importance of these rules of behavior, however, was that they were self-imposed and had the authority of male tradition.

In the Nick Adams stories, when Nick's father has "had" it, he picks up his gun and leaves. Hunting becomes for Ernest-Nick the male direction, and Nick's appeal at the end of "The Doctor and the Doctor's Wife" to *go with his father* is a plaintive cry for masculine assertion which is echoed down through the corridors of Hemingway's fiction. Hunting and fishing are continual symbols for the attempt of the Hemingway boy to identify himself with the father, attempts to return to the primitive family structure based on masculine authority and power which was destroyed by the Victorian-sentimental spiritualization of love, elevation of the woman to wisdom and authority, and reduction of the male to worse than the devil. The male was an ineffectual and misguided child who must be always watched, frequently scolded, and in general directed away from the base natural tendencies of malehood. Animals, the object of the hunt, in their natural and direct behavior become linked in the Victorian-feminine mind with all that is to be avoided and all that is base in human nature. It is rather natural, according to this line of thinking, that men should enjoy chasing them and, in part, emulating them in the chase.

Hunting and fishing become not only a means of escape and masculine identification for the Hemingway protagonist: but they also offer, in such Nick stories as "Now I Lay Me" and "Big Two-

Hearted River," opportunities for a release from anxiety—anxiety that is often produced from the continual effort of trying to be a man and trying to emulate a man's role when, as is the case for Nick, there is only a weak pattern to follow. There is pathos and tragedy in the intensity of the effort by Hemingway all his life to avoid his mother and embrace his father.

Further revelation of Hemingway's emotional background is given in the assessment of his father in "Fathers and Sons." How painful it is for Hemingway to approach directly this central problem of masculinity in regard to his father is indicated in the statement that "Nick could not write about him yet, although he would, later" (p. 588). Of course, Hemingway in writing this *is* writing about his father, but the difficulty of it is mentioned again as late as *For Whom the Bell Tolls*.[4] Revealing, too, in "Fathers and Sons," is the rather direct statement of Dr. Adams' weakness, which here is labeled "sentimentality"—the weakness which forced him to subordinate himself to the feminine world which destroyed him. "He had died," Nick says, "in a trap that he had helped only a little to set, and they had all betrayed him in their various ways before he died. All sentimental people are betrayed so many times" (pp. 587–88).

"Fathers and Sons" is a story largely told as a series of recollections by an older Nick, who is now himself a father, about his own youth. The associations in the story are significant. Nick's earliest sex experiences are tied together with hunting; as a matter of fact, in the incident described, they go on almost simultaneously. Nick has sexual intercourse with Trudy, a young Indian girl, while they wait (along with Trudy's brother Billy) for a squirrel to move so that they can shoot it with Nick's .22 single-shot rifle, a hunting piece given to youngsters so that they can learn to hit the mark. This incident is tied, in turn, to thoughts about his father's masculinity as expressed in hunting, but this memory of "soundness" is marred by a recollection of his father's unsoundness on the subject of sex. When Nick uses the word *bug-*

[4] *For Whom the Bell Tolls*, pp. 338–39.

ger to refer to a squirrel he has shot in company with his father, his father reprimands him with an explanation of the word's meaning. To Nick's questions, the father can only reply coldly, "It is a heinous crime." This "was the sum total of direct sexual knowledge bequeathed him by his father," the older Nick recalls with bitterness, except for one other discussion. Nick asks, "What is mashing?" and the father replies "It is one of the most heinous of crimes," and adds that "masturbation produced blindness, insanity, and death, while a man who went with prostitutes would contract hideous venereal diseases and that the thing to do was to keep your hands off of people" (p. 589). In the order of Nick's memory, this little lecture on sex, with its combination of Victorian primness and misinformation, serves as an ironic introduction to the scene of Nick's adolescent experimentation with Trudy.

Trudy—which, by the way, turns out to be the short form for Prudence and not Gertrude—turns up later in the Nick Adams chronology in "Ten Indians." In this story, in a humorously ironic reversal of her name, Prudence displays her promiscuity and betrays Nick's "love." "Ten Indians" reintroduces the theme of romantic love, which, like Dr. Adams' Victorianism, contrasts sharply with "natural" experience as represented by such elements as hunting and fishing, the Indians and their attitudes, and the setting in the Michigan woods. Going back chronologically to "Fathers and Sons" for a moment, we can observe Nick creating a melodramatic scene where he is protecting his sister's honor from the hypothetical sexual advances of an Indian boy. The boy has (as reported by Billy) simply suggested that he would like to do to Nick's sister what Nick has been doing with Trudy. Nick's Indian audience, Trudy and Billy, are astonished and uncomprehending in the face of Nick's righteous indignation and chivalric make-believe in response to this "threat" to his sister. Later, in "Ten Indians" the very free and simple attitude toward sex expressed by the Indian adolescents, reinforced by the animal comparisons made early in the story, makes Nick's conventionally romantic and self-conscious mourning of his lost love even more ludicrous than it is in itself: "Nick lay in the bed with his face in

11 •

the pillow. 'My heart's broken,' he thought. 'If I feel this way my heart must be broken'" (p. 434). Later still in the Nick Adams chronology, this satiric treatment of self-induced romantic sensibility is carried on into the story of Nick's break-up with a lower-class white girl, Marjorie, in "The End of Something" and "The Three-Day Blow."

In "Ten Indians," as in "Fathers and Sons," Nick's father is pictured as rigid, cold, and distant. His lack of humor and overtly expressed sympathy or love is contrasted in "Ten Indians" with the more natural, easygoing manner of the Garners, the family Nick rides home with from a Fourth of July celebration at the beginning of the story. Even Mrs. Garner enters into the banter regarding Indian sexuality and into the teasing of Nick about his Indian girl. The atmosphere at the Garners' home is relaxed, warm, and affectionate. Nick leaves Mrs. Garner lighting a fire to get supper, and he turns down an invitation to a warm meal to go home and have cold chicken, cold milk, and cold pie with his father. The conversation immediately becomes restrained and formal. His father reports having seen Prudence and suggests her infidelity. Nick, who is emotionally rocked by the news, tries to confirm his darkest suspicions, but he doesn't dare ask the question directly and is forced into stuttering and finally into a mumbled euphemism, "Were they happy?" "I guess so," answers the father without offering the least bit of help, and the only indication he gives of sympathy is the very indirect one of offering Nick another piece of pie.

In the stories that cover Nick's childhood, the emphasis is on the father's castration—castration by his wife specifically, but also by the genteel environment that robbed him of his manhood. However, the later stories of Nick's adolescence make clear that the tangled web of emotions that surround masculinity can be too easily oversimplified if we merely focus on sex or even on sexual role. There is much more at stake for Nick and Hemingway himself than simply sexual anxiety. The constant focusing and refocusing on the father in these stories, as well as later emphasis on the father figure, the "tutor" or professional, and assumption of the "Papa" role by Hemingway himself, would indicate that Hemingway's own father and the idea of "fatherhood" in general have far-reaching implications, serving as the foundation for an emotional structure that spreads out in many directions.

The father in the Nick Adams stories is first of all, of course, just that—a father. He is the possible source of love, comfort, and security. He is also, typically, a possible guide, teacher, and model. Every boy's father must take up the burden of living up to the stature of a hero, but Dr. Adams' failure in almost every respect would seem to reflect not only on his own shortcomings, but on the inflated romantic expectations of his son, a romanticism we have already seen satirized, and on his son's intolerance. This intolerance is recognized at the end of "Fathers and Sons," which is the last story to deal explicitly with the father. Even as an adult with his own child, the bitterness and shame that Nick feels for his father still rankles. At the conclusion of the story, however, Nick's young son, unconsciously, through his naive questions about his grandfather and the natural love and respect he expresses toward a man he hardly knew, acts as an intermediary and dissipates, at last, much of Nick's rancor. The young boy wants to know why they never go to pray at the tomb of his grandfather. When Nick indicates that the distance makes this impractical, the boy places Nick into a position parallel with Nick's father's by expressing the hope that Nick is never buried in a place where "I can never go to pray at your tomb when you are dead." Then the boy asks his father

"Couldn't we all be buried out at the ranch?"

"That's an idea."

"Then I could stop and pray at the tomb of my grandfather on the way to the ranch."

"You're awfully practical."

"Well, I don't feel good never to have even visited the tomb of my grandfather."

"We'll have to go," Nick said. "I can see we'll have to go." (p. 597)

The emotional catharsis of Nick's final reply is almost totally muted by the flat tone of what must be one of the most successful Hemingway short story endings.

However, the father becomes much more than just a person in Hemingway's scheme and comes to stand for much more than the disappointment of a young boy's heroic expectations. The father's life emerges as an archetypal pattern, a design for man's fate—even a prediction, personally, socially, and metaphysically. One formulation of Hemingway's mixed emotions regarding the father figure is the familiar hero-victim duality of almost all of his protagonists—a duality that in *Across the River* and *The Old Man and the Sea* Hemingway associates with his conception of the Christ figure. Another formulation of Hemingway's emotions regarding his father would certainly seem to be the contradictory expression of emotion through excess and restraint. Hemingway's interest in classical form, his tight stylistic control, his communication of emotional values in indirect and understated terms, and even his interest in "proper form" in the sporting and social sense may well have had their roots in the emotional restraint and emphasis on behavioral forms which characterized Hemingway's father. In opposition, these characteristics in Hemingway's life and work are the well-publicized excesses of rebellion: the emotional outbursts, the sexuality, the free use of language, the crude humor, the ill-concealed competitive hostility, and the interest in violence and abnormality.

The pervasiveness of such emotionally inspired conflicts in Hemingway's fiction may make us feel when reading it that we are handling a tightly sealed container that is about to explode. It is in the opposition of control and emotional potential that the real power of Hemingway's art lies—in a sense, his art is an exploitation of his own emotional turmoil translated into a precarious stalemate. When the container leaks, as it occasionally does, and the emotion is made explicit, not only is the power of the moment dissipated, but the entire artistic effect has been weakened. The irony lies in the fact that if the power were not so great, the leaks would not be so significant.

Man's courage and man's will are questions related to both

the life and the suicide death of Dr. Adams/Dr. Hemingway. They are questions made particularly crucial by the romantic idealism of a young boy, particularly if that young boy makes an effort, as Nick/Ernest does, to discover the world as it really is outside the protected environment of his middle-class home. They are also made particularly crucial if the boy goes to war and is wounded. Hemingway's view of man's powers is not so much dualistic as indecisive, a matter continuously under consideration. He can never really make up his mind whether man is defeated by his own lack of will, a matter of shame, or by those forces inside or outside man which involuntarily rob him of his will, a matter of sorrow. That man could triumph through the application of his will, regardless of the circumstances, was his hope. But it was a hope that conflicted with the circumstances of his father's death and led to a sense of shame. That man might be beaten and involuntarily deprived of his will was his great fear. It was a fear reinforced by the pride and love that he held for his father.

When Hemingway expresses concern for masculinity, he is being at various times a social critic, a moralist, and even a philosopher of sorts; but above all he is expressing a fear that courage will not work or come when needed and that he too will be victimized and destroyed. This fear must be at least partly responsible for the extensive concern with the processes of emotional victimization, the emotional effects of physical conditions, and the processes by which one human can emotionally disable another. (One critical slogan about Hemingway's work states that it is almost pathologically concerned with violence. This is not so. There is comparatively little physical violence in his fiction, just as there is little "action" in the normal fictional sense. What Hemingway, like Henry James, is concerned with is states of being. He is concerned with the threat of a violent world, or more precisely, the emotional effects of the threat of violence.)

The unstated question in Nick's mind as he sets out in his teen-age years to discover the world is, Will I find something so horrible or will something so horrible happen to me that I will

15 ◆

lose my selfhood, my self-volition, my ability to function? Later, in war, at the bullfight, and while hunting in Africa, Hemingway records the necessity not only to discover the sources and chart the ways of courage, but to certify it, to keep his hand on it—as it were, to make sure that it does not slip off unheralded in the night. This fear of victimization may be why, after creating central characters in his fiction who are victimized, he turns to create two central characters who are among the most heroic figures in modern literature, and why even in the most heroic of his characters, the nagging doubt that courage may not be enough, or may not come when summoned, is the real antagonist.

In his father Hemingway perceived man's fate. He saw in his father's life and death not just the narrow consequences of an artificial and inhibiting social environment or even, in the larger sense, the consequences of the workings of powerful natural forces beyond man's control, but the consequences of the mysterious workings of man's own nature. One layer of fear is stripped away to reveal yet another, and the ultimate threat lies in the question, How can you protect yourself from the self? In one story after another—such stories as "Big Two-Hearted River," "Now I Lay Me," "A Clean, Well-Lighted Place," "The Short Happy Life of Francis Macomber," "The Snows of Kilimanjaro"—the real question is the reliability of the self.

Hemingway was afraid, but it was no mean or petty fear. It was, rather, a profound recognition of man's condition, a recognition which can come only to those who have enough courage to begin with so that they are able to view the world with clear eyes. Hemingway's preoccupation with masculinity was not a petty, nagging doubt about a possible homosexuality, but a driven, urgent search for physical, moral, and spiritual survival.

The turmoil of love and hate, guilt and gratitude that tortures Nick in his relationship with his father (or perhaps one should say the *duty* to love and be grateful) is graphically summarized in another recollection included in "Fathers and Sons." Nick's father likes to work in the sun and perspires a great deal. "Nick loved his father but hated the smell of him and once when he had to wear a suit of his father's underwear . . . it made him feel sick" (p. 594). Nick can't stand it any more and hides the underwear under two stones in a creek, claiming that he lost it. His father whips him for lying. Later

he had sat inside the woodshed with the door open, his shotgun loaded and cocked, looking across at his father sitting on the screen porch reading the paper, and thought, "I can blow him to hell. I can kill him." Finally he felt his anger go out of him and he felt a little sick about it being the gun that his father had given him. (pp. 594–95)

In direct symbolic terms Nick reflects the frustration he feels in response to assuming manhood, with its accompanying standards of value and emotional response, within the pattern held up for him by his father. Significant too is the fact that here, as elsewhere in the stories, love is stated as a verbal formula preceding negative feelings which must always be disguised by metaphor.

In another passage in "Fathers and Sons," the emotional conflict centered on the father, which also embodies all the other conflicts we have discussed—male/female, Victorianism/realism, and repression/emotional freedom—is significantly tied to the act of writing. Writing is the way one "gets rid" of things, provided one can bring oneself to think of them. If one cannot write about such conflicts directly, it is always possible to write about the effects of them—the running, the searching, and the festering wounds:

Nick had loved him very much and for a long time. Now, knowing how it had all been, even remembering the earliest times before things had gone badly was not good remembering. If he wrote it he could get rid of it. He had gotten rid of many things by writing them. But it was still too early for that. There were still too many people. So he decided to think of something else. There was nothing to do about his father and he had thought it all through many times. (p. 589)

And, indeed, in one way or another, Ernest Hemingway was to say it all, over and over again. For the boy at the center of the early stories and the early novels never was whole, always hunted and haunted by what was left, geographically at least, behind, determined to be cut off from the confrontations between his mother and his father and the shame, and yet never erasing their memory. From these confrontations emerge the wandering and wounded Nick who is never able to find himself—a young man, who, when he escapes from home to take to the road, finds he cannot face emotional stress (as in "The Battler" or "The Killers") and in his shock finds himself running again—a young man who, in several stories, stops himself from thinking, only to think too much—a young man who returns again and again to the trout stream and the duck pond to look for the magical restoration of traditional sex roles which is never quite located except in a dim vicarious way in the reenactment of old masculine rituals.

The sentimental trap which destroys Nick's father, and against which Nick or his surrogate continuously struggles, is the trap created by a culture animated by the decadent remains of a Puritanism wherein patriarchy had given way to matriarchy, and the direct confrontation with sin had given way to anxiety over respectability. Feminine power and feminine standards were given constant reinforcement by a popular literature which largely consisted of the watered-down remains of the sentimental novel as formulated by Richardson. "Richardsonian Sentimentalism was degraded step by step to genteel sentimentalism, as the novel of seduction was deprived of its now unmentionable theme."[5] Nick's father's condition matches almost exactly the pattern set forth in the latter-day sentimental novel wherein the weakness of the woman (Mrs. Adams in her darkened room) is stronger than the male's strength, and the male is reduced in the end to the status of a dependent child.[6] To "take to the woods" is the last resource of the hurt child—to run away from home.

Hemingway was an inveterate reader as a boy, and much of what he read within the romantic-sentimental tradition was tied later in his writing to the Victorian climate of his childhood. The classics on the shelves of the Hemingway bookcases leaned heavily

[5] Leslie A. Fiedler, *Love and Death in the American Novel* (New York, 1960), p. 52.
[6] *Ibid.*, p. 65.

toward the Victorian novelists: Dickens, Thackeray, Scott, Kipling, and Stevenson. Less profound reading led young Hemingway to the more rabid romanticism of Horatio Alger, whose books he became addicted to and "took . . . seriously."[7]

The taste that controlled the offerings within the Hemingway household is indicated in the notation by Hemingway's sister that she and her mother loved Tarkington's *Seventeen*, which they felt helped very well to explain the teen-age oddities of Ernest's behavior. But whereas some current novels like *Seventeen* might find their way onto the bookshelves alongside the sets of classics, "the works of Jack London were conspicuously absent. My parents disapproved of the violence and the coarseness of his writing. They liked *John Halifax, Gentleman* much better."[8]

Hemingway's great achievement of injecting vigor and precision into American prose style must be seen not only as a reaction to the euphemisms of Oak Park respectability, but as a reaction also to his own youthful saturation in the romantic verbiage of his early reading. Repeated satiric allusions to romance (both as a set of literary conventions and as "life as we would wish it to be") in his writing make his own early seduction by the romantic and sentimental quite obvious. In "The End of Something" Nick's girl friend and her psychology are quickly classifiable as sentimentally romantic when she refers to a destroyed lumber mill as "our old ruin" and "like a castle" (*1st 49*, p. 206). Later, in the connected story, "Three-Day Blow" (a pun, by the way, on Nick's romantic and romantically considered wound), it is somewhat ironically revealed that Nick and his friend Bill are equally romantic in their reading taste. They express enthusiastic approval of *Forest Lovers*, a novel in which the hero and heroine "go to bed every night with the naked sword between them" (p. 216). In "Fathers and Sons" Nick acts out in his mind and emotions a fantasy chivalric defense of his sister's honor: "Nick had killed Eddie Gilby, then pardoned him his life, and he was a man now" (p. 592).

[7] Sanford, p. 154.
[8] *Ibid.*, p. 107.

19 ◆

Several of Hemingway's least sympathetic characters owe their difficulties to the fact that they read too much. Cohn in *The Sun Also Rises* (probably Hemingway's most foolish character) sees himself as a modern-day Sir Lancelot and finds that it is his duty to rescue his lady-in-distress, Lady Brett (who, of course, is hardly a helpless maiden), from her "betrayers." Cohn is the type of person who would guide his life by what he reads, and what he reads is exemplified by the romantic-adventure novel, *The Purple Land* (by W. H. Hudson and published in its best-known edition in 1916, suggesting that it may have been read by Hemingway as a teen-ager).

The usual Victorian attitude toward art was primarily negative. Its main concern seemed to be with the selection of decent subject matter and gilding it with a "poetic" veneer, avoiding at all costs the basic issues and difficulties of life. Thus, in Hemingway's youth historical novels dominated the best-seller lists, along with sentimental books about the very young (such as *Pollyanna* and *Penrod*) which were really written for adults (thus saving the dominantly female audience of the novel from any possible adult contaminations).

The Oak Park attitude toward art speaks with frightening clarity and familiarity in the words of Hemingway's mother in response to her reading of *The Sun Also Rises*: "Why does he want to write about such vulgar people and such messy subjects? With the whole world full of beauty, why does he have to pick out thoughts and words from the gutter? . . . I can't stand filth!"[9] The final break between Ernest and his parents was probably helped along to a large extent by the reaction of Ernest's parents to his second published book. The young author, probably filled with pride after a long hard struggle to get published, had sent a package of several copies of the hand-printed Paris edition of *in our time* to his parents. On reading the contents, his mother cried and his father, grim-faced and silent, wrapped up the books and sent them back.[10]

Like Krebs of "Soldier's Home," Ernest Hemingway had come

[9] *Ibid.*, pp. 240–41.
[10] *Ibid.*, pp. 218–19.

back home for a time after the war and then, understandably, left Oak Park behind for good. First, he went to Chicago and Toronto, and then to Europe for an extended residence. When Hemingway did return for brief stays in the United States, it was usually to those areas that in some way approximated the Michigan woods: Key West, Wyoming, and Idaho. As he left town, Hemingway the writer had three major concerns—concerns that were largely the result of the emotional environment of his childhood and the sharp contrast of that environment with the real and hostile world he had discovered as a young man: first, a deep consciousness of emotion and a concern with its honest expression; second, a concern with the individual and with felt values as a matter of individual quest; and third, a concern with male-oriented definitions of role and meaning.

One of the best metaphors for this tripartite concern is that developed by Wright Morris in *The Territory Ahead*: "He [Hemingway] is still, like his master Mark Twain, a boy at heart. While we pause to read what he has to say he is already off for the territory ahead before the world, or Aunt Sally, tries to civilize him. He can't stand it."[11] Like Mark Twain's Huck (with whom he has so often been compared), the Hemingway hero finds himself directly or indirectly living his life in firm opposition to Aunt Sally and the mores of respectability. Like Huck, the Hemingway hero is looking for a freedom that is essentially the freedom to be emotionally honest. It is not any wonder that *Huckleberry Finn* is the book that Hemingway put at the top of his list of American fiction. Huck's problem was very close to Hemingway's. Hemingway's life as a writer came to be a painful journey too, where one did one's best to discover what one "truly felt" rather than what one was supposed to feel. "Discovering what one truly feels" might serve as an excellent statement of the theme and central conflict in the bulk of Hemingway's fiction, while "communicating the felt experience truly" might serve as an excellent companion heading in dealing with his philosophy of composition.

[11] New York, 1963, p. 146. See also Young, Ch. IV.

This philosophy, or as one might term it, "Hemingway's doctrine of true emotion," is best expressed in a much-quoted passage from *Death in the Afternoon*:

In writing for a newspaper you told what happened and, with one trick and another, you communicated the emotion aided by the element of timelessness which gives a certain emotion to any account of something that has happened on that day; but the real thing, the sequence of motion and fact which made the emotion and which would be as valid in a year or in ten years or, with luck and if you stated it purely enough, always, was beyond me and I was working very hard to try to get it. (p. 2)

Emotion is central to the task that Hemingway defines for himself, and it is my contention that any discussion of the development of Hemingway's fiction must concern itself with the ways in which Hemingway attempted to express and control the emotions that gnawed at him and threatened to devour both him and his art.

In the quotation above, Hemingway distinguishes between emotion which can be manufactured by means of "one trick or another" in mass media writing and the emotion which is produced by the "real thing." Emotion as produced by the first process lacks validity (or, in modern psychological jargon, "authenticity") and the timelessness obtained by writing which has penetrated to the very core of human experience. On the basis of these criteria, the writing process for Hemingway starts with the problem of perception, "the real thing"; continues with the problem of honesty, avoiding "tricks"; and ends with the problem of the artistic mastery of one's form, stating your material "purely enough." The product for the reader is the true experience as he feels it to be true.

As made clear throughout *Death in the Afternoon*, the task that Hemingway looked upon as the most difficult and most pressing was that of perception, which he viewed not as an intellectual problem but as one of clarifying and straightening out one's own emotional responses. Although such a task has its specific origins in Hemingway's own childhood, it is also a task that faces all of us by the very nature of our time. The proliferation of sentimentality[12] (in conjunction with a continuing Victorianism) in our culture has created serious problems for the artist that are often overlooked. We are all very much aware of the fact that almost every conceivable situation has been made grist for a mill that produces a never-ending stream of drama, fiction, and even poetry wherein most of the language and relationships among people are pressed into a series of formulas; the formulas are designed to produce entertainment only as ego-directed emotional satisfaction and escape into pseudo-problems. In such a culture the serious writer faces the incredible job of trying to avoid the boobytraps of a language made almost denotatively sterile by clichés and sentimental abuse, and at the same time forging a document that presents an original vision of reality with the power to evoke an honest emotional response. The serious writer's main task must be to free himself from his own conditioning in order to see.

Although throughout much of his lifetime Hemingway saw himself in actual competition with other writers, living and dead, his success came not as a triumph over others' great accomplishments in literature, but as a triumph over that product of the abuse and the deterioration of literature, the cliché. Hemingway gave weight once more to the written word. Significantly, Hemingway saw the cliché in both language and situation as representing a

[12] Sentimentality is a gross form of emotional reassurance. It tells us that everything is really all right and that suffering, although sad, is only temporary and not really serious. It tends to measure all things in relation to man's basic needs and holds that emotion, as an end, has more value than the honesty of the means used to generate it. For most of its audience to some degree, sentimental writing involves a condition of suspended disbelief used to gain relief from reality. Characteristic of sentimental literature is its ability to bring emotional benefits without demanding emotional payment: emotions generated by sentimentality flow toward the self rather than toward others.
   Sentimentality has a long history and many conventions. It can be associated with the courtly love tradition, the medieval romance, the English sentimental novel, English Romantic poetry, with Gothic novels, plays and poems in eighteenth- and nineteenth-century melodrama, the nineteenth-century novel of sentiment, and, I am sure, other genres and types besides those that I have named. In contemporary life, sentimentality has proliferated into popular literature of all kinds and into advertising. Wherever it has appeared, however, it has relied heavily on the creation and repetition of stock response materials ("emotional triggers") which are centered around the emotional values of injustice to the self, manifested as self-pity, victimization, and martyrdom.

loss of emotional impact. Meaning in fiction was for him essentially defined as "felt experience." To compete, to go beyond what had been done posed the task of refreshing the power of narrative in order to affect the reader to the center of his bones, to make the reading experience akin to the living experience.

In the Hemingway doctrine, therefore, there is not only a similarity to Eliot's "objective correlative,"[13] with all of the implications of similarity in technique between these two writers (ellipticality, the dramatic uses of imagery, and the continual use of irony), but a close connection with Ezra Pound's conception of the poet as maker, as the re-creator of "factively" reproduced experience. It was Pound's aim, also, to penetrate in the *Cantos* behind the sham of second-hand history, to present the "thing" itself, and force the reader to live the life that the poet presents to him on the basis that it is more genuine and vital than the experience produced by watered-down abstraction, decorated "respectabilities," and popular pablum. In a general sense, both Hemingway and Pound attempt to produce a primary, rather than a secondary document. The artist does not describe, he creates.

[13] T. S. Eliot, *The Sacred Wood* (New York, 1960), p. 100. It is a mistake, although sometimes inescapable, to talk about emotion existing in an author, in the words of an author, or in a reader, as if each brand of emotion were contained in a different kind of bottle. Emotion in literature is carried through an active and intradependent relationship among author, text, and reader. Emotion, therefore, is part of the experience of reality that an author is attempting to communicate; emotion is potentially the result of certain uses of language; emotion is part of the experience created or re-created by the author's language; emotion is also the way a reader reacts to the words he reads, which, in turn, is dependent on the reader's relationship to his reality.

The ability of the artist to predict response, as of course he must, and thus to communicate emotion is partly intuitive (how I feel, therefore how you feel) and partly statistical (that is, the sum of samplings of reader responses to the author's own and to other works of literature). Thus, the author can be successfully analytical of his own emotional responses and at the same time educated beyond his own emotions to a more or less successful recognition of emotional norms. "On the basis of the present-day knowledge about emotion, it may be said that emotional habits are learned (not inborn), and further, they are learned through the mechanisms of *conditioning, identification,* and *socialization,*" says Sidney M. Jourard (*Personal Adjustment* [New York, 1963], p. 85). For a general review of the current psychological work on emotion, see the "Introductory Essay" by the editors, Warren G. Bennis *et al.*, of the essay collection, *Interpersonal Dynamics* (Homewood, Ill., 1964).

As in much of the best twentieth-century fiction, the level on which Hemingway's fiction usually operates (that is, the level on which emotion is generated) is not the narrative level, but a level more often associated with poetry—the level of experience produced above and beyond the words themselves through the powers of imagery, irony, metaphor, and associated modes of expression. Of all these devices used for the expression, direction, and control of emotion, irony is perhaps the most pervasive and important. At this point in the development of Hemingway criticism, it has become almost impossible to deal with any story or novel without dealing with the implicit pattern of irony which has transformed much of what readers and critics thought, in years past, were rather flat and journalistic reports to the level of significant literature.[14]

Thus, the importance of irony in Hemingway's work can hardly be overstated. It affects his sense of the comic, his use of allusion, and his employment of verbal wit, and it leads him into various associated modes of satire and parody. It is irony also that leads him into his worst failures of emotional control when his attack on sentimental attitudes becomes so extreme that it causes him to approximate the same emotional excesses in his own work.

There are two other broadly based modes of expression that will be examined in the following chapters. The first is the use of games as a metaphor or structure for the controlled expression of emotion. Hemingway's natural affinity for masculine sports and games leads him, in turn, to the bullfight and a study of traditional structures for the expression of emotion. This study produces the final mode of control, tragedy.

All of these structures for the communication of emotion (or for writing in such a way that a valid living experience is proffered for creation by the reader) arise naturally out of the circumstances

[14] E. M. Halliday in "Hemingway's Ambiguity: Symbolism and Irony," Robert P. Weeks, ed., *Hemingway: A Collection of Critical Essays* (Englewood Cliffs, N.J., 1962), was the first publicly to call attention to the extreme importance of irony in Hemingway's work. "The extent to which the ironic method has packed his [Hemingway's] fiction with substrata of meaning has not yet, I think, been adequately appreciated in published criticism" (p. 64).

of Hemingway's own emotional conflict. Irony becomes the direct expression of the conflict, which in all of its terms can be summarized as the conflict between appearances and sensed reality, and is a natural vehicle for the re-creation of the emotion itself, since the terms of the ironic contrast can be presented, without comment, to the reader's own sensibilities. Other devices such as literary allusion perform much the same function—for example, the obviously sentimental may be employed within a realistic context, or the continuity and depth of man's experience as represented both in and by the Bible itself may be contrasted with the shallow self-concern and sentimental illusions of fictional characters.[15]

In addition to their more specialized applications as metaphors for escape, release, or security, games and their special relation to the emotional condition of Hemingway and the modern male in general make them a natural vehicle for the Hemingway treatment of the male as traditional hero. Tragedy, which in the Hemingway scheme is really an extension of the game structure, becomes a final means for the attempt to resolve the male-female, hero-victim, and repression-expression aspects of the Hemingway conflict. The castigation and torture of the early antihero (grouping loosely the alienated and suffering protagonists, Jake Barnes, Nick Adams, and Frederic Henry) is overcome by those later protagonists who make a place for themselves and gain heroic stature in their ability to act, risking their affections for ideals that extend in significance far beyond their own immediate satisfactions.

Although the following chapters maintain a rough chronological order in relation to the publication of Hemingway's works, and although several of the chapters are devoted to full-scale reinterpretations of individual novels, I am primarily concerned with several major topics under which I examine the various techniques used by Hemingway to express and control emotion in his fiction. These topic headings are comedy and satire, game structure, irony

[15] Robert W. Lewis, Jr., in *Hemingway on Love* (Austin, 1965) explores in great detail the extensive ironic literary paralleling of the materials of *The Sun Also Rises* with the book of Ecclesiastes.

and terror, and tragedy and allegory. Since these topics are not strictly chronological in relation to Hemingway's work, I have felt free to move back and forth, to a certain extent, throughout all of the works in my selection of supportive examples.

In "Roles and the Masculine Writer," I consider *The Sun Also Rises* as a social comedy and move on to define and further explore Hemingway's humor (as well as satire and literary allusion) in "Dark Laughter." Although such modes of expression are not confined to Hemingway's early period, in their most exaggerated forms humor and satire are most commonly found in the early work, marking lapses from the discipline that Hemingway imposed upon himself more severely as he got older. In "Game: A Structure for Emotional Control," I define Hemingway's use of the game structure and explore its origins, going on, in the remainder of that chapter and in "Learning to Play the Game Well," to examine *A Farewell to Arms* in light of the game metaphor. In "Control and Loss of Control Through Irony" and "Suffering and Loss Without Tears," I examine in detail Hemingway's uses and misuses of irony (irony is also discussed to a certain extent throughout the book), as well as the mode of terror, the use of multiple protagonists, and other control devices. In these chapters my examples are drawn primarily from the major short stories, although I do touch on most of the major novels as well. The two chapters before the concluding chapter are chiefly concerned with Hemingway's conception of tragedy as expressed first in *For Whom the Bell Tolls* and then in *The Old Man and the Sea*. I also discuss allegory and certain kinds of stylized forms and prose patterns in *The Old Man and the Sea*.

ROLES
AND THE MASCULINE WRITER

♦ ♦ ♦ LIKE FIELDING, who launched his novel-writing career
in protest against the blatant falsity and emotionalism of the first
sentimental novels, Hemingway launched his own career in protest
against the emotional excesses and rampant self-pity of his own
time, first in a parody of emotionalism in *The Torrents of Spring*
and then in a satire of self-pity in *The Sun Also Rises*. Unlike Fielding's, however, Hemingway's attack was not directed at specific
works (aside from the parody of *Dark Laughter* in *Torrents of
Spring*) as much as it was at emotionalism in general and the entire
"romance" attitude toward life which had moved from literature to
pervade the entire cultural value structure. Love between man and
woman is one of the themes that recurs in every one of Hemingway's major novels except the last one and is explored very specifically in a number of his short stories; it will become obvious as
we examine these works in some detail that Hemingway was vi-
tally concerned with re-establishing what he felt were the proper
roles of man and woman in their relationship to each other. The
courtly love–feminine tradition demanded that the love object be
removed; Hemingway insists on close physical contact as a prerequisite to love. The feminine tradition insisted that love be based
on a "spiritualization" of the relationship, and on the emotions of
yearning or desire (which must remain unfulfilled); Hemingway

depicts love as being founded on sexual intercourse and requiring that satisfaction be given and gained. The feminine tradition rejects pleasure for the "joy" of suffering; Hemingway embraces pleasure as the substance of love (which, although based on physical satisfaction, is given and received on many different levels). Furthermore, the feminine tradition in literature (in conjunction with those other cultural forces we term *feminism*) tends to confuse the roles of one sex with the other, so that the man is the weaker sex and the woman the stronger, the woman the leader and the man the dependent. Hemingway views the roles of man and woman as given, deriving from biology, and the masculine tradition as more ancient and general than the feminine tradition.[1]

In connection with this Hemingway counterattack, we might note that the two favorite stereotypes of sentimental literature have been the "martyr-victim" and the "all-wise mother"—women studiously avoided in Hemingway's fiction. Instead of the "martyr-victim," Hemingway offers the girl who frankly enjoys sex and who is genuinely able to give of herself, ungrudgingly, without a sense of sacrifice. The "all-wise mother" becomes the "all-around bitch," the aggressive, unwomanly female.[2]

Hemingway's emphasis on the masculine point of view is easily

[1] The classic study of the courtly love tradition is C. S. Lewis's *Allegory of Love* (New York, 1958).

[2] Maria and Pilar, in *For Whom the Bell Tolls*, might be seen as exceptions to the above descriptions. Maria, however, although victimized in a sensational way before the novel's action begins, is not seen in the novel itself in the role of victim. On the contrary, her role is that of an emerging personality. Just as an unhealthy sex experience has "killed" her, so does a healthy sex experience give her back her life. A victim of mass rape, she loses her identity; a recipient of an individual's genuine love and concern, she regains it. She is a person of limited background, but still a recognizable identity with needs and an existence important to Jordan beyond his own life. Pilar, of course, is a wise mother figure, but almost a reversal of the expected "mother-knows-best" role in that she is crude and profane and is on occasion also wrong. Furthermore, throughout the entire novel she is guided by the wishes of the male protagonist. It is significant for the thesis I develop in this chapter regarding role-confusion to see that she becomes a man only by default when Pablo renounces his own manhood; when another man, Jordan, takes over, she becomes a woman again. Although she remains aggressive and opinionated, she never becomes "mom"; Hemingway is at great pains to reinforce the idea that she is all the while a lusty, passionate girl inside.

the most characteristic aspect of his writing, and although it is only one among many elements in his work used to channel emotion into non-sentimental directions, it serves to unify them all. Firmly within the masculine tradition are the self-reliant hero, the heroic encounter within conventionally masculine settings, the lusty and direct encounters with life rather than intellectualizations of experience, the dramatizations of the circumstances leading to emotion rather than the discussion of emotion, the continual satirization of pretense and illusion, and the emphasis on virile and direct language.[3]

This approach may embody a superficial view of life, but we may cry "Bravo!" instead of "For shame!" as we wade through a history of fiction weighted down with drawing rooms, assignations, and hand-wringings. But it may not even be true that simplicity and directness necessarily involve simplemindedness.

A good place to start looking to see whether simplicity is equivalent to simple-mindedness is Hemingway's first major novel, *The Sun Also Rises*, wherein he launches his sharpest attack against the modern confusions of male and female roles and his most sustained satire of sentimental illusion. It is true that there are many obvious things about the book. One of them is that it is the story of a male who becomes a man even though his male equipment does not work, and a female who never becomes a woman even though she is blessed with the best equipment available. But there must be some things about the novel that are not quite so obvious, for although this book has been one of the most frequently glossed American novels, I do not think that anyone has yet really touched on the spirit of the novel as Hemingway surely intended it. This is probably because so few people have given Hemingway credit for having any sense. If the reader is of the opinion that Hemingway never stood back from his experiences to make judgments about

[3] This tradition at the inception of the novel was carried on by the picaresque narratives, such as Nash's *The Unfortunate Traveller* and Fielding's *Tom Jones*; today, such picaresque novels as Heller's *Catch-22* and Bellow's *Henderson the Rain King* carry on the burden of the masculine tradition in the legitimate novel. It is interesting that Hemingway never wrote a novel in this vein.

them, but only reacted to and recorded his experiences like a stimu-
lated literate amoeba, then the reader is bound to feel, as many
do, that this novel is primarily of historical interest—a "journal of
the lost generation"—and that the hero is merely some kind of projection of the author's ego.

So it is that most critics have viewed the novel as a contrast between an in-group (those who behave well) and an outsider (he
who does not behave well) in a time of moral and spiritual chaos
that requires the individual to define his own values. Jake, the narrator (usually closely identified with Hemingway's own point of
view) is thought of, despite a lapse or two, as being admirable in
his stoic acceptance of his sexual disability and its consequent emotional frustrations. He, along with his friend, Bill Gorton, his love
interest, Lady Brett, her fiancé, Mike Campbell, and a minor character, the Count, make up the in-group that more or less adheres
to what has come to be known as the Hemingway "code." At opposite poles on the behavior scale outside the group, but connected
to it, are Romero the bullfighter, an almost perfect personification
of the "code," and Robert Cohn, an almost perfect personification of
the "code" violated.

Further, the novel has been often seen as a kind of modern
"sexual tragedy" that symbolizes a general breakdown of social
order and cultural values (T. S. Eliot's "The Waste Land" is a frequently cited parallel). This is closer to the spirit of satire in the
novel. I would differ only in declining to see the characters in the
novel as sad; they are certainly confused and they are certainly sad
about themselves, but to us they should appear to be rather foolish.

There is no doubt that they have their sexual problems. Jake, like
the Fisher King, is sexually impotent; Brett assumes a male role in
appearance, dress, and manner, and at the same time behaves like
a nymphomaniac (confusing?); Mike Campbell, the fiancé, is ignored while Brett, in love with Jake, without any attempt at secrecy
(she even shows Cohn's letters to Mike), has affairs with Robert
Cohn and then Romero. Mike, in the meantime, continually makes
lascivious remarks to and about Brett in public, but remains impo-
tently falling-down drunk. Robert Cohn lives with a woman, Fran-

ces, who dominates and maintains him like a mother. Bill Gorton is a bachelor who plays the field, and the Count is a bachelor who is "always in love." Other added touches of sexual chaos are the presence of the homosexuals with Brett upon her initial appearance in the novel, and the joke engagement of Jake early in the novel to a prostitute with bad teeth who is later taken up by the homosexuals (and is almost danced to exhaustion as one homosexual follows another in a parody of the courtship ritual).[4] Finally, there is the super-irony of the confrontation of Jake, the impotent, and Brett, the nymphomaniac.

There is, of course, a general validity in these collective views of the novel's themes and structure, but as I have indicated, there is in my mind a crucial question concerning the assumed relation of the author to his characters in this novel. It is generally thought, with few dissenters, that the author's sympathy is with the "insiders"—that is, he is actually predicating a code through them that he endorses (and continues and modifies in the fiction that follows *The Sun Also Rises*).[5] This question of an author's "distance" is one that critics have often run afoul of, particularly in dealing with contemporary authors whose physical presence so frequently complicates our thinking about their work. It has particularly complicated our thinking about Hemingway's work, making *The Sun Also Rises* and *For Whom the Bell Tolls* social or historical documents that they were never intended to be, and probably making *Across the River and into the Trees* a worse novel than it is and *The Old Man and the Sea* a better one than it is. A warning about the distance

[4] Mark Spilka, "The Death of Love in *The Sun Also Rises*," in Carlos Baker, ed., *Ernest Hemingway: Critiques of Four Major Novels* (New York, 1962), p. 20. Spilka's article is probably the best ever written on this novel, but he takes Jake and Cohn much too seriously.

[5] Robert Penn Warren, "Ernest Hemingway," in John W. Aldridge, ed., *Critiques and Essays on Modern Fiction* (New York, 1962)—the basic essay on the Hemingway "code." Warren, very properly, gives a great deal of emphasis to discipline; I cannot agree, however, with the idea of Jake and Brett as "initiates." The idea of the "code" has been expanded and altered by many others; among the most interesting and complete re-examinations of the code is that presented by Earl Rovit in his fine book, *Ernest Hemingway* (New Haven, 1963) (see his chapter, "The Code: A Revaluation"). For my interpretation of the code and why Hemingway formulated it, see pp. 73–81.

Hemingway may have from his material in *The Sun Also Rises* might be taken by noting the numerous satirical sketches he wrote as a journalist and the fact that his first published novel, *The Torrents of Spring*, was a blunt satirical parody. Charles A. Fenton makes it clear in his book *The Apprenticeship of Ernest Hemingway* that from high school sketches all the way through his later parody of Anderson in his first novel, Hemingway's most typical mode of expression was *satire*—a fact to which no one, except Fenton himself, seems to have given any importance.[6] Some hint might also be taken from the title of the novel, a sardonic blast at those who take themselves too seriously (see pp. 42–43).

If, as I think, Hemingway does not back the in-group and its behavior, the whole focus of the novel and its structure changes. Jake becomes less admirable (as the most admirable member of the group), and Cohn less a villain for his violations of the group's sensibilities. Major and minor characters alike (with the possible exception of Romero, who assumes a special status that I shall discuss later) become possible objects for satirical scrutiny rather than subjective projections of various Hemingway attitudes.

[6] New York, 1958. I count some twenty-four direct and indirect references to Hemingway's uses of satire reported by Fenton. Hemingway's first published writing in the high school paper *Trapeze* was heavily influenced by Ring Lardner. Fenton notes that Hemingway's "careful adaptations of Lardner had been an invaluable opening exercise in some of the technicalities of idiomatic prose, as well as a profitable experiment in various levels of humor, burlesque, and satire" (p. 26). Later, even in the straight reporting of his job on the Kansas City *Star*, there was an opportunity for writing which allowed for the "now characteristic, undercut Hemingway climax, full of unstated, ironic implications" (p. 44). Still later, when working for the Toronto *Daily Star* and *Star Weekly*, where he had a great deal more freedom as a feature writer, Hemingway presented himself in his material primarily as a humorist: "Humor continues to be at least an important ingredient in all of his work for the magazine and, to a lesser degree, the *Daily Star*, during the next four years. His style and attitudes matured as he ranged experimentally through all the various levels of burlesque, mimicry, satire, and irony. All of these qualities have been important in his fiction" (p. 81). Fenton notes further in regard to this period that "the war, quite clearly, was a genuinely compulsive factor in all Hemingway attitudes in 1920. His instinct toward satire had been sharpened by his experiences in Italy and by the disillusioning contradictions he observed in Chicago and Toronto" (p. 84). A break in Hemingway's employment by the Toronto paper came when he went to Chicago to write for a promotional house organ, *Co-operative Commonwealth*, and while holding down a nine-to-five job wrote on his own in the evenings, firing out "satirical

We might best look at the book as Hemingway's own version of the "Book of the Grotesque," for, like Anderson, Hemingway treats his characters with a mixture of sympathy and ironic detachment. There is no "norm" established in the novel except by implication; essentially, a rainbow pattern of abnormality is shifted back and forth to evoke a number of ironic contrasts, one with another. Most of these contrasts can be seen as anti-sentimental in nature. Rather than a sad and desperate "sexual tragedy," this is really a sexual comedy,[7] wherein all the possible deviations from the sentimental pattern of love are depicted alongside the traditional, sentimental patterns themselves (with a few ragged edges, it must be admitted). And all is presented as realistically as possible, with perhaps the same rebellious spirit that led Sinclair Lewis to depict the absurdities and ironic contrasts of a different scene.

In *The Sun Also Rises* we have the extreme irony of a man, Jake Barnes, who gains his wholeness by renouncing the sentimentality that has really crippled him more than his physical wound—the sentimental self-deception that leads him to propose that Brett and he "just live together" to help ease his anguish for her. We also have a man, Robert Cohn, who is led to make a strutting fool of himself by engaging in the classically defined ritual of sentimental courtship (even continually pomading and combing his hair) with a girl who is trying her best not to look like a girl and who has gone beyond that kind of sentiment to a more immediately rewarding state of continual self-pity and self-justified indulgence.

rewrites of world news to *Vanity Fair*" (which were not published). Two short sketches, one ironic and the other satiric, were published during this period in New Orleans by the *Double-Dealer* (p. 101). Quitting his job in Chicago and going back to work for the *Star Weekly*, Hemingway turned once again to satirical sketches and feature articles (p. 113). Finally, at the end of his book Fenton notes that "the interludes of buoyant humor and ironic wit" were basic to Hemingway's success as a correspondent and "he exercised them constantly." After his newspaper apprenticeship in the months that followed, "Hemingway was inclined to think of himself at least in part as a humorist. . . . and as late as July, 1925, when he was working on the first draft of *The Sun Also Rises*, he regarded that manuscript as in part a humorous one" (pp. 260–61).

[7] See *D.I.A.*, p. 7. Hemingway sees comedy as a parody of form, as something that pretends to be serious.

Cohn thinks Brett is "awfully straight"! Even to the layman, her initial appearance and entrance must suggest more descriptive terms from abnormal psychology than any one person really deserves: *narcissism, masochism, sadism,* and *transvestism* are enough for a good beginning. Poor Cohn is either killed or cured by his adherence to the gospel of romance; the novel does not specify which. But there is no doubt that he is a humorous character and not a villain.

There is, of course, a certain element of sadness in the comedy of Cohn's slapstick blunders (knocking everybody down and then trying to shake hands is really Chaplin-esque), his posing ("I'm just worried I'll be bored" when going to the bullfight), and the absurd contrast of his peacock preening and his doormat ability to be continually stepped on. But as with the circus clown or the Chaplin character, the sadness of Cohn's predicaments should not spoil the fun. After all, like Rollo in the Katzenjammer Kids, "He only brings it on himself."

As I say, aside from the absolutely convincing quality of the characterization, the only reason I can think of for the inability of so many readers to see the comedy here is the tendency to take Jake, Brett, and company much more seriously than the author does. The same type of character as Cohn has been comic ever since Chaucer and Elizabethan comedy—his name is really Sir Ernest Wishwash Lovefolly. Even Lady Brett, with her mixture of lust and self-pity, has a distant relative in Fielding's Lady Booby.

Why should we take any of these characters and their so-called "code" seriously? Just because they do? That should make it even more humorous. Self-pity is satirized so heavily at times it brings the novel to the edge of farce. Mike, Jake, Brett, and Cohn absolutely wallow in it. The really funny thing is that the "code" forbids the expression of emotion.[8] Jake lies down on the bed and weeps because the dark is different from the daytime. You may be sympathetic if you like, but the name of this particular black pit is still self-pity. Mike is continually drunk; wallowing in and enjoying his

[8] See Arthur L. Scott, "In Defense of Robert Cohn," *College English,* XVIII (March, 1957), 309–14, for an excellent discussion of this point.

bankruptcy and his "lost" status, he sulks and snaps at the first target of opportunity. The fact that he really does nothing at all but
drink or sleep it off makes it seem odd that so many readers have
become snappish along with him and would like Cohn "to go away,
like a good fellow." In the meantime, feeling particularly low, Brett
is informing her loved-but-cannot-have one, Jake, that to make herself feel better (to hell with Jake, or Mike, or Cohn, or anybody)
she has just *got* to have Romero. Nothing short of this new toy will
do the trick of temporarily raising her spirits. So she makes Jake
pimp for her (which is sad and acidly humorous—Jake is more like
Cohn than many readers are willing to believe) and take her back
to destroy the one symbol of clean honesty that Jake at the moment
has. (She is completely unaware of Jake's emotional involvement
with Romero, as she is completely ignorant of, or chooses to ignore,
everyone else's emotions throughout the novel.) The "code" comes
to resemble the structure of farce; it is simply a self-delusion used
to make oneself feel right while doing the wrong thing. To herd together, to scapegoat others, and to make it work on the basis of
some set of "principles" is a typical human technique for self-justification of pride and selfishness. That the code is such a sham is one
of the great ironies of Hemingway's treatment of these characters.

In the center of the "in-group" barricade is, of course, Lady
Brett, who to a great extent is not only the center of the conflict but
the central character in the novel. Hemingway treats her with a
delicate balance of sympathy and antipathy. She displays a number
of attractive qualities which are often attached to the traditional
heroine, including beauty, wit, and pluck, and Hemingway reveals
to us that her current unstable condition has been caused, at least
in part, by two devastating experiences with romantic love. (His
picture of Brett and her husband on the floor with a gun between
them is a wonderful multiple irony, joining a number of other romantic images satirically employed in the book and reminding us
also of the forest lovers in the story "The Three-Day Blow.") To
the shockable reader, Brett is the center of the novel's "sordidness";
to the young at the time of the novel's publication, she was the literary prototype of the liberated woman (having actually been pat-

terned after one); and to the stubbornly romantic, she remains, regardless of her faults, the heroine who is tragically victimized by the modern world. Indeed, one can classify readers into types rather easily by the way they react to Brett—matching quite well the power she seems to have for segregating the characters within the novel itself.

However, despite the extenuating background for her current irresponsibility and despite her undeniable attractiveness, Brett is clearly in Hemingway's mind "a case," a waste of a fine spirit and a fine body. Regardless of her admirers both in and out of the novel, she *is* a Circe, as that damned literary fellow, Cohn, observes, and is the closest thing to a villain that the novel contains. She embodies all the sins of character that Hemingway publicly abhors and sometimes unconsciously displays, which may account for a certain amount of ambiguity in the attitude he has toward her and even toward her sins. Nevertheless, she is one of the primary targets for the satiric attack of the novel's title, since having decided she is "lost," Brett feels that she cannot be held responsible for her desperate behavior and the grief that she causes. She is out of the same mold of self-pity that later produced a hundred B movie heroines who are "jinxed" and "no good for anybody, even myself."

In response to her negative challenge, Jake, Mike, and Cohn (as well as Romero) all come to measure their manhood against her as a kind of catalyst. And their manhood is not measured by *cojones* (another misleading cliché of Hemingway criticism)—at least not in the usual sense of this vague Spanish colloquialism—but on the basis of the strength to see themselves clearly and the strength to bind themselves to an ideal worth living by.

That Mike and Cohn fail in these terms has already been demonstrated. Jake, however, is a developing character whose awareness and commitment is shaky until the end of the novel, where there is some evidence that he becomes self-aware and really aware of Brett for the first time. I have already spoken of the self-pity he is drawn into in the first section of the novel where his intercourse with Brett is largely that of trading sighs for what cannot be. Book

I ends with a fairly good summary of their previous meetings: "'Oh, darling,' Brett said, 'I'm so miserable.' I had [Jake thinks] that feeling of going through something that has all happened before." (p. 64.) When one reads at the end of the passage (p. 65), "The door opened and I went up-stairs and went to bed," there is a strong suggestion that there will be a repetition of the suffering that Jake underwent the night before, when he left Brett, only to have her come up to his apartment at four-thirty the next morning, briefly parting from the Count waiting in his limousine in the street below, to see Jake and to report on her evening with the Count and his impressive ten thousand–dollar proposition. After she has left a second time, even after he has come face to face with what she really is, Jake cannot lose hold of the sentiment that had gripped him before her appearance:

This was Brett, that I had felt like crying about. Then I thought of her walking up the street and stepping into the car, as I had last seen her, and of course in a little while I felt like hell again. It is awfully easy to be hard-boiled about everything in the daytime, but at night it is another thing. (p. 34)

Jake's feeling of going through something that has happened before and his suffering because of the way Brett steps into the car are all elements of comedy—if we can keep our distance.

Day is the time for those who have at least some measure of awareness to measure their feelings and values against the reality of things, and it may be that those who build their daytime bridges to reality with the strongest awareness are those who are troubled least with "night thoughts." Thus it is that a character in Hemingway's fiction may secure his stability (as in "Big Two-Hearted River") or redeem his sense of proportion through contact with nature.

It is this function that the pastoral interlude in the first part of Book II performs for Jake. Akin to the contrast pointed out by Carlos Baker between the priest's mountains and the narcotic, self-indulgent cities of the plain in A Farewell to Arms,[9] a sharp con-

[9] Hemingway: The Writer as Artist (Princeton, 1963), Ch. V.

trast is drawn between the clarity of the day experience on the Spanish fishing trip, and the confused chaos of the nightmare of Pamplona (it is stylistically—and in terms of a weird, disconnected content—a true nightmare). In Pamplona there is a constant conflict of egos floundering about, creating friction, betrayal, and degradation. In the mountains the characters feel free. Perfect harmony exists as Bill and Jake share with each other. It is the only real demonstration of "love" in the novel, and the fact that it comes between man and man, rather than man and woman, does not necessarily imply that Hemingway prefers men or that he feels women can be dispensed with. Instead, it is a further element of criticism directed toward the confusion of roles and the corrosive power of romantic illusion which have destroyed the simplicity and directness of the relationship between man and woman.

When Harris the Englishman comes, there is simply an expansion of sharing. All three men are not only intensely aware of their own and one another's well-being, they are all committed to an internal ideal of behavior based on their awareness. This is almost directly opposed to the jealousy and strife in Pamplona, and significantly, at the center of all of the trouble is Brett, the woman who refuses to accept her role as a woman. The only valid internal ideal held by the group in Pamplona is that of the aficionado held only by Jake, which Jake betrays by being seduced through his false sentimentalization of Brett. He is overcome, despite the dirty role she wants him to play, by feelings of yearning generated in a situation that is a parody of courtly love. He cannot have her; therefore he wants her. However, the lover here is not frustrated by circumstances that have committed his loved one to someone else (she is extremely available), but rather by his own physical disability. A great love story is being enacted by a man who has lost his maleness and a woman who dresses and talks like a man and who is filled with lust. What is more romantic than being asked to pimp for the woman you have put on a pedestal? The power of self-delusion is powerfully reinforced by the number of times Brett hits Jake on the head with her velvet hammer only to have him come back for more. *Tristan and Isolde* has been transformed into a comic Punch and Judy show.[10]

It is only after returning to nature once more in San Sebastian to wash out his soul in the ocean and assess his gains and losses that Jake, to paraphrase his previous statement of philosophy, finds out truly what he has bought and what he has paid for (p. 148). His illumination comes after he receives a telegram from Brett asking him to rescue her (she has cut off her affair with Romero) at a hotel in Madrid. It is a summons to a task that is a hideous parody of knight-errantry—the fair maiden is really a whore, and the castle in which she has been imprisoned is a second-rate hotel; the dragon who keeps the gate is an unpaid bill for two weeks of adultery with a squire almost half her age. Jake sends Brett a telegram in return announcing his arrival time, and with the bitterness of true self-perspective says to himself: "That seemed to handle it. That was it. Send a girl off with one man. Introduce her to another to go off with him. Now go and bring her back. And sign the wire with love. That was it all right. I went in to lunch." (p. 239.) "And sign the wire with love" is his realization of the folly of self-indulgence, lack of awareness, and commitment to an illusion. It is only by keeping this change in perspective in mind that the full irony of the final scene can be apprehended. Athough remaining to a degree sympathetic and loyal, Jake allows his bitter detachment to become more and more obvious. The climax and point of the novel is that Jake finally becomes his own man. No one should believe that he joins together again with Brett, agrees with her that she has "acted well," and goes off on the merry-go-round once more. As far as Madrid is concerned, "all trains finish there" (pp. 239–40).[11]

The elements of Brett's repetitions in the last scene are interesting variations on the theme of egocentricity. Her only real acknowledgment of Jake as a human being with emotions comes toward the end of the scene, first with the question, "You like to eat,

[10] Robert W. Lewis, Jr., has examined the courtly love pattern which recurs throughout much of the early and middle period of Hemingway's work.

[11] For the interpretation of this line and for the insight that this moment is the turning point for Jake, I am indebted to Rovit, pp. 155–58.

don't you?" and next the request, "Don't get drunk, Jake. You don't have to." In context, both appear to be feelers toward confirming whether the old sentimental magic is still working on Jake—"Am I really tearing you up inside?" Until this point, she displays a mixture of two emotions: self-pity for the loss of Romero and self-righteousness for her sending him off. Her most frequently repeated statement is that she is not going to talk about it. She continues to beat the drum of her great love and sacrifice on the brain of her companion, however, and at the thought of how good it feels not "to be one of these bitches that ruins children" (p. 243), she is overcome by a sense of her own nobility and bursts into a fit of crying. Now at this point the reader can join in her sense of martyrdom, her faltering attempts to repress emotion, her nearly unrecognized act of courage, and her sense of the loss of the one good thing that has entered her shattered life. If the reader does, then he must regard *The Sun Also Rises* as a sophisticated soap opera. The reader had better look at the details of Brett's character and behavior as Hemingway has drawn them. Then Brett's statement at the climax of her self-dramatization, "You know it makes one feel rather good deciding not to be a bitch," becomes almost comic except that the self-deception is so disastrous for others. When she says, further, that "It's sort of what we have instead of God," Jake sums up her choice to be lost and to glory in it when he replies, "Some people have God. Quite a lot." But of course, God has never "worked well" for her; how could He? So Jake suggests another martini as a more acceptable alternative.

The contrast between Jake's state of mind and awareness and Brett's is nicely set up in the last paragraph of the novel. She is resting *comfortably* against Jake in a taxi, while at the same time Jake perceives that *outside* "it was very hot and bright, and the houses looked sharply white" (p. 247). Brett's attention is still inward, as reflected by her physical position, and her emotions still directed toward pity for herself and what she cannot have but wants: " 'Oh, Jake,' Brett said, 'we could have had such a damned good time together' (p. 247). And we know exactly what a damned good time he would have had too. The kind of good time he has already had, plus the happiness given to Mike, and Cohn, and Romero. For of course it is not just Jake's incapacity to have sex that encourages Brett to tromp all over him. To her, Jake is a valuable piece of property, a home base for self-pity that she can return to until the loss of Romero, or whoever it might be, has lost its poignancy.

However, Jake is no longer crouched into himself, as he was at the table in Pamplona, there wallowing.[12] He sees the sharp white of the houses (a clarity of vision reminiscent of the fishing trip and San Sebastian—but this time *in Brett's company*) and the raising of the traffic policeman's baton (a gesture of control and an indication that for Jake, at least, self-pity and illusion have been put in their place). " 'Yes,' I said. 'Isn't it pretty to think so?' " (p. 247) are Jake's last words, and implicit in his tone are the indications that the emotional price for such pretty pretenses is far too high in terms of value received for him to pay any longer.

In my mind, therefore, *The Sun Also Rises* is a satire of sentimentality wherein contrasts of various levels of awareness are presented, and various types of mistaken commitments are ironically and sometimes humorously used to make the point. The novel is an attempt to apply an outside perspective to the internal vice of self-indulgence and its consequent vice of irresponsibility. The author tries to make this theme clear in his contrast of prologue quotations: the "You are all a lost generation" with "One generation passeth away, and another generation cometh; but the earth abideth forever . . ." The former quotation by Miss Stein (as he notes in *A Moveable Feast*) irritated Hemingway, and he tried to balance what he considered a glib slogan with the quotation from Ecclesiastes. "All generations were lost by something," he recalls thinking at the time (pp. 29–30). (Later, Hemingway excised the Stein quotation, perhaps feeling that his readers were too often remembering the quotation and missing the satire. This would be particularly galling to him, since he had, by this time, developed a strong antipathy for Stein's ego.) There are always circumstances that can be used as excuses for self-pity, but it is important to see that the char-

[12] Pp. 222–23. Bill identifies the period at Pamplona as a "wonderful nightmare"; Jake sits and gets drunk but does not "feel any better."

acter most seriously crippled by circumstance in the novel, Jake, is the character who emerges at the end as the most clear-sighted. Jake learns the lesson that all Hemingway protagonists learn: to live with dignity requires that a man be hard on himself. If a man is lost, it is because he has lost himself by preferring illusion to reality, self-deceit to self-honesty.

The battle that Jake fights with himself is only the first of a series of battles fought by the protagonist in every Hemingway novel that was to follow. With the possible exception of *To Have and Have Not*, the internal struggle of the male is so central to each novel that every other element, whether structure, theme, character, symbol, or irony, must be considered as an extension of that struggle. If there is such a thing as a "key" to the interpretation of Hemingway's work, this is it. Any interpretation that attempts to ignore this struggle and focuses exclusively on the historical accuracy of the setting, or the depth of characterization of the supporting roles, or the pattern of symbol runs the risk of being irrelevant. For Jake, as for Frederic Henry, Robert Jordan, Colonel Cantwell, and Santiago, the essential thing is to "know oneself," and to "know oneself" is to discipline oneself toward a solid basis for honest feeling. Very little that is unrelated to that effort toward self-discipline matters.

In Hemingway's fiction the unit of ultimate moral responsibility is the individual. The beam of his attention is nearly always so sharply focused on the protagonist that other people, singly or in groups, seem to exist only in the reflection of his light, having their place only insofar as they work for or against the moral achievement of the protagonist. Seldom does Hemingway use the device of a multiple point of view, and usually, as in *To Have and Have Not*, so unsuccessfully that we must assume that the author's moral imagination can only operate as a projection of his own condition, either as a projection of the failure to achieve self-discipline ("The Snows of Kilimanjaro"), or more often as a projection of success in achieving it ("The Short Happy Life of Francis Macomber").

Groups are only very dimly perceived in Hemingway's work. They usually exist as forces, lacking definite character or shape and therefore lacking specific responsibility. And it is this inability to pinpoint, to locate the group, to bring it to a face-to-face moral accounting that often gives the group in Hemingway's work such an ominous cast. "The army," "the Party," "the government" are nebulous shadows in the mind of a Frederic Henry or a Robert Jordan, threatening chaos, confusion, misunderstanding, red tape, and waste. But worst of all, though groups present dangers that can go so far as to bring the individual to his death, they offer no redress, no target for retribution, and no real opportunity for the individual to defend himself. When, on occasion, a group does become positive and tangible, it takes its immediacy and force from the personality of the male protagonist as its leader, becoming really an extension of his character—as the guerrilla band in *For Whom the Bell Tolls* becomes a positive force under the leadership of Jordan in direct contrast to the ineffective amorphousness of the Republican Army.

Despite the needling Hemingway received throughout his career from the Marxist critics and others about his so-called narrow range of vision (his failure to be "really serious" in his fiction about politics, economics, or social caste), he apparently realized very early that the materials most organic to the human condition were extremely simple, and the more simple and basic they were, the more likely they were to hold true (*D.I.A.*, p. 2). A key part of this realization was that meaning and value must be considered in terms of the individual, not in terms of the role of generations, classes, political parties, or social movements. Hemingway was certainly anti-Marxist: almost everything in his work points to the idea that joining together with other men in mass movements tends to dissipate the energies of the individual, rather than making the efforts of the individual count for more. It may be that for a moment in his career Hemingway himself was uncharacteristically carried along by the group. Brought to life in the middle of the Great Depression, Harry Morgan, in *To Have and Have Not*, may mumble at his death, "a man alone ain't got no bloody fucking chance," but Jake Barnes, Frederic Henry, Robert Jordan, Colonel Cantwell, and Santiago give the world another message: Anything a man does, anything a man *really* does, he does from the courage of his own breast. There is no help—no cavalry over the hill, no god in the machine, no salvation in membership.

Although we must never confuse the artist with his creation, each protagonist is, nevertheless, a kind of surrogate artist, functioning as Hemingway the artist is functioning: he is attempting to know a part of reality truly and well as a result of achieving emotional honesty. The emotions of the protagonists create values, which in turn create meanings. The battle of the self (the focus of *The Sun Also Rises*) is prerequisite to the achievement of valid and meaningful relationships among people (*A Farewell to Arms*) and to valid emotional commitment to other men (*For Whom the Bell Tolls*). Hemingway's concern with overcoming a false, and achieving a true emotional structure within the individual does not mean, as some have insisted, that he ignores the importance of social responsibility. It is, rather, that he understands very well that the true and valuable society begins with the true and valuable man. Supporting roles in Hemingway's major novels lead, first, *to* the individual in support of or in opposition to his search for truth, as Miss Van Campen in *A Farewell to Arms* stands in opposition to Catherine's attempts to lead Henry to a fuller understanding of the nature of love, or as the major, Rinaldi, and the priest lead Henry to a fuller understanding of the nature of war. Second, certain emotional commitments flow *from* the individual to the characters or society that surrounds him as a function of the relative success of his search, as Henry, while becoming more firmly aware of the nature of war and love, becomes more firmly committed to Catherine.

It is understandable, therefore, that in Hemingway's works certain supporting roles tend to recur, with many of the same general characteristics on each appearance as a result of performing, roughly, the same general functions in regard to the protagonist. Among these is the "tutor" or "professional," who functions as a teacher or model to help the protagonist achieve awareness or worthy commitment. A conspicuous example is Romero, who provides an example of a thoroughly honest and courageous commitment to the thoroughly unsentimental and manly profession of bullfighting. Another of Hemingway's stock characters is the foil, who provides examples of conspicuous failure in awareness and/or commitment, such as Cohn (or Pablo in *For Whom the Bell Tolls*). Further, there are the contributing characters, who are characters from whom the protagonist does not learn—although he may do so to some extent—as much as he finds rapport with them. This latter group includes the "good women," such as Catherine Barkley in *A Farewell to Arms*, and masculine friends, such as Bill Gorton in *The Sun Also Rises* and Rinaldi in *A Farewell to Arms*.

But though the protagonist may get some help on his moral journey, and though he may form attachments that are worthy of his commitment, he is ultimately alone and ultimately responsible. Except for Nick Adams, Hemingway's protagonist is essentially without family and, except for brief periods, without home and comfort. There is no church or permanent shelter for blessing, no country or community that surrounds him with a strength beyond his own strength. Though he may strive all his life with every fiber of his being to love or to make love possible, when love is in sight, it is snatched away from him. All things that are good are temporary; all things that threaten destruction and death are permanent. Knowing these things, it is the Hemingway protagonist's lot to fight anyway. He may not win. But he will fight.

DARK LAUGHTER

♦ ♦ ♦ IN MANY RESPECTS, *Across the River and into the Trees* is more akin to Hemingway's early work than his later. Like *The Sun Also Rises*, it has many facets that have been taken far too solemnly. Again, a far greater identification has been assumed between the author and his central character than is actually the case. *Across the River* is a return to the novel of "pity and irony." The problem with both novels has been that many readers have too often embraced the pity and neglected the irony.

That Hemingway ever thought of himself as a humorist, of all things, and worked extensively with burlesque and satire certainly contradicts the public impression of the man as it was conveyed during his middle years by *Time* and *Life*. For those of us who lived during this period of time, it is almost impossible to erase the impression of Hemingway the blowhard, of Hemingway posturing with movie queens, bullfighters, and big fish, or of Hemingway the hard drinker who made pompous male pronouncements in men's magazines. It was an invidious and unfortunate legend which emphasized the worst in both the man and his work, making his writing popular for the wrong reasons and obscuring the real depth and quality of his art. He seemed shallow, ostentatious, anti-intellectual, and, most particularly, humorless.

For much of the reading public, however, here was a writer after their own hearts. An important writer, at last, who put life into simple direct terms, who never had a thought in his head but wrote, instead, from the gut. For others, he became a source of constant irritation, especially as his popularity grew and he became one of the best known of American writers: he was good enough, despite his *Esquire*-like heroines, his guns, blood, and tough talk, so that he could not be entirely erased from the rolls of the literarily respectable. But many critics were certain that he would eventually fade or fall—his view of life was too superficial, and he would eventually be destroyed in the flap of his own flamboyance.

There is no record that Hemingway ever went out of his way to ingratiate himself with anyone. And it is entirely possible that more critics, reviewers, and scholars may have despised Hemingway than any other modern writer of similar stature. For some of these, every book published by Hemingway became a test case. They had predicted his decline for so long that they could view the course of his career in no other way. *To Have and Have Not* confirmed the downward trend in quality that some had already detected in *Green Hills of Africa*, but the appearance of several outstanding short stories during this period put the verdict in some doubt. When *For Whom the Bell Tolls* appeared, some critics claimed a Hemingway victory, and some, defeat. At last, after the war years and the spectacle of Hemingway irregulars "liberating" Paris, the crack-up that some had so anxiously awaited came. Almost everyone seemed to agree that *Across the River and into the Trees* was a disaster of magnificent proportions.

Critics seemed to lick their chops as they pounced on Hemingway's unabashedly personal and maudlin picture of his own middle-age in the character of Colonel Cantwell. Here was the inevitable end of the alienated boy protagonist—the aging, sick, and misunderstood professional soldier. Almost every element of the novel seemed to fulfill every hope for a Hemingway failure. Every mannerism, trick, and eccentricity that had so irritated some readers had now been magnified by Hemingway himself to the point where they seemed to parody themselves. Even those readers who wished Hemingway well found some difficulty in bearing up under the weight of Cantwell's version of the adolescent gang and its secret passwords, his tear-jerking bravado and nostalgia, and his love affair conducted (again, with adolescent overtones) by proxy with a painting. Few readers had the fortitude to watch the Hemingway protagonist mooning and yearning for the physically unattainable courtly-love princess who was half his age, without squirming in their seats.

For anyone who had observed Hemingway's constant application of self-discipline, his constant fight (despite significant lapses) against sentimentality, and his usually careful guardianship of his own more tender emotions, *Across the River and into the Trees* was certainly puzzling, to say the least. The man who had learned at such great cost to channel his emotional conflicts into severely structured dramatic patterns expressed by a style famous for its restraint had apparently lost his control and simply poured out his griefs and anxieties directly onto the page. The result was not literature, but was very close to a true confession.

However, the book does hold an important lesson for the student of Hemingway's work. Over and over again, Hemingway notes that good writing must begin with direct experience. He continually mocks those who, like Willa Cather writing a war scene from watching the movie *Birth of a Nation*, attempt to express what they themselves have not experienced. The writing process was for him the translation of the personal to the objective, which means that almost everything Hemingway wrote treads the narrow line between a personal journal and fiction. In attempting to find "that formula" wherein his emotion can be recorded so that it is our emotion also, he is forced to walk the tightrope of artistic success while his own emotions threaten to spill him into the yawning pit of emotionalism which threatens below. What we as readers tend to forget is Hemingway's own sharp awareness of his predicament. Too often we fail to recognize the extent to which Hemingway could objectify, as well as express, the very emotions which pressed him to his typewriter. The very great style that Hemingway laboriously hammered out for himself was only one response among many to the artistic problem as he perceived it, and of course "style" is itself a general term that encompasses a number of techniques and devices.

The one Hemingway response that has been most neglected above all others is his use of humor. When a writer is famous in our age of mass media, the man keeps getting in the way of the artist, and our image of Hemingway was of a man who, with little self-directed humor, took himself too seriously. It is little wonder that when lay reader and critic found in Colonel Cantwell an absurdly serious pomposity, they made the equation and took both the novel and its writer in full seriousness.

In a review of the Caedmon recording, *Ernest Hemingway Reading*, Kermit Vanderbilt suggests that Cantwell is meant to be the very joke that he is. If it is possible to push the Hemingway man-legend out of our sights for a moment, Colonel Richard Cantwell can emerge as the comic figure closest to Hemingway's heart: the poor soul who, with romantic self-delusions (here again, as knight and lover), takes himself far too seriously. As Vanderbilt points out, "his surname is an obvious pun on what he talks well," and the more Hemingway allows him to rant, the more Cantwell's loss of rank (he is a demoted general) appears justified. The "braggart and bogus philosopher . . . resembles the classic *miles gloriosus*," just as the aging-lover Cantwell reminds us of the *senex-amator* figure.

As for the young Renata of the long, dark hair, she plays his spurious Mary Magdalene. She fancies that his mutilated hand is the hand of Christ, and apparently hopes to be born again ("renata") by listening to his cant, which she mistakes for wisdom, as does he. ("How many times have you been hit on the head?" his doctor asks.) She also thinks of him as Richard the Lionhearted, while he reaches for his glycerin pills and washes them down with 15–1 martinis.[1]

My point in quoting Vanderbilt here is not to attempt to show that *Across the River* is a good novel, which it is not, but to try to show that what concerned Hemingway as a result of his own emotional conflicts was not expressed only in the direct, projective

[1] "The Last Words of E. H.," *The Nation*, CCI (October 25, 1965), p. 285.

way that so many readers have insisted on. As any skilled writer can, Hemingway was able to express his emotions in a number of ways, and frequently at the same time. Certainly, Cantwell is in part Hemingway romanticizing his own position, mourning his own middle age, and sentimentalizing his continued desperate concern for virility. But wary of the danger of emotionalism, Hemingway turns back on such expressions of sentimentality in this novel to ridicule them for what they are.

Taking Vanderbilt's direction in regard to *Across the River* and pursuing it further, we can see that a number of other details in the novel begin to make more sense. In the absurd picture of Richard the Lion-Hearted launching his attack on the two sailors who have insulted his honor and his ladylove, we are reminded both of Cohn, in *The Sun Also Rises,* and Don Quixote. There is a tart humor in this acting out of an adolescent daydream (the display of manhood in the presence of one's girl) at the age of fifty which is tinged with sadness. Cantwell's continual nostalgia is balanced by the Sancho Panza realism of his usual companion during the reliving of his youth, the very literal- and limited-minded T5 Jackson. And Jackson, the chauffeur of Cantwell's "over-sized luxurious automobile," decides, like Sancho, that it is best to humor the patrone who seems to alternate, inexplicably being "a mean son of a bitch" at one moment and "so God-damn nice" the next. As they journey about the countryside, Cantwell's encounters are by turns pathetic and funny. His absolute judgments and exaggerated dignity provide the quixotic touch, as when he sees a couple in a bar, he immediately classifies them as spiritual enemies, "post-war rich" and mistress. He salutes the pair in response to their stares, and with high sentence announces his calling to arms: "I am sorry that I am in uniform. But it is a uniform. Not a costume" (p. 38). His exaggerated dignity can also be seen very clearly in his pronouncements, which despite a certain conscious mockery on his part are often ludicrous in their egocentric solemnity. "Now, Daughter, let us resume the having of fun," Cantwell says at one point, much in the manner of a king to his subjects.

Cantwell's role as a Quixote-like figure is extended by his insistence on hearing only what he wants to hear, such as his doctor's telling him that he is "in good shape" despite his battered head (suggesting that like Quixote, he is not "quite right"). Cantwell also makes the people around him play the roles that he has assigned to them. Membership in the Order and the mock titles he bestows reflect a severely idiosyncratic view of the world and a romanticizing of himself and his "trade." Cantwell is happiest when, significantly, his mythical world comes alive enough for him and his companions so that a "spell" is created. Much of his energy is devoted to keeping the spell alive when he is in the company of the Gran Maestro and Renata. He is most irritated when a nonmember threatens to destroy his momentary illusions or when he, himself, is overtaken by his own truculence.

Cantwell's romantic image of himself becomes most ridiculous when, again like a teen-ager, he acts out the role of a man in constant danger. Here the satire of sentiment certainly can hit home, since almost all of us, at one time or another, have been led to solemnize and dramatize our lives in response to the romantic stimulus of popular literature or the movies. Like the hero in a bad Western, Cantwell "keeps his security" by sitting in corners in bars and restaurants and castigating himself whenever he fails to note the arrival or departure of customers. Failing to notice that several people had left Harry's bar, he thinks, "I'll get killed that way," and one is forced to conclude that not all giants are to be found disguised as windmills.

Richard Cantwell creates a world and a role, as all of us create them. If the world and the role are foolish, it is in part that Cantwell is caught, and we have yet to be exposed. Jake Barnes and Frederic Henry search painfully to find themselves and, ironically, end up, as a result of the nature of the world they live in, finding the traditional role of hero in a romantic dream created in middle age by their surrogate, Cantwell.

Certainly, *Across the River and into the Trees* is at least in part a satire of a middle-aged man who takes himself too seriously, but it is also a satire of a middle-aged man who doesn't take himself seriously enough, for one of the continuing themes of the novel is age—what it is and what it means; the most pervasive ironic motif is adolescence (a time, as Hemingway has always seen it, of romantic illusion). Colonel Cantwell falls in love with a teen-ager, yearns for her like a teen-ager, necks and pets with her in a gondola under a blanket, sees himself as a movie hero, rants against established authority, seeks approval from his peers, has difficulty controlling his emotions, makes faces in mirrors, walks with an exaggerated cocky strut, and feels sorry for himself. A major conflict in most of Hemingway's novels is the attempt by the protagonist to straighten himself out, to distinguish not so much by the mind as by the emotions what is real and what is illusion. One of the major illusions of age is to feel that we are still young. Each of us must learn, and it is a hard lesson that almost every instinct rebels against, to put aside his youth or bury it as Cantwell literally does, or one will become as foolish and self-deluded as Cantwell has been. Whether one is young like Jake Barnes or old like Colonel Cantwell, sentimentality is always the tender trap.

As many readers of the novel have pointed out, its subject is purgation, but it is a purgative for the author as well. By attacking those tendencies he despised in himself and by drawing a caricature of his own emotional condition, Hemingway achieves the position of disinterest that he is searching for, much as James Joyce in *Portrait of an Artist* and Ezra Pound in "Mauberley" rid themselves of the emotional baggage of their past so that the writing of *Ulysses* and *The Cantos* is made possible. To the extent that both *The Sun Also Rises* and *Across the River* may be seen as combinations of satire and pathos, they perform largely the same function, leading in one case to *A Farewell to Arms* and in the other to *The Old Man and the Sea*. Both "preliminary" novels deal with protagonists who are unable to achieve objectivity from their own illusions, both men find loving difficult, both find sexual intercourse limited or impossible because of physical disabilities, both love women who are more symbolically love objects than physical objects, and both fight a battle within themselves to gain equilibrium and to get outside themselves. Both try to learn to achieve that distance from themselves which will allow them to master themselves. The struggles of Jake Barnes and Richard Cantwell are fitting preliminaries to the attempts at tragedy in the novels that follow in each case, not because distance is a prerequisite for the tragic hero in relation to the objects of his concern, but because it is prerequisite for the author of tragedy in relation to the objects of his concern.

The worst parts of *Across the River and into the Trees* give testimony to the fact that when Hemingway's emotional conflicts are too directly expressed, when they are attached to his own condition too closely, his writing becomes inferior and even, at times, painful to his readers. Much of Hemingway's poorest writing comes, therefore, at times when he uncharacteristically fails to process or dramatize an emotional reaction, and it is at such times that the emotion remains Hemingway's, to the reader's embarrassment, and is not translated into those sequences of "motion and fact" which allow the reader to recreate the emotion for himself.

Throughout Hemingway's career, he sought (both consciously and unconsciously) various modes and structures for expression that would allow him to objectify his own feelings. In his early years, he almost instinctively turned to wit and humor for this purpose. The nonverbal high school student may express his frustrations and anxieties in sullen hostility; the verbal student, in exuberant witticisms uttered in or out of class. Hemingway was considered a wit among his classmates. He and his friends initiated elaborate verbal games, rituals, and jokes (a pattern that he carried on also through his adult years), and his high school writing was largely composed of Lardner adaptations which shot barbs at himself, his classmates, and his community.

Most of this early humor is only gently satiric (explicitly critical), but through the years of journalism and then serious writing, Hemingway's humor became increasingly "dark"—"dark" in the sense of morbid and/or destructive, and "dark" in the sense of obscure. Some of the material that is overtly presented in joke form by Hemingway is very close to what was called several years ago the sick joke. A good example of this is the short story "An Alpine Idyll." A Swiss peasant puts his dead wife out into his woodshed where she freezes stiff from the winter cold. Her face is mangled by the peasant's habit of using her mouth as a hook from which to hang his lantern while in the woodshed. The body is finally brought into town to be buried. The shocked parish priest tries unsuccessfully to communicate a sense of wrongdoing to the uncomprehending peasant, who stubbornly maintains that he did love his wife. The joke ends with the kind of punch line an adolescent might use at a mixed party, when one character asks the narrator, "Say, how about eating?" and the narrator replies, "All right." The masculine bravado here is on the level to be found in the challenge of goldfish-eating.

Constance Cappel Montgomery has said that Hemingway was known by at least one early friend as quite an oral storyteller (p. 163). Several Hemingway pieces have twists to them that are reminiscent of what used to be called smoking car humor. For example, "A Very Short Story" refers to an actual occurrence in Hemingway's life. What amounted to a Dear John letter, complete with implications of another love interest, was received by Hemingway shortly after the war from Agnes von Kurowsky who, of course, is said to have been the model for Catherine in *A Farewell to Arms*. Hemingway's brother has indicated in his book that it was his impression that this was Hemingway's first big love affair. The events which may have occurred almost literally to Hemingway are so condensed in "A Very Short Story" that they are forced into the form of an anecdote.[2] We can surmise that the material was painful to Hemingway at the time the sketch was written and that its primary purpose was to cauterize the emotion. It is perhaps the weakest sketch in the collection of sketches it was published with, for the events are only summarized to be capped with an ironic, anti-sentimental outburst: "A short time after he contracted gonorrhea from a sales girl in a loop department store while riding in a taxicab through Lincoln Park" (*1st 49*, p. 240).

[2] This story first appeared as one of the sketches in the Paris edition of *in our time*.

The story remains today as one that meant a great deal more to Hemingway, turning an emotional crisis into a sardonic joke, than it does to us.[3]

Much of Hemingway's more overt humor strikes the reader as being awkward and boisterous. There is the embarrassment, too, of watching the professional slip and become for a moment unprofessional. Literary art is a kind of showmanship wherein an illusion is maintained with impersonal consistency. The audience always wants to know how the magician does it, what the matinee idol is "really like," but if the audience finds out, the reaction is likely to be close to contempt.

Despite all of his self-discipline, the temptation toward gross humor was difficult for Hemingway to resist. At the beginning, his humor acted much like an escape valve for the tremendous pressure that he placed on himself. *Torrents of Spring*, Hemingway's most notorious lapse from his self-imposed artistic standards, was one long joke, a literary trash collection of parodied odds and ends, caricatures, and literary slapstick which enabled Hemingway to dispose of his frustrations, jealousies, and peeves in an undisciplined way. He explained that he "wrote it after I had finished the first draft of *The Sun Also Rises* to cool out."[4] He should have written and burned it. Later he became more and more suspicious of such impulses and finally became so guarded about what should appear in print that he would not allow *Esquire* to reprint some of his old stories in an anniversary issue because he did not feel that the material was worthy of his reputation.

We are familiar enough in a general way with Freud's discussion of the relation between wit and the unconscious to recognize as a truism the idea that what we joke about most often is what we really take most seriously. We also recognize as true the premise that for a male in our society, laughter is a much more acceptable expression of emotion than tears. In his clinically oriented dis-

[3] This story was the one which upset Hemingway's parents the most among the materials of Hemingway's first published book.

[4] As quoted by Charles Poore in his preface to *The Torrents of Spring*, reprinted in *The Hemingway Reader* (New York, 1953), p. 24.

cussion *Beyond Laughter*, Martin Grotjahn states that "laughter is based on previously mastered anxiety" and that it "helps us to repeat the victory and in doing so to overcome residual anxiety which is not quite assimilated."[5] Perhaps, since his humor is so often obsessively motivated, Hemingway's idea of what is funny is often too "dark" to be widely appealing. Jake Barnes' condition is on the one hand "tragic," but at the same time, particularly in connection with a nymphomaniac, a condition that can be very funny. But perhaps it is the kind of joke that only a soldier with a soldier's anxieties can really laugh at. There is evidence that Hemingway's own wound involved a temporary cessation of his ability to have sex.[6] The resulting anxiety, along with the male role anxiety from his childhood, leads to a complex literary response in *The Sun Also Rises* which mixes both mockery and sadness. If the reader insists on tears alone, it is because he prefers sadness.

It would be a mistake to draw any direct one-to-one connection between Hemingway's subjects for humor and his anxieties, but the reader of Hemingway's work has long since perceived that behind much Hemingway comedy lies a deep concern for maleness and sexual potency, a concern that is perhaps as much an expression of a cultural emotional climate as it is of Hemingway's own emotional condition. The topics of his more overt humor are (not necessarily in order of frequency) death and maiming, romantic illusion, sentimental stereotypes, sexual impotency, and sexual perversions. Doctors, critics, writers, politicians, inept athletes, pseudo artists, homosexuals, and middle-aged women comprise the list of figures most often treated comically.

Some of the stories that Hemingway certainly intended to be at least partly humorous have been handled very solemnly by some critics; other stories, hardly representing Hemingway's best work, have been largely ignored. A story that has frequently been passed over with only a reference to its part in the maturation process of Nick Adams is "The Light of the World." One of the few writers

[5] New York, 1957, p. 202.
[6] Montgomery, p. 117.

to give much space to it is Constance Cappel Montgomery, who points to the derivation of the title from Matthew 5:14: "Ye are the light of the world. A city that is set on a hill cannot be hid." Her suggestion is that the irony of the title might indicate that "all of the sordid people in the train station are 'the light of the world,' or . . . that the truth spoken by Alice 'cannot be hid'" (p. 94). With a somewhat darker view of Hemingway's use of irony in relation to sexual matters, other possibilities suggest themselves. Since this is a story of sexual deviation and deviates which implicitly compares various means of sexual release, the overwhelming concern of the characters is with sex, which is thus discovered by Nick to be the "light" or motivating center of the world. At the same time, it appears impossible in the story to hide from the world one's sexual identity or preferences.

The story opens grimly with an atmosphere reminiscent of "The Battler" and "The Killers," but the threat of physical violence in the opening paragraphs is translated into the psychological threat of abnormality. The world that Nick and Tom enter as they walk into the train station of a small Michigan town could be called "sordid," but "grotesque" would be a more appropriate term for the sideshow the boys are about to witness. As they enter, "nobody was talking and the ticket window was down," and everyone is in position: three whores with "silk dresses that change colors," two ordinary peroxide-blonde whores, six white men (including a homosexual cook), and four Indians. Enter, stage left, "two tough kids" who are greeted at the door by the cook. The cook is taunted by one of the other men, to the great amusement of one of the whores who "must have weighed three hundred and fifty pounds" and who shakes all over as she laughs, mumbling "Oh, my Christ . . . Oh, my sweet Christ." Another lumberjack, referring to the "biggest whore . . . and the biggest woman" Nick had ever seen in his life, tells Nick under his breath that it "must be like getting on top of a hay mow" (*1st 49*, p. 484). The two know-it-all boys have just walked through the looking glass: "I swear to Christ I've never been anywhere like this," Tom says, and trying to be adaptable, makes a vulgar joke. "Ho! Ho! Ho!" laughs the big whore, shaking all over. "Oh, can't you be decent?" scolds the cook.

But this wild comedy is only a preface to the comedy of the "serious drama" that now unfolds. An argument develops between the largest whore and one of her comrades over who really knew a fighter named Steve Ketchel. The situation becomes more and more ludicrous as the smaller, peroxide-blonde prostitute describes her love affair with Ketchel in such glowing, romantic terms that everyone in the audience becomes "very respectful" to her feelings. At last, after her sad story of self-sacrifice and her marriage to Ketchel "in the eyes of God," everyone "felt terribly. It was sad and embarrassing" (p. 487). For reasons we can only guess at, the Indians, who have not made a sound, have gone outside.

Then Peroxide is called a liar by the large prostitute, Alice. She gravely counters with her own bit of nostalgia, which is almost threadbare compared to Peroxide's melodrama. While crying so hard that she can hardly talk, she offers the brief, endearing comment made to her by Ketchel that she has held close to her heart all these years: "You're a lovely piece, Alice." Peroxide counters in turn that Ketchel didn't talk that way, but the reader is convinced that Peroxide's stagey dream of the past is less genuine than the meager compliment so carefully hoarded by Alice.

The fierce emotional battle of the two women so devoted to the flesh over such a trivial claim to romantic fame brings another ironic possibility to the title: no matter how buried in flesh, lust, and sordid circumstances, sentiment will out. Since Alice is literally a mountain of flesh, it is fitting in regard to the biblical reference that what emerges is her light. The title may apply also to the fact that Nick, who has been preoccupied with Alice's presence throughout the story, finds her increasingly more attractive; her sex appeal seems to grow (in a grotesque reversal of sentiment in itself) and becomes so attractive to him that Tom, sensing Nick's fascination, gets him to leave the station. The two depart while Nick is still weighing her disadvantages versus her advantages, "But my God she was big. . . . She certainly had a nice voice," and at the same time, Tom is fending off the cook.

The story ends with a burlesque-house punch line, a pun on the word *"going"*: "'Which way are you boys going?' asked the cook. 'The other way from you,' Tom told him" (p. 489). Significantly, the story was one that Hemingway liked very much himself but which he felt "nobody else ever liked" (*1st 49*, p. vii). It is easy to see why such subject matter might not be to the taste of some readers, but the inclusion of such "offensive" materials in themselves is for Hemingway a common anti-sentimental technique. In intimate connection with Hemingway's sense of humor is a dark delight in the "unsavory." A great enjoyment comes to him in shocking old ladies of both sexes.

This two-pronged attack on sentimentality, an unsavory subject treated ironically, is demonstrated in another humorous story, "God Rest You Merry, Gentlemen." No darker subject for a joke could have been chosen than this one—a boy who has a desire to "purify" himself by castration cuts off his own penis not knowing what *castration* means. The heavy-handed irony of the title points both to the reader and to the incompetent doctors: "let nothing you dismay," gentlemen. The reader is involved as a member of a society that through its Victorian prudishness has set the stage for the possible bleeding to death of this boy. On Christmas day, because he took Aunt Sally's Sunday school lessons seriously, he is bleeding for a false sense of shame—a travesty and perversion of the motives of Christ who bled on the same day centuries ago. If the joke is a sick one, Hemingway diagnoses the sickness to be ours, turns, and in effect asks us, "How do you like it now, Gentlemen?" When the more competent of the two doctors tries to talk the boy out of his shame for his body and his request that the doctors castrate him, the boy replies in a precise echo of the emotional blindness and deafness of Mrs. Adams (in "The Doctor and the Doctor's Wife"): "No. I won't listen. . . . When you talk like that I don't hear you" (*1st 49*, pp. 492–93).

One might argue, as Carlos Baker and others have, that the backbone of such stories as these is an inevitable advocacy of normality. But this view is really stating the case backward. Typical in his moralist-satirist position, Hemingway proposes no social models; he is, rather, a writer of reaction, recovery, and counter-attack. A large percentage of Hemingway's initial instincts as a writer was destructive; his laughter was often malicious, and sometimes hateful, scornful, or spiteful. He may be said to advocate normality, but only as a vicious and dedicated soldier can be said to advocate peace. Alternating in much of his early writing between the fundamental satirical modes of ridicule and disgust, the only clearly advocated virtue is the virtue of direct experience, and very little that is recorded of that experience in Hemingway's writing fails to shock, or twist the arm of "normality." "Normality" in this sense might be considered a cultural agreement to reduce condition and response to an absurdly simple formula: the Emperor must have his new clothes. For the spectator who sees the joke as Hemingway does, his initial laughter may come at the expense of the naked Emperor or his willfully blind subjects, but in the end, his laughter must come as a crow of victory and a celebration of the freedom of his own psyche. When he wins, Hemingway does not triumph over society so much as he triumphs over the self in spite of society.

Hemingway may laugh at almost anything (including some things his readers may not be inclined to laugh at, at all) and even laugh at himself, but one thing he does not laugh at is the projection of the self who is successful in gaining freedom from the myth, the lie, the sentimental formula through the courageous application of self-discipline. Jake Barnes may begin as a joke, and remain in part the object of ridicule as long as he is self-deluded, but he ends up very nearly sanctified. However, though the creation of the objectified self lies at the heart of all of Hemingway's artistically successful efforts to resolve his emotional conflict, his overt efforts at humor usually represent relative failures. Such stories as "God Rest You Merry, Gentlemen" and "Mr. and Mrs. Elliot" can be seen as *direct* self-indulgent attempts to purge the emotions of the writer.

Nowhere is this personalness better demonstrated than in Hemingway's grosser applications of humor and wit to his fellow writers. It may be that Puritan self-examination and a rigid conscience, rather than mere animosity, made it impossible for Hemingway to forgive others their weaknesses, just as it seems impossible for him to forgive himself. Some further insight into Hemingway's emotional connection to his own writing may be induced from the fact that most attacks can be divided into one of two categories: parody of, or disparaging references to, the author's writing itself, or references to a sexual maladjustment of one kind or another. The "standard meter of Paris," Hemingway's phrase for unvarying honesty, seems to stretch from healthy heterosexuality at one end to a healthy, experience-oriented prose at the other.

The force of Hemingway's own self-discipline in conjunction with the inevitable frustrations and insecurities of the beginning writer led him frequently in the early years to what might be generously termed an overdeveloped sense of competition. Whereas a writer such as Gertrude Stein probably got no more abuse from Hemingway than she deserved (particularly in response to her calculated jab below the belt in calling Hemingway a coward), other writers appear much less deserving.[7] Much of the parody in *The Torrents of Spring* was directed, often viciously, toward the flabby sentimentality of Sherwood Anderson's *Dark Laughter*. The fact that Hemingway, who was generally a kind man himself, should have so badly hurt Sherwood Anderson, who had been so kind to him on numerous occasions, simply because he "felt that it was his duty to criticize any inferior work that Anderson might produce,"[8] is evidence for the metamorphosis of the driving moral energy of Hemingway's early environment into an uncompromising sense of literary standards. Such callousness also indicates the extent, during the period of *The Torrents of Spring* and *The Sun Also Rises*, to which sentimentality had been recognized as the enemy. Much injustice, however, exists in Hemingway's expectation that Anderson should have been able to separate himself dispassionately from his own writing—a separation which Hemingway was never able to accomplish himself.

[7] Baker, *Hemingway: The Writer as Artist*, p. 44.
[8] *Ibid.*, p. 43.

Some poetic justice can be found in the almost exact parallel of E. B. White's later parody of the sentimentality in *Across the River and into the Trees*. Like Anderson, Hemingway had lapsed into certain distinct mannerisms of style and technique that in this particular novel existed almost unto themselves. The subject matter was too slim to be carried by a rhetoric that had previously sustained far more significant drama than the last thoughts and gestures of an aging colonel. Hemingway's first reactions to the White parody were defensive and carry the irony of the situation even further: "The parody," he stated to A. E. Hotchner, "is the last refuge of the frustrated writer. Parodies are what you write when you are associate editor of the Harvard *Lampoon*. The greater the work of literature, the easier the parody. The step up from writing parodies is writing on the wall above the urinal."[9] Possibly realizing the irony of this, his second reaction was to out-parody White's parody into Hotchner's microphone. The result is the touching story of an eighteen-year-old colonel who has an eighty-six-year-old girl friend. Following a shooting spree on the Grand Canal in Venice, the young hero has a forty-eight-day drinking bout in Harry's bar, and misplacing his elderly countess, he turns to a younger girl, who, tragically, has a heart condition. Oversensitive to human suffering, he leaves her on the island they have eloped to and swims off into the sunset. The parody ends with an appeal to the reader's tenderness and generosity, since some of the profits from the book will be used to support a foundation established in the name of the heroine.[10]

Hemingway's less overt humor is most often expressed as part of an extensive pattern of double-entendre, pun, literary allusion and parallel, and ironic echo. As distinct from his grosser parodies, Hemingway's uses of contemporary and past literature within this pattern are often extremely subtle and hard to document. For this reason, critics when writing about such influences are more likely simply to mention the authors' names than to trace the influence in detail. One of the few critics to trace such an allusive pattern

[9] *Papa Hemingway* (New York, 1966), p. 70.
[10] *Ernest Hemingway Reading* (Caedmon, TC-1185).

is Robert W. Lewis, Jr., who deals rather explicitly with the many uses of the Bible in *The Sun Also Rises* and, in particular, shows that many verses from Ecclesiastes (taking the lead from the epigraph) provide an ironic counterpoint to the characters and situations of *The Sun Also Rises*. The very existence of such a parallel was probably amusing to Hemingway, and, although Lewis does not make a point of it, several of the correspondences that he notes can be seen to have humorous overtones. Ecclesiastes 3:18–19, which points out that men are like beasts ("they themselves are beasts. For that which befalleth the sons of men befalleth beasts . . ."), adds a note of sardonic humor to Jake's role as a steer. When these sexless animals are gored by the bulls at Pamplona, Bill Gorton in ironic parallel to Jake's punishment at the hands of his "bull" friends—Mike, Cohn, and Romero—comments it "must be swell being a steer" (p. 133). Jake, as Lewis points out, also performs the function of herding his friends around, introducing Brett to Cohn and to Romero, and acting as peace-maker, or to quote Jake himself in regard to the steers: "To quiet down the bulls and keep them from breaking their horns against the stone walls, or goring each other" (p. 133). In this sense, Jake, the steer, becomes identified with the "sexless" priest, or the Preacher (several verses indicate that the Preacher is not literally sexless). The sentimental tenacity of Jake, Cohn, and the others who rush to the destruction offered by Brett is given sardonic dimension in "Thou knowest not what is the way of the spirit" from Ecclesiastes 11:5; Brett's power to destroy and Jake's final escape from that power may be echoed in Ecclesiastes 7:26: "And I find more bitter than death the woman, whose heart is snares and nets, and her hands as bands: whoso pleaseth God shall escape from her; but the sinner shall be taken by her." Lewis points out other parallels, aside from those few that I have adapted for my own purpose here, but, as is often the case when pinning Hemingway down in regard to such a possible source of inspiration, Lewis is on thin critical ground, and he knows it: "Ecclesiastes once more provides the text and enlightening parallels that Hemingway must have been aware of" (p. 33).

The Sun Also Rises, although in a much more restrained fashion, is laced with literary allusions, as is its burlesque counterpart, *The Torrents of Spring*. In the former novel there are many echoes of Laurence Sterne's *Sentimental Journey Through France and Italy* which, in themselves, must have provided Hemingway with some amusement. Making the association even more comic is the fact that some of the strongest parallels are between sections of *A Sentimental Journey* and the sequence in *The Sun Also Rises* wherein Jake picks up and escorts a prostitute to a Paris restaurant.[11] Since the organizational plan of *The Torrents of Spring* roughly resembles that of Fielding's *Joseph Andrews* (and quotations from the preface of *Joseph Andrews* head each of the chapters in *The Torrents of Spring*),[12] there is a possibility that *A Sentimental Journey* actually contributed the basic plan for the more comic first manuscript of *The Sun Also Rises*—a humorous classification of types. Early in Sterne's novel a list of various types of travellers is presented, and it is possible to match some of the types with some of the characters in the Hemingway novel, so that Cohn might be the Vain Traveller, Mike the Delinquent and Felonious Traveller, Bill the Inquisitive Traveller, and Jake the Sentimental Traveller. In a statement that might hold true as well for the reader of the Hemingway novel, Sterne says, "It is sufficient for my reader, if he has been a traveller himself, that with study and reflection hereupon he may be able to determine his own place

[11] The existence of parallels between Sterne's novel and *The Sun Also Rises* was brought to my attention by a colleague, James Hinkle. Citations from *A Sentimental Journey through France and Italy* are from the volume edited by Gardner D. Stout, Jr. (Berkeley, 1967).

Georgette, in *The Sun Also Rises*, offers her hand to Jake who rejects it; Yorick's lady, in *Sentimental Journey*, tends to pull her hand away. Both ladies are from Brussels. Georgette asks Jake, "You're not Flamand?" and the French captain asks the lady in *Sentimental Journey*, "*Apparamment vous etez Flammande?*" Jake picks up Georgette because of a "vague sentimental idea," and Yorick exclaims to his lady, "To think of making love by *sentiments!*" The theme in *The Sun Also Rises* of getting what you pay for (as a metaphor for the investment of emotion) is echoed in Yorick's statement: "It will always follow from hence, that the balance of sentimental commerce is always against the expatriated adventurer: he must buy what he has little occasion for at their own price" (p. 78).

[12] Montgomery, p. 166.

and rank in the catalogue—it will be one step toward knowing himself" (pp. 82–83).

There are times when a reader can take an obvious hint from a title, a paraphrased sentence, or a name and, if he feels it is worth the trouble, trace such literary parallels for himself. At other times, the reader has little or nothing to guide him and must be content with the feeling that there is something familiar about what he is reading. "Mr. and Mrs. Elliot" can be taken as a gross attack on Victorian morality, or the story can be seen as a gross attack on T. S. Eliot. Further examination readily reveals that Gertrude Stein is also mocked: "Mrs. Elliot was quite sick. She was sick and when she was sick she was sick as Southern women are sick" (*1st 49*, p. 259). The allusions become somewhat more subtle when we take the hint from the title of the story and find that the relationship between Mr. Elliot and his wife is defined in part of Eliot's poem, *The Waste Land* (particularly the typist seduction scene). The resulting equation is somewhat comic, although vicious: T. S. Eliot plus Gertrude Stein equals sterility.

Mrs. Elliot runs a tea shop, and Mr. Elliot falls in love with her "dancing to the gramophone," and after they are married, Mr. Elliot wrote "a great number of poems and Cornelia typed them for him" (p. 261). They take a château in Touraine, but find that they are living in "a very flat hot country very much like Kansas" where a "hot evening wind blew." Meanwhile (like Joyce), Elliot had taken to drinking white wine and lived apart in his own room. Elliot "wrote a great deal of poetry during the night and in the morning looked very exhausted." (This echoes Eliot's line "I read, much of the night, and go south in the winter"—possibly partly explaining also why Mrs. Elliot is a Southern woman.) Meanwhile, Mrs. Elliot and her girl friend "now slept together in the big mediaeval bed." This relationship may tempt us to think of Mr. Elliot turning to his wife, and in the words of *The Waste Land* asking, "Who is the third who walks always beside you? . . . I do not know whether a man or a woman . . ."[13]

In the Hemingway story "The Three-Day Blow" there is a gen-

[13] *The Complete Poems and Plays: 1909–1950* (New York, 1952), p. 48.

eral humorous applicability of the novel titles brought up in the discussion between Nick and his friend Bill. *Forest Lovers* and *The Dark Forest* refer to the affair between Marjorie and Nick which has just been broken off in the preceding story, "The End of Something." Nick and Marjorie have been, in fact, forest lovers, and the romance of these novels puts a comic perspective on the sentimental view of love that Marjorie has in the first story and that Nick has in the second. Nick's main problem in the second story seems to match another title that is discussed, *Fortitude*, since he finds it difficult to resist the temptation to return to Marjorie and hopes with boyish sentimentality that he might run into her again if he goes into town Saturday night.

More subtle and much less certain are possible references to the contents of the novels. Both *Richard Feverel* and *Fortitude* have protagonists who suffer through painful and "tragic" love affairs as boys and young men, and both novels have heroines who die, in a sense, for the "lost" love of the protagonist in each case. The mood of these novels, therefore, comically highlights the self-pity of Nick, who is "drinking to forget," and the humor of his increasingly drunken sense of bereavement expressed in the rhetoric of high tragedy:

Nick said nothing. The liquor had all died out of him and left him alone. Bill wasn't there. He wasn't sitting in front of the fire or going fishing tomorrow with Bill and his dad or anything. He wasn't drunk. It was all gone. All he knew was that he had once had Marjorie and that he had lost her. She was gone and he had sent her away. That was all that mattered. He might never see her again. Probably he never would. It was all gone, finished. (p. 221)

The bookish melodrama of Nick's thoughts can be given further humorous, anti-sentimental dimensions through the application of *Fortitude*, the story of a boy who is always alone, an outsider, and who learns to face life, at last, with courage. Walpole's novel might very well have been one which engaged Hemingway's sympathies at one time, especially since the boy turns out to be a successful writer and the boy's mother, in a rough approximation of Mrs. Adams' condition, is an invalid who never leaves her room.

However, despite Walpole's popularity, it seems unlikely that Hemingway would depend on his readers' detailed knowledge of the novel to make a point. Such a possible use of the older writer's novel does lead us to the likelihood that there are a number of near-private jokes sprinkled throughout at least some of Hemingway's writings.[14]

Sometimes crude, sometimes subtle, the humor in Hemingway's work is uniformly directed toward ridiculing the illusions and emotions of sentimentality. When he attacks with a sledgehammer, the too obvious need to shock and the too obvious need to declare personal superiority can be embarrassing, but are at the same time revealing of the intensity of Hemingway's own emotions.[15] The conflict in Hemingway between childhood environment and adult experience leads to such outbursts as this expression of scorn in *Der Querschnitt* (February, 1925): "And in the end the age was handed/The sort of shit that it demanded." Alongside this piece of juvenilia, the achievement in *The Sun Also Rises* (October, 1926) stands as almost incredible in its wealth of finely wrought detail and carefully controlled irony.

[14] One such near-private joke brought to light recently by Sheridan Baker concerns some wordplay with "Francis Macomber": "Hemingway, who liked to make the Swahili *m'uzuri* into sentences about Missouri and Arkansas, has also made himself as 'Bwana M'Kumba' into 'Francis Macomber' (M'Kumba seems to be Hemingway's transcription of *mkubwa*, 'chief'), drawing another slightly effeminate portrait of what he did not like in himself, christening the irony in 'Chief' an effeminate 'Francis.'" *Ernest Hemingway: An Introduction and Interpretation* (New York, 1967), p. 101.

Earl Rovit in his book notes that in light of "Mark Twain's abuse of the guide Ferguson in *Innocents Abroad*, it is possible that Hemingway is having a private joke in his naming and employment of this character [in *A Farewell to Arms*]" (p. 180).

Much Hemingway wordplay is so ambiguous and uncertain, as well as possibly distasteful, that much of it will probably never be discussed in print. Dark-minded students have often called my attention to the pattern of diction in "Chapter III" (*1st 49*, p. 203): "Buckley," "one leg over," "potted," "They all came just like that." Hemingway's habits would seem to confirm their suspicions.

[15] I should mention that there are also those passages in Hemingway's work in which the humor is handled with such a light touch that they may very easily be passed over completely. Such a passage is the one concerning Ettore in *A Farewell to Arms* (discussed below, pp. 92–93). Another is the first part of Chapter XIII in *A Farewell to Arms*, which describes Henry's arrival at the American hospital. It was not until I heard this latter passage read aloud that

But the heavy-handed humor of Hemingway's youthful writing is more than a masculine declaration of independence, it is often the by-product of an informal course of study. His early burlesques and parodies not only reflect a close interest in language and style, but also reveal a great talent for perceiving detailed connections between literary technique and effect. The next stage in Hemingway's development as a writer manifests itself as an increasing concern for the serious and the formal. This time his analysis is not directed toward the writing of others, but instead, in an attempt to understand the emotional values implicit in experience itself, toward the emotional mechanism within the tragic and tradition-laden drama of the bullfight.

the full impact of the repetition and the skillful blend of pain, clumsiness, and confusion came through to me. The doubtful elevator, the garlic breath, the hospital which, although empty, has no room for its first patient (who is reaching the end of his patience), and the befuddled nurse who can't act without official directives are all elements of a fine comedy. The full comic effect of such passages may be dimmed by a silent reading, which doesn't give full value to the sounds that Hemingway obviously cultivated. (The "Ettore" passage improves considerably when read aloud also.) This raises the question of how much we may be missing by our failure to give full value to the "tuned" aspects of Hemingway's prose, particularly in the longer works which are seldom read aloud.

GAME
A STRUCTURE FOR EMOTIONAL CONTROL

◆ ◆ ◆ BEHIND HEMINGWAY's very skillful uses of image and metaphor lie the personal fears and joys expressed by the author in response to a continual self-dramatization of the will beset by temptations to weakness and self-indulgence. Although Hemingway very explicitly rejects the standards of his home and birthplace, he is never able to cast aside that energy toward proper conduct which characterized the atmosphere in which he grew up. It is hardly any wonder that the most common mode of thought for the Hemingway protagonist is some form of argument, some form of self-trial.

The drama of the self, whether illuminated by the arc lights of Henry's lunchroom or the sunlight on the deck of a blood-spattered motor launch, hesitates always between weakness and strength, victimization and heroism, tears and stoic calm. The tension between these directions forms the emotional and ethical center of Hemingway's work, leading to the extremes of solemn self-justification on the one hand, or bitter self-mockery on the other. It is this tension which is responsible for that constant underlayer of irony which, to the alert reader, makes so much of Hemingway's fiction appear schizoid, both as a loss of contact with everyday reality and as a division into several conflicting personalities.

When we put together the published reports of Hemingway's

personality, two distinctly different men do indeed seem to emerge. One is generally well-disciplined and well-organized even in his fun, a man who is quiet, shy, and secretly generous. Then there is the Hemingway who is the grandstander, full of egotism, wordy and vain, prone to cute tricks and clever poses, a man so supersensitive that a long friendship can be cut off in a single sullen instant of resentment. Certainly the two Hemingways overlap, but the separation is more constant and distinct than the modern author's defensive need for a public mask will allow for or even the polarities of friendship and enmity can fully explain. Whether Freudian in our orientation or not, we are almost forced to view this split in terms of ego and superego, son and father. Most overtly, this split is reflected in the rigid discipline and terseness that characterize the best short stories in contrast to the flabby wordiness, cuteness, and painful display of ego so prominent in *The Torrents of Spring, Death in the Afternoon,* and *Across the River and into the Trees.*

Less overtly, and I think more importantly, there is that split which occurs within the work itself, involving on the one hand that "self" which is always onstage, always a focal point for attention and judgment. This is the self that is risked, that can be laughed at or applauded, that can demand and get sympathy or admiration. However, the self onstage is seldom left to fend for itself. Usually, it is supported or checked, interpreted or excused by another "self," standing between the audience and the footlights.

Contributing to this theatrical effect of Hemingway's work is the constant and explicit audience consciousness. Sometimes appearing in the work itself and sometimes assumed to be the reader, an audience is prerequisite to the meaningful presentation of the protagonist's ordeal. Hemingway's younger brother has pointed out that "Ernest was never very content with life unless he had a spiritual kid brother nearby. He needed someone he could show off to as well as teach."[1] When Hemingway most obviously plays to his audience in the role of pragmatic moralist, he may give what amounts to an illustrated lecture. This relationship with the reader

[1] Leicester Hemingway, *My Brother, Ernest Hemingway* (New York, 1963), p. 117.

more often develops in the nonfiction, but there are passages in the novels that stop the narrative for a pronouncement from a worldly-wise and somewhat weary older brother. It is not surprising that these passages, such as the baseball analogy to life in *A Farewell to Arms*, are among the most often quoted, reinforcing as they do the image of the gut-thinker.

Generally, the theatrical apparatus is constructed so that the son is sacrified onstage, while the father hovers nearby in spirit, vicariously participating in the pity of it all, yet preserving an outside overview of the son's ordeal as necessary in light of the nature of the world and the limitations of the son. This technique of the divided point of view, which includes both a storytelling persona and a protagonist (who also may be a narrator), varies in its explicitness. In the Nick Adams stories which deal with childhood and early adolescence and in *A Farewell to Arms*, the story is told in retrospect by the protagonist. Thus, Hemingway is able to assume both the "father" and the "son" roles and both an objective and subjective point of view at the same time. In a sense Hemingway is thus twice removed from the emotional turmoil at the center of the story.

Many readers have noted how often Hemingway's settings are either literally stages or reminiscent of a stage by being spotlighted, raised, or segregated for the audience's view. In addition, the recurrence of certain stock characters may make us feel, as we read through the whole of Hemingway's fiction, that we are viewing the various productions of a repertory company. The fundamental lack of connection characteristic of the Hemingway protagonist may remind us that he is more like an actor called in to play a role than a "normal" human surrounded by family and daily routine. He lives in hotels, travels from place to place, owns very little, and maintains few permanent ties with people. He is more often like Frederic Henry, who promises Catherine that she will never have to meet his parents, than like Santiago, who, thinking of his return to shore, is impelled to declare, "I live in a good town" (*O.M.*, p. 115).

Most of Hemingway's central characters are at one time or another self-consciously dramatic; many even think of themselves as actors or are thought of as actors by other characters. Jake Barnes' tendency toward self-deception and public performance is defined and subtly mocked in the affair with the prostitute Georgette, which resembles a play within the larger play of his self-dramatized relationship with Brett. Like Hamlet, Jake educates his emotions and nurtures them by giving them theatrical structuring and dimensions. Frederic Henry both thinks of himself and is thought of as an actor. As is often the case, *actor* here becomes equivalent to *faker*, and the older Frederic Henry self-critically recalls and underlines the acting of a shallower, emotionally stupid younger self. In "The Killers," one of Hemingway's most obviously theatrical stories, Max's recommendation that George "ought to go to the movies more" and that the movies "are fine for a bright boy like you" suggests a mockery of the "reality resistance" of both the shocked audience of the killers in the story and the reader-audience outside, as well as providing an ironic edge to the theatrical brutality of the killers themselves (*1st 49*, p. 381). Mockery, as we have already seen, is just as clearly indicated in the self-conscious role-playing of Cantwell in *Across the River* and his display of his colonel's "costume." Even the shell-shocked Nick of "A Way You'll Never Be" becomes a travelling sideshow. He is forced to become an actor as his only escape from the unbearable consequences of emotional honesty in the face of war. The role that he creates for himself is ironically one of a morale-builder, that is to ride around on a bicycle in an American uniform (although he is in the Italian army) to make the Italian troops believe that other Americans are coming to help. "It's perfectly all right for you to look," he tells his nervous audience of Italians. "You can stare, if you like" (*1st 49*, p. 509).

This whole scheme of self-dramatization, which Hemingway uses both to attack the self and to sympathize with it, is intimately related, of course, to his employment of the game metaphor. The game player, also, takes a role in front of spectators, often with accompanying costume, prescribed actions and lines, and characteristic apparatus and setting. Not only are various games used as subject matter to a greater or lesser degree throughout Hemingway's fiction, but more important, as many readers have observed, life itself is often perceived as a kind of game, and many protagonists are presented as game heroes.[2]

The game metaphor is essentially a method for ethical dramatization, for distilling and isolating the forces which in ordinary life are too diffuse to be perceived clearly. Game competition has rich metaphorical possibilities which were undoubtedly attractive to a moralist with a tendency to view life through sensation: the game creates a small, independent world, with its own sharply defined structure of physical consequences, its own laws, its own tribal customs and rituals, its own hierarchy of participants, its own set of conflicts and emotions, and its own set of rewards and punishments.

Again, self opposes self, since most of the games that are of particular interest to Hemingway are, significantly, individual sports wherein the participant competes against himself as well as serving as his own umpire or judge. The rules governing these "blood sports" rest on a character goal almost uniquely confined in our day to games—honor. In few other contemporary activities outside such individual sports are infractions of the rules considered so serious. Nevertheless, if the stakes are high enough, as they can be in hunting or bullfighting, the temptation to cheat in one way or another can be overwhelming, as it is to Macomber to run from the lion he has wounded rather than to finish him off. This infraction of the rules turns into a major crisis in Macomber's life, and it is important to see that it is his own self-condemnation, rather than pressure applied by his wife and Wilson, which leads him back into danger to recapture his self-respect.

[2] "Today in the social sciences, two languages compete for primacy: the language of the 'game' and the language of the 'myth.' Game languages follow the model of the physical sciences by defining all terms operationally and in formal terms. '. . . Analysis of social interaction is made in terms of moves and countermoves. . . . In all these fields the trend toward miniature systems is indicative of the model of a tight situation, rigidly defined, where individuals can be assumed to conform to a set of rules which can be completely specified,'" from Bennis *et al.*, p. 18 (including a quotation from K. W. Back, "The Game and the Myth," *Behavioral Science*, VIII [1963], 68).

On the other hand, the sense of honor of the participant may be so great that like the bullfighter, Manuel Garcia, in "The Undefeated," he may lose his life in solitary pursuit of his commitment even though he knows beforehand that an honorable performance will probably cause his death. Although, like Garcia, the winner may take away from his victory nothing more tangible than his honor, it is the most important thing he can preserve: it epitomizes the meaning of his life, and for the observer, it can represent the meaning of being a man.[3]

The moral imperatives under which the game hero operates as well as the qualities of character that he must express in response to those imperatives are traditional and are neither coined by Hemingway nor, of course, confined to his writing alone. Derived from experience, rather than codified in some intellectual way, the two main sources for them would appear to be Hemingway's own inheritance from his father and his observation of behavior under the stress of violence as recorded in *Death in the Afternoon*. These moral imperatives are not only implicit for the reader of Hemingway's work, but are implicit also for the Hemingway protagonist himself, who often derives a sense of these imperatives by observation within the game situation, much as a son may learn without explicit verbal instructions from his father.

Death in the Afternoon, although ostensibly a guidebook to the bullfight, is really Hemingway's record of his own deliberate exploration of the game metaphor and its fundamental ethical and aesthetic terms.[4] The many roles of Hemingway, or the many selves

[3] Hemingway was also obviously attracted to particular games because of their masculinity, as well as their violence and elements of real risk. Activities such as hunting, fishing, boxing, and bullfighting are by tradition kept within the province of the male, and through the violence, suffering, and death inflicted upon man and, even more important to some observers, upon animals, they are strongly antithetical to feminine sentiment.

[4] The one characteristic that ties the miscellaneous materials of *Death in the Afternoon* together is that everything is strongly directed against sentimentality. To some extent the book seems to be aimed toward irritating and provoking its readers. Of the three major, short-story-like anecdotes in the book, two are primarily about homosexuality, and the third, "A Natural History of the Dead," is a bitter parody of sentimentality about nature. Then too, Hemingway could not have picked a country, Spain, or a spectacle, the bullfight,

of the writer, are all tied together in a rather complex way into the figure of the bullfighter, his behavior, and his relation with his audience. First of all, the matador is a hero in a very traditional sense who risks his life as the result of a commitment to an ideal of behavior. To some extent he is both a priest and holy knight who attempts to renew with each armed acting out of dangerous sacrifice the sense of man's mastery over himself and his environment. Second, the matador is a performer, an actor within a tragic drama whose actions have meaning only as they are observed and shared by a qualified audience. Third, the matador is an artist who has freedom to act within a certain form to create a work of beauty with the materials of real violence, suffering, and death, with the opportunity to communicate a deep aesthetic apprehension of the "simplest things" to his audience. Finally, the matador is a player of the game who succeeds or fails ultimately on the basis of his own self-imposed integrity, and whose success is measured not on the basis of whether the bull is killed or not (it always is), but *how* the bull is killed. The greatest possibility is that through skill and courage, artist and hero can combine with a courageous bull and a sensitive audience to produce, at the moment of death, a moment of transcendent unity. It is a moment that suggests man's origin and destiny, triumphs and sorrows, possibilities and limitations.

"Honor," "courage," "pride," and all the other attributes of the archetypal hero discussed and illustrated in *Death in the Afternoon* can be reduced in the end to one underlying imperative and character trait—self-honesty. The basic conflict in the book which operates on several levels of interpretation—heroic action, artistic integrity, or game situation—is set up between those who are "sincere" and those who use "tricks."[5] (An additional conflict is the implicit one of the sensitive versus the insensitive observer.) Hem-

less endemic to the American emotional climate. In the arena in Spain, Hemingway found himself about as far from the province of Aunt Sally as a Midwestern American boy could put himself. That he had Aunt Sally in mind is testified to by his inclusion of a cardboard likeness of her in the book as a foil for his pompous humor.

[5] Pp. 54 (writers' faking), 91, 163, 193, 200, 210, 223—all are among the more specific references to "sincerity" versus "faking."

ingway finds that, for the informed observer, true or false emotion is produced depending on whether the bullfighter really puts himself in danger or fakes it. In art, as in life, one knows what is moral by how one feels afterward (p. 4); to see the "real thing" is to know it is real by the way one feels while watching it. There is that faena[6]

that takes a man out of himself and makes him feel immortal while it is proceeding, that gives him an ecstasy, that is, while momentary, as profound as any religious ecstasy; moving all the people in the ring together and increasing in emotional intensity as it proceeds, carrying the bullfighter with it, he playing on the crowd through the bull and being moved as it responds in a growing ecstasy of ordered, formal, passionate, increasing disregard for death that leaves you, when it is over, and the death administered to the animal that has made it possible, as empty, as changed and as sad as any major emotion will leave you. (pp. 206–7)

Just as the matador is both artist and hero, so too the aesthetic and the ethical are joined in the establishment of a standard of judgment which consists of the emotional apprehension of the "trueness" of the performance. Hemingway finds that in bullfighting as in life or literature, if the members of the audience "prefer tricks to sincerity they soon get the tricks" (p. 163). Not only is this emotional apprehension akin to a religious revitalization, a ceremony of purgation and rebirth, but, as has been pointed out many times, it is very similar to the emotional workings of tragedy set forth by Aristotle in the *Poetics*. What is important is to see (for example, in the passage quoted above) how in Hemingway's thinking the game metaphor is associated with classical drama and classical aesthetic standards. In Hemingway's sense of tragedy, however, it is the bullfight, not Greek drama, which is primary. The Hemingway protagonist is not cleansed by his own death, but lives to be changed emotionally by the sacrifice of someone or something that has come to stand for life. This sacrifice can have no meaning without a genuine emotional investment, and the self-honesty which is prerequisite to genuine investment is Hemingway's point.

[6] The last act of the fight, which includes a series of passes with a small cape over a pointed stick called the muleta and the actual killing.

The connection between Hemingway the artist and Hemingway the man of action has, of course, created a popular legend as well as a counterreaction of criticism and mockery. The fact that Hemingway was a performer does not necessarily impeach his honesty. Furthermore, the connection between hero and artist that Hemingway made in his own mind has a significance for the reader of his works that goes beyond the showmanship or muscle-flexing of the mass-media "Hemingway." For one, the connection is seen to be pervasive and organic, rather than simply philosophical and verbal, regardless of the fact that in his writing Hemingway occasionally succumbed to faking and sometimes failed to win his own internal battles. For another, art and experience have a connection far more intimate than mere observation or imagination in a detached sense can provide.

Green Hills of Africa might be seen as Hemingway's own testing ground for the game fundamentals he apprehended in the bull-fight and recorded in *Death in the Afternoon,* thus underlining his constant attempts to integrate his life and art, to investigate personally and certify the truth of the emotions he sought to communicate in his fiction. Particularly interesting in certifying this connection between art and life, as well as the connection between the two books, is a passage in *Green Hills of Africa* where Hemingway inadvertently switches from hunting imagery to bullfight imagery in a time of crisis.[7] In this fictionalized account of an African safari, Hemingway tells himself (matching the self-versus-self conflict of his major novels) time after time that if he doesn't kill cleanly he will quit hunting. When he is led into a "petty" external competition with a friend, he works continuously to defeat the unworthy emotions of jealousy and spite which are generated in him by this false moral focus. When at the end of the hunting he is again bested by his competitor, Karl, the white hunter, Pop, puts the perspective of competition back where it belongs as an internal conflict when he says, "You can always remember how you shot them. That's what you really get out of it" (p. 293). Thus, the winner *does* take

[7] Noted by W. M. Frohock in *The Novel of Violence in America* (Dallas, 1958), pp. 181–82.

something; he may lose the largest kudu, but he can gain himself. The integrity of the artist is explicitly joined to the integrity of the game protagonist in another passage from the same book in which Hemingway proposes that a fourth or fifth dimension can be achieved in prose provided the writer has "an absolute conscience as unchanging as the standard meter in Paris, to prevent faking" (p. 27).

It may be, as many claim, that Hemingway erected this value system because of a cultural vacuum, a vacuum some literary historians point to as a result of the disillusionment following World War I and the cynical settlements that scuttled the Wilsonian rhetoric of the war. Other literary historians say that Hemingway's need to erect a personal value system is part of a pattern that has involved all serious American writers and that arose owing to our lack of traditions, a lack which has put American culture in a continual "frontier situation" wherein each individual must find his own standards of conduct. The existentialists, many of whom have come close to claiming Hemingway as an associate member of that loosely organized school of thought, point to the historical, gradual decay of the belief in God. They see the necessity for individually determined conduct as springing from the dehumanization of general values through the substitution of scientism for God.[8]

Whereas the causes of ethical chaos may be accurately described in such arguments, Hemingway's reaction to the chaos has been, I think, falsely interpreted. Hemingway did not feel the need to build so much as he felt the need to perceive. He did not seek to build a unique value structure by which he judged his characters and their behavior and presumably, thereby, convincing his readers that here was a personal code worth living by. On the contrary, the chaos caused problems of perception, and as his declared purpose for attending the bullfight (*D.I.A.*, p. 2) would indicate, Hemingway felt it was his task to penetrate beyond the surface confusion

[8] For Hemingway's relation to the Existentialists, see William Barrett, *Irrational Man* (New York, 1962), pp. 44–46, 283–86; John Killinger, *Hemingway and the Dead Gods* (New York, 1965); and Richard Lehan, "Camus and Hemingway," *Wisconsin Studies in Contemporary Literature,* I (Spring–Summer, 1960), 37–48.

of modern life to find the basic values that had always remained at the heart of our Western civilization. For Hemingway, the artistic problems posed by modern culture were primary: to see, to feel, to organize, and to communicate a sense of life were preliminary to any statement about life's meaning. In this sense Hemingway's approach approximates that which is expressed by Thoreau in his *Journal*: "The man of science, who is not seeking for expression but for a fact to be expressed merely, studies nature as a dead language. I pray for such inward experience as will make nature significant" (V, 135), and "Men commonly exaggerate theme. . . . My work is writing, and I do not hesitate, though I know that no subject is too trivial for me, tried by ordinary standards; for, ye fools, the theme is nothing, the life is everything" (IX, 121).[9]

Hemingway, I am sure, viewed himself as a kind of artistic explorer into the fundamentals of living. Contrary to popular belief, what he was concerned with was not something new, but something old—How could he hope to write what was to be always true if he could not first discover what had always been true? The critic who has best perceived this basic truth about Hemingway's search for tradition is Sean O'Faolain, who in his book *The Vanishing Hero* makes his point this way (referring to several examples of description from Hemingway's first two novels):

These are not "accidental trappings of time and place." They are things that are always true, everywhere. They are generally true, not true in a particular time and place. Always Hemingway seeks for these universal things. . . . I place Hemingway, in his own modest way, in the great and now almost defunct classical tradition.[10]

It may be that one reason Hemingway so disliked T. S. Eliot, the self-proclaimed redeemer of tradition and the universal, was that he felt Eliot's adaptations of traditional materials were simply

[9] *The Journal of Henry D. Thoreau*, ed. Bradford Torrey and Francis H. Allen (Boston, 1949). Despite remarkably similar ideas regarding art and nature, Hemingway could not read Thoreau (at least up until the time of his writing *Green Hills of Africa* [see p. 15].) See also Baker, *Hemingway: The Writer as Artist*, p. 178.
[10] New York, 1957, p. 142.

tricks (by a man he looked upon as too sterile himself ever to discover directly the essentials of life)[11] used to fake a discovery of reality. Tradition, in the Hemingway sense, was not found in the past, to be borrowed from or revived, but implicit in the present. Tradition as a survival of universal truths was to be arrived at not by decoration, but by an honest and thoroughgoing realism—penetration, not emulation.

Discovery of the fundamentals of human behavior in games, of course, is very much like discovering them in surviving folk materials or myth. One major difference, however, is that since many of these activities, such as hunting, fishing, and bullfighting, have remained primarily in the province of the adult male, their roles, rituals, and rules have not atrophied through popular treatment. Games have remained vital and vigorous in contemporary experience despite the frequently outraged voice of sentiment which will always condemn many of these activities as barbaric and primitive. Perhaps they are, or perhaps it is that they underline situations and traits that are too characteristically human and real to be palatable.

I turn now to Hemingway's first extended use of the game metaphor. Whereas Jake in *The Sun Also Rises* is a study of a man's struggle to gain awareness and self-honesty, Hemingway's next protagonist, Frederic Henry, is a study of a man who struggles to gain awareness and finds it only when he finds a worthy commitment. An exploration into the problems of gamesmanship, *A Farewell to Arms* focuses on Lieutenant Henry's attempts to discover the full implications of two culturally defined activities, war and love, that he is only partly aware of as games. His problem, in short, is finding the right game to play.

In the characterization of young Frederic Henry, Hemingway again stands back from his own experience and turns it around, so that what has haunted him personally is now, in part, an object of regret and even ridicule. One might say, as commentators often have, that Hemingway never grew up. But that is precisely the point: Hemingway as reflected in his works, like so many Ameri-

[11] See *D.I.A.*, pp. 139–40.

can novelists, is always growing up, always becoming a man. His central characters are nearly always developing characters; the adults who refuse to be honest with themselves and refuse to see things as they really are—the cases of arrested self-centeredness—make up the true juveniles in Hemingway's scheme. A way of defending oneself is to attack oneself, or a part of oneself. From ages sixteen to fifty-five, from Nick Adams to Colonel Cantwell, the iron hand of Papa leads the juvenile or exhibitionist into a fiery purgatory that will not tolerate the naive, the superficial, the casual, or the careless.

The really hellish thing about Frederic Henry is that he is a perfectly normal young man, a nice guy. This very normality is the basis for an ironic treatment that is barbed both in the direction of the young protagonist and in the direction of the reader (compare the same ironic treatment of the young waiter in "A Clean Well-Lighted Place"). Like many young men, Henry is rather selfish, rather casual about the suffering of others, somewhat indifferent to the consequences of his actions, willfully a victim of his own self-indulgence and completely unconvinced of the possibility of his own death.

His main fault seems to be a general unawareness—a deadly sin within the Hemingway canon. He is, to use the Hemingway epithet applied to such people, a tourist through life and the war he has enlisted in. Frederic Henry is somewhat like a fraternity boy, a party boy, who has been motivated by an ill-defined idealism and a vague romantic urge to join the Peace Corps, only to find that he is not the star of the show. He wears his officer's uniform with a casual pride, just the right touch of nonchalance, and takes advantage of his position to attack the local contingent of nurses, as if his role required it of him. And since, fortunately, it is the Italian army that he is attached to as an ambulance officer, there is drinking and whoring even close to the front. Frederic Henry's situation at the beginning of *A Farewell to Arms* is very much like an American teen-age male's dream of overseas duty.

In his early encounters with the British nurse Catherine Barkley, Henry is the casual, uniformed boy on the make, but down deep inside he is really a decent sort. In other words, what makes Henry so sinister is his All-American-Boy lack of guile. He demonstrates an attitude and pattern of behavior that any Rotarian would privately endorse. He fully intends (he spells it out quite clearly) to take a girl, who is described in terms of a helpless, trembling Henry James bird, and crush her in his hands very casually as part of the game that every young, virile lad must play. It is a backhanded tribute to Hemingway's irony here that most readers don't seem to even blanch at the prospect. A further sinister element is Henry's rather bland and unexcited approach to the calculated betrayal of his neurotic young nurse—if he were drooling with lust, he would be more forgivable.

A Farewell to Arms is not a war story or a love story so much as it is a modern morality drama, the story of the developing consciousness of a young American within the characteristic twentieth-century context of war. *Consciousness* here has a somewhat special meaning in that the development of Henry's character is not indicated so much by changes in the quality of thinking, as it is by changes in the quality of seeing. Hemingway's technique in this novel is very similar to that employed by many contemporary poets who use imagery rather than argument or exposition: the landscape in *A Farewell to Arms* is the landscape of Frederic Henry's mind. The problem or central term of the novel's conflict defined very explicitly at the beginning of the novel in the words of the priest as that of "seeing" (p. 70). Since Henry, at the beginning of the novel, is selfish and ego-centered, his perceptions of his surroundings are vague, limited, and detached.

His youth, his egotism, his callow playacting approach to life are all indicated in his view of the war: "Well, I knew I would not be killed. Not in this war. It did not have anything to do with me. It seemed no more dangerous to me myself than war in the movies" (p. 37). The voice here of the older and wiser Henry looking back on his previous condition is tinged with both regret and wry prophecy—in effect, "Little did I know at the time what war was really like and how it would affect me." Although unpleasant details are brought home to the reader, the burden is not so much antiwar, as it is anti-Henry. These details are presented in such a callous, incidental way (using the same ironic understatement Hemingway had previously perfected in the *In Our Time* sketches of the war), that they reflect discredit on the observer: "At the start of the winter came the permanent rain and with the rain came the cholera. But it was checked and in the end only seven thousand died of it in the army" (p. 4). Particularly unpleasant in their implications regarding Henry's condition, as well as establishing the absurdity of the war itself, are those observations of the war early in the novel which bring carnage and destruction into a context reminiscent of a quaint Italian operetta: there is priest-baiting in the mess hall, a mobile house of love up the street, the Italian infantry which moves back and forth retreating from and then recapturing the same territory, and an Austrian artillery which seems to be less than serious, bombarding the town in which Henry is stationed, not "to destroy it but only a little in a military way" (p. 5).

Within the self-imposed prison of the self, Henry is unable to connect with or react to external conditions or other people very strongly, but he is able to take himself rather seriously. He reacts sullenly to the joking of his Italian roommate, Rinaldi, and is aloof or uninterested when in the company of fellow officers or his own enlisted men. He thinks that the smooth running of the business of his ambulance section depends "to a considerable extent on himself" until he finds on returning from leave that "evidently it did not matter whether I was there or not" (p. 16). His position emotionally, when concerned with others at all, is best described as apathetically defensive. When the priest asks Henry whether he loves God, he replies "No," and the priest continues: "You do not love Him at all?' . . . 'I am afraid of Him in the night sometimes.' 'You should love Him.' 'I don't love much'" (p. 72). Then the priest defines love. It is not, he says, what Henry does on leave or at the government-provided whorehouse at the front; rather, the priest says, "when you love you wish to do things for. You wish to sacrifice for. You wish to serve" (p. 72). Here the priest defines a commitment beyond oneself, beyond the unfeeling, unattached condition of Henry at this point in the novel, a commitment Henry will achieve later with the English nurse, Catherine Barkley.

But for the present, love to Henry is but a subgame, a role defined by the larger game of war. Henry takes the soldier's motto of loving them and leaving them: "I knew I did not love Catherine Barkley nor had any idea of loving her. This was a game, like bridge, in which you said things instead of playing cards. Like bridge you had to pretend you were playing for money or playing for some stakes. Nobody had mentioned what the stakes were. It was all right with me" (pp. 30–31). Henry defines himself well as a man so cut off from real participation in anything that he must pretend there are stakes, no matter what the pretension may be, so that some sort of artificial sense of life can be generated. Rinaldi, the Italian doctor who is Henry's only close friend, confirms Henry's inadvertent self-diagnoses. We are alike, he says, "You are really an Italian. All fire and smoke and nothing inside. You only pretend to be American" (p. 66). Henry is an actor in the worst sense. He is indeed, as Ferguson later calls him, "a snake with an Italian uniform" (p. 246).

The emptiness on the inside of Henry parallels the abstract, dreamlike world of the outside. Nothing at this point has meaning or makes any connection between the inside and the outside except immediate physical sensation. Following his thoughts about pretending at love as one would play bridge, Henry insists that Catherine kiss him. There follows a paragraph of several pertinent contrasts:

We kissed and she broke away suddenly. "No. Good-night, please, darling." We walked to the door and I saw her go in and down the hall. I liked to watch her move. She went on down the hall. I went on home. It was a hot night and there was a good deal going on up in the mountains. I watched the flashes on San Gabriele. (p. 32)

Catherine has recently lost to the war the man she was going to marry. She has been deeply wounded emotionally, and her sudden outbursts and changes of behavior cause Henry to think of her, rather dispassionately, as "a little crazy." It is obvious to the reader that she is extremely vulnerable and a good deal more immediately involved in the relationship than Henry is. In the paragraph cited above, her emotional withdrawal from a situation that she knows she is already committed to contrasts sharply with Henry's casual impersonality. As a matter of fact, all of Henry's perceptions, of different things, have here, typically, the same flatness: Catherine's leaving, his enjoyment of her walking, his going home, the heat of the night, and even the distant manifestations of the war are all of the same cloth. The two major aspects of life during the course of the novel, love and war, are lumped together in the same package with trivialities. It is ironic that two such conflicting human manifestations should have such equal impotency. Later, during the course of an after-dinner wine party at the officers' mess, the same flatness of perception is reinforced with the significant exception of the direct physical sensation of the wine: "The priest was good but dull. The officers were not good but dull. The King was good but dull. The wine was bad but not dull. It took the enamel off your teeth and left it on the roof of your mouth" (pp. 38–39). There is some irony in the fact that the dullness of his general opinion of things while intoxicated matches almost exactly the dullness of his perception of things while completely sober.

Lieutenant Henry's lack of awareness is again reinforced in his relationship with the priest, but is also given further dimension. It is the priest who perceives Henry's capacity for commitment, "to do things for . . . to sacrifice for . . . to serve" (p. 72). And when Henry insists that he does not love, it is the priest who insists, "You will. I know you will. Then you will be happy" (p. 72). Then, in terms that echo Hemingway's statement about intuitively recognizing the "real thing" in watching the bullfight, the priest tells him that with this kind of happiness, "You cannot know about it unless you have it" (p. 72). But this early in the game, regardless of his capacity for commitment, Henry prefers to insulate himself or immerse himself in sensations. Rather than going to the cold, clear, and dry mountains where the priest invites him to stay with his family during Henry's leave, Henry instead goes "to the smoke of cafés and nights when the room whirled and you needed to look at the wall to make it stop, nights in bed, drunk, when you knew that that was all there was . . . and the world all unreal in the dark . . . sure that this was all and all and all and not caring" (p. 13). It is the priest also who sees that even after Henry is wounded, the reality of the war has not yet penetrated his consciousness. Henry is wounded, but for him it is some sort of impersonal accident (at least he thinks of it as such)—just something that has happened to him. "Still even wounded," the priest says on his visit to the field hospital, "you do not see it. I can tell" (p. 70).

What Henry apparently does not see is that war is a destroyer of love through its fundamental irrational violence, and war is a destroyer of the individual through its obliteration of the individual's dignity and importance. The priest calls attention to the former in trying to get Henry to see what love is as compared with the lust that accompanies war (Rinaldi calls the girls at the Villa Rossi "war comrades," they have become so familiar), and the priest calls attention to the latter by pointing to the dignity of the individual found in his home province of the Abruzzi—"it is understood that a man may love God. It is not a dirty joke" (p. 71). The point is that at the beginning of the novel Henry's even perfunctory commitment to the war has robbed him of both his capacity for love and his capacity to act and react as an individual—but he is unaware of this. He has not perceived that as a game war is absurd, for what rules there are have nothing to do with winning or losing, as the novel constantly points out, and are constantly contradictory and self-defeating. Until the incident at the bridge, Henry goes on trying to make war meaningful, as his attempts, within the chaos and absurdities of the retreat, to follow "orders" make clear.

War is a particularly good controlling metaphor for all those things that we have come to associate with "mass man"—the bureaucracy, the indifference, the brainwashing and propaganda, the tyranny of an overgroup devoted to the "abstract good" (and sanctified by that devotion)—in short, all those things that are accepted as normal in wartime (particularly in the modern mechanized warfare that commenced with World War I). All these are the very things that are the substance of the nightmare societies pictured, for example, in Orwell's *1984*, in Huxley's *Brave New World*, or perhaps even more to the present point, in Kafka's *The Castle*. It is ironic that it is so difficult for us or for Henry to perceive this effect: the worst thing about war, even more terrible than the physical suffering, because it is more subtle and insidious, is that the individual (and along with the individual, morality and responsibility) is lost and that the loss serves little purpose except to feed irrationality. All who have been in the army of any country know that the first abiding principle of service is the loss of individual volition, a literal beating down of identity, a submersion into the general, and an unquestioning submission to the impersonality of "orders."

These are the elements that surround Henry, yet because he is an officer and is with a support unit, they are not quite so obvious to him or to the reader. Henry is not unconscious of some of the inconsistencies of the war "game" at the beginning of the novel, but their emotional impact on him is negligible. He tends to wonder a good deal about what is going on and what will happen in the war, and it is interesting to see how often his speculations are made in terms of individuals—Napoleon, or Napoleon contrasted with Vittorio Emmanuele (pp. 36, 118)—or in terms of armies or parts of armies considered as individuals with individual traits and weaknesses. But throughout the part of the novel concerned with the war, we can observe the growing frustration of an individual attempting to assess the incomprehensibility of madness acted out on a mass scale, a madness so overwhelming in its scope that it is beyond the grasp of the individual caught up in the web: "Perhaps wars weren't won any more. Maybe they went on forever" (p. 118). When Henry is in the hospital, he finds that the only meaningful reading is the baseball scores; the other game has no score. In a passage invariably quoted from the novel, Henry rejects the jargon of war which is used to anesthetize the individual to the "sacrifices [which] were like the stockyards at Chicago if nothing was done with the meat except to bury it" (p. 185). Like baseball scores, "finally only the names of places had dignity" (p. 185).

But all these reactions of frustration reflect the turmoil of an individual still committed to the proposition that there is meaning somewhere in the pattern, although it may be unavailable to him. Before the attack in which the enemy shelling is to wound Henry and take him away from the front for several months, he crouches in a bunker with his ambulance drivers waiting for the time that they will be needed. The drivers talk about the coming attack. One notes that there aren't enough troops for a real attack; another suggests that "It is probably to draw attention from where the real attack will be" (p. 48). Do the men who are going to participate in this pretense know they are going to be bait—simply objects, pawns to be manipulated in someone else's game? "Of course they don't," another replies; "They wouldn't attack if they did" (p. 48). Then the drivers turn to a discussion of various troops that have refused to attack, including the story of a "big smart tall boy" who is allured by the glamour of the crack troops, the granatieri, enough to join up to show off to the girls and to associate with the carabinieri (MP's), who later shoot him for not attacking when he is ordered to. Not only is he shot, but his family is deprived of their civil rights and the protection of the law—"Anybody can take their property" (p. 49). At this point one of the drivers tells Henry that he should not let them talk this way. But Henry does not mind as long as they "drive the cars and behave" (p. 49). His attitude of commitment to the absurdity contrasts sharply with the awareness of the ambulance driver Passini in the exchange that follows.

"I believe we should get the war over," I said. "It would not finish it if one side stopped fighting. It would only be worse if we stopped fighting."
"It could not be worse," Passini said respectfully. "There is nothing worse than war."
"Defeat is worse."
"I do not believe it," Passini said still respectfully. "What is defeat? You go home." (pp. 49–50)

When Henry continues to insist that being conquered is worse, Passini makes the same charge indirectly that the priest is to make later in the hospital: "There is nothing as bad as war. We in the auto-ambulance cannot even realize at all how bad it is. When people realize how bad it is they cannot do anything to stop it because they go crazy. There are some people who never realize" (p. 50). Many, including Catherine and later Rinaldi, "go crazy," but Lieutenant Henry is not to find this same depth of emotional realization of the war until he becomes personally involved in the absurdity of the bridge.

The story of Lieutenant Henry's discovery begins with his being hit by fragments of a trench mortar shell. Before that, he was a "nice boy," as Catherine calls him, who argued that "defeat is worse" than war and who thought of the war as no more dangerous to himself "than war in the movies." But when he is hit, he finds that he is really in the war after all: "I tried to breathe but my breath would not come and I felt myself rush bodily out of myself and out and out and out and all the time bodily in the wind. I went out swiftly, all of myself, and I knew I was dead and that it had all been a mistake to think you just died" (p. 54).[12] He is not dead, but any doubt that may remain about how close death has come to him is erased when he turns to the man next to him in the bunker. When Henry touches him, he screams and then biting his arm, the man pleads deliriously for the pain to stop, until he dies. Reaching down to examine himself, Henry puts his hand on his knee: "My knee wasn't there. My hand went in and my knee was down on my shin" (p. 55). The terror and shock and suffering are relentlessly conveyed by the realism of the detail. The effect on Lieutenant Henry's over-all attitude is never directly stated. It is, if stated at all, best phrased by Colonel Cantwell in another novel, *Across the River and into the Trees*, who suffered the same kind of wound under similar circumstances in the same war: "Finally he did get hit properly and for good. No one of his other wounds had ever done to him what the first big one did. I suppose it is just the loss of the immortality, he thought. Well, in a way, that is quite a lot to lose" (p. 33). It may be, therefore, that Lieutenant Henry has lost what Colonel Cantwell has called his "immortality." He has volunteered

[12] The stylistic technique here demonstrates an interesting attempt to reproduce the emotional impact of an experience. The passage is similar to the much-criticized intercourse passages in *For Whom the Bell Tolls* where rhythm and repetition of carefully selected words are used to reproduce the impression of a very difficult to describe emotional state.

to serve in a war without really knowing the stakes, the price he may be called on to pay. Commitment is morally less significant without a true sense of the risk involved; one is not really putting anything on the line if he thinks he is never going to lose. Nor is he really "alive" without risking something. Like so many young men, Henry is unaware because he is wrapped up in himself—bored. And the young are bored when everything comes too easily; "you don't appreciate," the older generation cries, and we never do until we become losers. It is interesting to see that the wounding draws Henry into a game that he has been playing with one hand tied behind his back, whereas Nick Adams' big wound takes him out of the game: "Rinaldi. . . . You and me we've made a separate peace." The unnamed protagonist of "In Another Country" is another Hemingway character in the same war who is taken out: "We only knew then that there was always the war, but that we were not going to it any more" (*1st 49*, pp. 237, 367). But Henry has to go back, for he has a great deal more to learn about the war game before he is through with it. For Nick and the other protagonist, withdrawal is an accident; for Henry, it must involve a decision.

There are several ironic contrasts implicit in the story of Henry's wounding that are of some help in assessing its impact. Henry and his men are noncombatants who are waiting to perform an act of mercy in carrying the wounded to medical help. Instead of this, Henry ends up being carried in an ambulance himself, suffering the discomforts (the pain, the bumps, the slowness, and the hemorrhage of the man in the stretcher above him) of one of the men Henry would have perfunctorily transported if not himself wounded. The shells coming in from the Austrians are indiscriminate; they do not seek out the infantryman and leave the ambulance driver unharmed (just as when someone shells a city, he does not neglect the women and children and select only the soldiers or arms factories to destroy—a stupidity, as Passini would term it, which only makes sense in a pattern of stupidity). Henry is seriously wounded, not in the process of attacking, but in the process of eating. And of course, it is Passini, who so hates war, who is killed. These ironies may raise certain questions in Henry, at some level of consciousness, just as they most certainly do in the mind of the reader: What kind of game is this? Who understands the rules and the objectives that demand such a risk and such a price? Fittingly, Henry's first step to full awareness comes with the shock of physical sensation. He has become personally involved on an indisputable level of consciousness, like it or not. The next level involves a fuller realization of what war can do to others.

Henry's period of convalescence at the American hospital in Milan is primarily the story of his increasing attachment to Catherine Barkley. His connection with the war is a meager one, established through the newspapers and one or two conversations with other soldiers. At his distance from it, the war seems to take on less clarity than ever. The Italians are losing tremendous numbers of men in their offensive, and even if they go on to capture Monte San Gabriele, there are "plenty of mountains beyond for the Austrians" (p. 118). He meets a British major on somebody's staff who declares that "it was all balls." At headquarters "they thought only in divisions and man-power. They all squabbled about divisions and only killed them when they got them" (p. 134). Again, Henry encounters the contrast of the mass with the lost individual. As an individual having been touched personally by the war, Henry is now able to stand back in an ironically impersonal perspective and get a dim glimpse of the entire meat grinder. Finally it gets to the point, as I said before, that the baseball news is all Henry can read, even though he does not have the slightest interest in baseball (p. 136).

One other indicator of Henry's growing disillusionment during his stay at the hospital is the satirical treatment of Ettore, the "legitimate hero" who finds the war game very satisfying. Henry runs into Ettore and several other acquaintances at a bar while killing time away from the hospital waiting for Catherine. Ettore responds to the baiting of his companions, including Henry, who ask him all the right questions: "How many [medals] have you got, Ettore?" "How many times have you been wounded, Ettore?" "Where were you wounded, Ettore?" These are questions that probably have been asked and answered a dozen times before, as we can induce from Catherine's label of him as a bore, and from Hemingway's wonderful touch of including Ettore's name at the end of almost every question that leads him on, to provide just the right tone of mockery, a mockery unperceived by Ettore but available to the reader.

Ettore seriously recites his entire repertoire of accomplishments yet one more time with continuing and undiminished enthusiasm. He's got five medals and, Oh boy, aren't they great for making the girls think you're fine. But wound stripes are better: "Believe me, boy, when you get three you've got something" (p. 121); he goes on to show his scars and describe the circumstances in detail. He points out that the real pros touch their stars, as he does, whenever anybody mentions getting killed. And when a friend, in leaving, says "Keep out of trouble," Ettore of course takes it literally and seriously announces his dedication to his profession through clean living (pp. 122–23). A further hint of irony is found in the almost perfectly complementary situation of another man in the group, an opera singer, who is so bad, despite his unbounded enthusiasm for his own singing, that everywhere he sings audiences throw things at him. Then too, Ettore provides the perfect foil to Henry's lack of engagement—overenthusiasm. Ettore has decided to play the wrong game well, and his very enthusiasm for it condemns war as ludicrous, particularly so with the hint of Babbitt that Hemingway inserts into the boy's inflection. Such a pressing to full enthusiasm and use of dialect are old satiric devices.

Thus, although the passage concerning Ettore may be on the surface only a passage of humorous banter, the implications of the banter are grim in regard to the subject at hand, war and Henry's attitude toward it, and in mulling over Ettore's enthusiasm, the reader may well be reminded of the more harsh satirical treatment by Hemingway of similar kinds of enthusiasm. A good example is found in one of the sketches in *In Our Time* where the unidentified speaker sets up "an absolutely perfect obstacle" that was so "absolutely topping" that whenever the enemy tried to get over it, "we potted them from forty yards" and "we were frightfully put out when we heard the flank had gone, and we had to fall back" (*1st 49*, p. 211).

Of much more serious impact on Lieutenant Henry's feelings toward the war are the dramatic changes he finds in his friends following the summer offensive. After he has returned to the front, he checks in with his commanding officer, the major, who now looks "older and drier" (p. 164). He is, as the priest comments later, now "gentle." The theme of "how bad it is" which had been taken up by Passini and the priest at the time of Henry's wounding is now taken up again upon Henry's return, this time by the major—an unexpected certification of the same sentiments previously expressed by the socialist driver and the priest. Just how bad it is comes through gradually to Henry when the major tells him that he is lucky that he got hit when he did and (an even more telling blow) when he states that "if I was away I do not believe I would come back" (p. 165).

More shattering still is Henry's reunion with his friend Rinaldi. Rinaldi is one of several Hemingway characters who has often been badly treated by Hemingway critics. He is usually taken at face value, accepted on the basis of what he says about himself—a dangerous practice in criticism, as in life. A hard professional, flippant and cynical, he speaks of himself (and Henry) as having "nothing inside" (p. 66). But as usual in Hemingway, the negative emotions are the most apparent. What we tend to see most directly is Rinaldi's cynicism about himself and his life, the anger, the depression, and the frustration that come from the overwork of a surgeon in a bloody war. Like the best bullfighters, however, Rinaldi combines his cynicism with a tremendous devoutness, a devoutness seen only obliquely. He is tough, but he is also sensitive; throughout the initial scenes with Henry, he shows a great affection for him. In what happens to Rinaldi during the summer, there is good evidence, to my mind, for the fact that here is a man who cares a great deal about people in general.

Driven beyond physical endurance by the enormous demands put on him by the offensive, he has also been driven to the wall emotionally. The picture of Rinaldi as Henry finds him on his return is not just that of a man almost shattered from exposure to the pain of others. He cannot think, for to think means to feel: "No, by God, I don't think; I operate" (p. 167). If he can turn himself into a mechanical man, keep busy, work all the time, perhaps he will not have time to feel. But now the offensive is over: "I don't operate now and I feel like hell. This is a terrible war, baby. You believe me when I say it" (p. 167). If this means that Rinaldi is simply a one-dimensional man, simply a cynical surgeon, simply a foil for Henry and his devotion to Catherine, it would not be that war is so terrible; it would not be that everything that was so funny, so full of life before the summer is now flat and dead. No man destroys himself with such vigor as Rinaldi is seen destroying himself here just because he has run out of work, unless that work has taken on more than just professional dimensions. For a surgeon such as Rinaldi, the incessant burden of life and death that the war has forced upon him has more impact than just that on his professional pride. Rinaldi's emotional destruction is the product of an emotional investment, never stated, but implicit in his behavior toward Henry and in his present wild irrationality. Neither is he a failure. He does not demonstrate to Henry the uselessness of a commitment, the failure of "the ideal of service," but rather the failure of war to allow love to exist except at a terrible price.[13]

Drink, he says to Henry, "Nothing is worse for you. . . . Self-destruction day by day. . . . It ruins the stomach and makes the hand shake. Just the thing for a surgeon" (p. 172). Then turning to the priest, trying to make the mess "like the old days," he cannot bait him as before. He can only call out wildly, "To hell with you, priest!" (p. 173). Paranoically, Rinaldi suspects everyone is trying to get rid of him. He also suspects that he has syphilis, although the major doubts it.

"The snake of reason" acts more like a wounded deer. Rinaldi has been pushed to the edge, and we might hypothesize from the pain that his change has caused us that the effect on Lieutenant Henry is a powerful one indeed.

[13] See James F. Light, "The Religion of Death in *A Farewell to Arms,*" in Baker, ed., *Ernest Hemingway: Critiques of Four Major Novels*, p. 39.

Henry's evening is not over, for following his exposure to the changes made in the major and Rinaldi, he encounters one more changed friend. Because of his calling, the priest, like Rinaldi, has made an increasingly heavy investment of emotion in the war. Indicative of this investment is a decrease in his sense of self. The baiting by the men at the mess used to make him blush, but having possibly been called on to give the last rites to numberless young men in their last agony, "the baiting did not touch him now" (p. 173). Although he prays that something will happen to stop the war, he does not believe in victory any more. He sees that "many people have realized the war this summer" and "officers whom I thought could never realize it realize it now" (p. 178). If everyone could see it, perhaps both sides would just stop. In such a statement we see the desperate hope of a tired and depressed young man. Henry adds to the priest's discouragement by suggesting that it is only in defeat that we realize war, that we can become Christian, not technically, but only "like Our Lord" (p. 178). Since the Austrians have won by beating back the advance, they will not stop fighting. What is there to hope for? "What do you believe in?" the priest asks Henry. "In sleep," he replies. There has been a change in Henry's thinking somewhere along the way. No longer does he argue that victory is necessary, fighting is necessary, or that defeat is worse than war. Henry no longer believes in victory or defeat, and as for victory, it may be worse (p. 179). So that by the end of this evening, this depressing evening, it may be that when Henry says "sleep," he means more than that he is just tired.

It may mean that he sees at last that in the war game everyone loses and that the goal he has been committed to is really as empty as the rhetoric that describes it: that everything in war was in vain. The next day, while Henry is riding with Gino, the patriot, it becomes apparent to the reader that he has come a long way since the beginning of the novel. It may be that he has always been embarrassed by the kind of language that Gino uses, but his mental declaration is formulated with a depth of bitterness and perception inconsistent with the Henry we observed before his wounding: "the things that were glorious had no glory and the sacrifices were like the stockyards at Chicago if nothing was done with the meat except to bury it" (p. 185).

With neither mind nor heart any longer even distantly devoted to the process of war or to victory as the lesser of two evils, it is only Lieutenant Henry's physical presence on the scene that must be accounted for. Complete withdrawal cannot be accomplished, however, until the other party to the contract, the Italian army, in some way invalidates the contract Henry is bound to whether it is meaningful to him any longer or not. There is no doubt that without the incident at the bridge or one like it, Henry would have continued to serve despite his disillusionment until the end of the war or until he was killed. We await the coup de grace.

The battle police at the bridge operate very well as symbols of the enforcement of non-meaning. They stand for everything that Henry has come to realize is false and irrational about the war. The main quality in the passage that stands out about these carabinieri is their complete, self-confident ignorance: they have no idea whatsoever of what it means to be under fire. Henry notes on two separate occasions that "the questioners had that beautiful detachment and devotion to stern justice of men dealing in death without being in any danger of it" (pp. 224–25). Here, in spades, is the ultimate absurdity of commitment to the irrational that Henry has been part of. With growing awareness, however, he perceives their stubborn blindness: "They were all young men and they were saving their country" (p. 224). In their pursuit of the cliché, they shoot everyone they question, for the questions are not really requests for information, but the recitation of the litany of war.[14]

The absurdity of the game that Henry has pledged himself to is revealed in the contrast brought out here between the rules, rituals,

[14] There is much irony in the parallel of Henry's previous shooting of the deserting sergeant and also in the anxious desire of the driver, Bonello, to "finish off" the sergeant, inasmuch as Bonello himself later deserts to the enemy (the last of the series of desertions is, of course, Henry's own). Further irony is gained when we see how closely Henry's irritation at the lack of defenses by the Italians matches the later patriotic enthusiasm of the carabinieri at the bridge. Following Henry's outburst against the lack of rearguard action, the driver Aymo is killed by a trigger-happy Italian rear guard. The series of senseless shootings begins with Henry's shooting of the sergeant, moves to Aymo's

rhetoric, and values of the pretense, and the reality which at its worst can involve panic, cowardice, brutality, suffering, destruction, and death. All the human elements, the pity and the terror of the *individual*, are lost on these minds which find war glorious and filled with purpose. The basis of game, as we have defined it, is its framework of rationality; the very basis of war as seen here is its irrationality. While the Austrians and Germans roam the countryside unopposed, the Italians have applied the most immediate practical solution: they have decided to shoot all of their own officers.

These elements of reality and unreality are nowhere better contrasted than in the interview (observed by Henry) between the battle police and the "fat gray-haired little lieutenant-colonel" who is taken out of the retreating column for "questioning":

"It is you and such as you that have let the barbarians onto the sacred soil of the fatherland," [said the battle police].
"I beg your pardon," said the lieutenant-colonel.
"It is because of treachery such as yours that we have lost the fruits of victory."
"Have you ever been in a retreat?" the lieutenant-colonel asked.
"Italy should never retreat." . . .
"If you are going to shoot me," the lieutenant-colonel said, "please shoot me at once without further questioning. The questioning is stupid." (pp. 223–24)

Reason is lost. This is the country of the slogan. Unlike Henry, the colonel has no choice except to try to give his death what dignity he can. Not only is a human life destroyed for no good reason, but a valuable professional has been stupidly thrown away. For Henry, younger and more objective in his position, an alternative to a stupid death does present itself, and he takes it, dashing down to the water to escape. Turning from the state of acceptance and then disillusioned compliance, he begins, from this moment, to move actively toward a game worth playing.

death and the shooting of the lieutenant colonel at the bridge, and ends with the threatened shooting of Henry himself. Both of these ironic patterns, with an accelerating rhythm of absurdity, reach their climax in Henry's decision to abandon his commitment to the war.

LEARNING
TO PLAY THE GAME WELL

◆ ◆ ◆   THERE ARE THREE movements that dominate *A Farewell to Arms*. The first is the movement away from the commitment to war which I have just discussed. The other two are combined in the love story of Catherine and Henry. In Henry's movement toward a full commitment to Catherine, there is the accompanying growth of what has been called the "sense of doom." This constant foreshadowing of misfortune or death that accompanies Henry's growth in his ability to love can be looked at in two ways.

First, this growing sense of doom can be considered another manifestation of Hemingway's anti-sentimentality. *A Farewell to Arms* is an attempt by Hemingway to write a "true" love story, one in which the protagonist, Frederic Henry, progresses from a false sense of love as a "courtship game" to a true sense of love as "total involvement." That is, Henry enters into the "game" as Hemingway conceives of it, involving genuine risk; Henry begins by playing at love and ends by participating in it.

Contrary to its treatment in *A Farewell to Arms*, love in sentimental fiction is usually considered the sovereign method for gaining happiness, a happiness generally treated as eternal and indestructible. Trouble, conflict, and risk accompany the attainment of the love object, but seldom accompany securing it, maintaining it, or facing its reality. In other words, emotional benefits are received, but the price is seldom paid. The price of commitment in reality, as Hemingway pointedly demonstrates in *A Farewell to Arms*, is loss and the fear of loss: "If two people love each other there can be no happy end to it" (*D.I.A.*, p. 122).

The second way of regarding this sense of doom is to regard it as akin to the necessary movement toward disaster which is one of the few ingredients that is agreed upon as essential to tragedy by most definers of the term. A fine description of this movement is given by Jean Anouilh in his preface to his version of *Antigone*:

That's what's so handy about tragedy—you give it a little push so it'll start rolling—nothing: a quick look at a girl passing in the street who raises her arms, a yearning for honor one fine morning, when you wake up, as though it were something to eat, one question too many in the evening—that's all. After that, you just leave it alone. You're calm. It's been punctiliously oiled from the start.[1]

As slight as the gestures described by Anouilh may be, they are all gestures leading to a firm commitment. Like a finger or an eyebrow raised at an auction, a contract has been signed, a risk taken. So it is with Frederic Henry the first day he sees Catherine in his hospital room in Milan:

I heard some one coming down the hallway. I looked toward the door. It was Catherine Barkley.

She came in the room and over to the bed.

"Hello, darling," she said. She looked fresh and young and very beautiful. I thought I had never seen any one so beautiful.

"Hello," I said. When I saw her I was in love with her. (p. 91)

Henry has just signed a contract to a commitment that will eventually overcome every other consideration in his life. When Catherine dies at the end of the novel, the two strands of emotion, love and threat of loss, have grown from the very ordinary and almost trivial beginning we have just witnessed to a climax wherein complete emotional commitment is achieved only to be followed by a disaster equally complete.

But before tracing Hemingway's achievement in developing these two strands of emotion to see how he has endowed them

[1] As quoted in and translated by Oscar Mandel, *A Definition of Tragedy* (New York, 1961), p. 40.

with so much potency, I shall probe further into the necessity of the disaster which ends this novel. In examining the outcome of Hemingway's emotional buildup, we may very well ask if there is any necessity at all reflected in Catherine's death. Is not her death simply a biological accident? Surely, we ask, this death cannot be implicit in the love itself—might not Catherine just as well have continued to live, if the author so chose to have her live? But I think we miss Hemingway's point if we ask these questions. The concept of tragedy that Hemingway begins to evolve in fiction with this novel does not involve a matter merely of a flaw in character, nor does his concept of tragedy revolve around a particular set of circumstances related in any direct sense to cause and effect (nor is this Anouilh's point either). Necessity, according to Hemingway, is born of life itself; it is inherent in the human condition. Life must end in death, and all commitment must end in loss. These two ideas are the essence of Hemingway's tragic vision. Anyone, suggests Hemingway, who has the courage honestly to commit himself will become a loser: "you will find no man who is a man who will not bear some marks of past misfortune" (*D.I.A.*, p. 104). The equation is proportionate: the more heroic or courageous the man, the more sizable and necessary is the disaster which will eventually overtake him.

He points out further on the same page in *Death in the Afternoon* that "there is no remedy for anything in life. Death is a sovereign remedy for all misfortunes." That is to say, life or the natural circumstances of living exist in constant opposition to "game," man's emotional structures and goals. There can be no happy end to love because in some way or another life *must* break through what man has built in order to destroy it—if not through death, then through separation, loss of affection, or physical degeneration. There are a hundred thousand ways that love can be lost, and no man can build a wall high enough to keep them all out. Knowing this, should a man play the game anyway? Should he run his course, glancing back over his shoulder, committing himself to an all-out effort, realizing all the while that he can never win?

Catherine need not die as any logical consequence of circumstances. But love must die. The game is logical, man-imposed, man-created; the circumstances of life are not. By having Catherine die, Hemingway has simply created a more unified way of dealing with the truth that must come about in one way or another and of bringing both axioms, regarding life and commitment, to bear on Henry's commitment at the same time:

Now Catherine would die. That was what you did. You died. You did not know what it was about. You never had time to learn. They threw you in and told you the rules and the first time they caught you off base they killed you. Or they killed you gratuitously . . . But they killed you in the end. You could count on that. Stay around and they would kill you. (p. 327)

The game of life, the "outer game" where knowing the rules does not matter, is not the Hemingway game. In the game of life you lose by playing, and the harder you play, the more you lose. This larger game wherein man is just a pawn in a pattern outside his own control is the biological trap that Henry speaks of when Catherine tells him she is with child (p. 139), the same trap that the ants find themselves in in the "ant allegory" (pp. 327–28) which follows the passage quoted above. What is most natural to this world is disaster, death. The center of Hemingway's concept of tragedy is the conflict between the game man creates for himself with his own will (a context that is meaningful for man but always temporary) and the game man is forced to play wherein his will counts for nothing, a context of non-meaning which permanently threatens destruction. (This continuing division throughout much of Hemingway's work between physical areas defined as meaning or non-meaning has a kinship to the classical division between the order expressed by the civilization of the walled city, and the chaos expressed by the barbarian in the surrounding wilderness— an interesting connection in light of the many other classical elements found in Hemingway's work. The central principle of Hemingway's "walled city" is also law—man created game.)

One of the main elements in *A Farewell to Arms*, fittingly designed to carry the sense of doom, the forecast of necessary disaster, is Hemingway's symbolic use of rain. And as many critics have noted (particularly Carlos Baker),[2] the opposing symbol, standing for what I have called "created game," is that of "home." The rain is a particularly well-chosen symbol for what Hemingway had in mind, for it is an atmospheric gloom that is both natural and unavoidable. "Home," on the other hand, must be extremely temporary and makeshift for these two lovers, Catherine and Henry; it is a matter of creating an atmosphere of genuine love in a shabby hotel room, a hospital room, or a room rented in someone else's house. Materially a very flimsy thing, this man-created atmosphere of home is in *every* case, whether in Italy or Switzerland, opposed by the oppressive inevitability of the rain. Those (like Ray B. West, Jr.) who see the temporariness of home here as signifying the "lost generation" are cutting this symbol much too short. Home is temporary because all human happiness is temporary, a flimsy island that must sooner or later be washed away with the tide. Nature must win, and the use of rain as a symbol of this necessity is given special poignancy in the fear of the rain that is expressed by Catherine early in the novel:

". . . I'm afraid of the rain."
"Why?" I was sleepy. Outside the rain was falling steadily.
"I don't know, darling. I've always been afraid of the rain."
"I like it."
"I like to walk in it. *But it's very hard on loving.*" [Italics mine.] . . .
"You're not really afraid of the rain are you?"
"Not when I'm with you." (pp. 125–26)

Henry asks her several times why she is afraid of it, and finally she gives in and tells him that it is because sometimes she sees herself dead in it and sometimes she sees him dead in it. The basic tragic conflict of the novel is nicely summarized in the desperation of her concluding cry:

"It's all nonsense. It's only nonsense. I'm not afraid of the rain. I'm not afraid of the rain. Oh, oh, God, I wish I wasn't." She was crying. I comforted her and she stopped crying. But outside it kept on raining. (p. 126)

[2] See Baker's *Hemingway: The Writer as Artist*, pp. 101–16.

It continues to rain "outside" on each occasion that they establish a home together until Catherine dies and Henry leaves the hospital and walks to the hotel, alone, in the rain.

In *A Farewell to Arms* there is not only the antagonistic non-meaning of nature that we have just seen expressed in the omnipresent rain, but there is also a non-meaning, an irrational threat, expressed through man. Man is, of course, part of nature, despite his efforts to separate himself from its necessity. Man can become a force aligned with irrationality if he is unaware. The aware man can, with courage, create a temporary, small island of meaning by committing himself to a worthy ideal which brings with it a pattern of behavior that is in itself meaningful. The non-meaning of nature, its lack of relevance to man's purpose is, in a sense, simply given; it is the non-meaning created by man himself that often produces the greatest ironies in Hemingway's fiction, perhaps because man need not be unaware, because something could be done. Since lack of awareness is often a matter of being blinded by one's own ego, the most unpleasant people in Hemingway's fiction are the selfish, the petty, and the egotistical.

Miss Van Campen, the head nurse of the American hospital, is a fairly good example of the unaware character who makes more than just a token appearance. Significantly, she feels that her present duties are really beneath her. (In both *Across the River and into the Trees* and *A Moveable Feast* ambition is categorized specifically as a cardinal sin, as it would be in Hemingway's scheme, since it is concerned with glorification of the self rather than performance of one's job as honestly and courageously as possible.) Miss Van Campen's ambition is particularly damning in her profession, and it leads eventually to the stupidity of her charge that Henry has inflicted jaundice on himself to escape going back to the front (p. 144). With no empathy and with the self-righteousness of her kind, she vindictively has Henry's leave cancelled. She is, of course—very much like the more impersonal irrationalities of the war and the natural world—an enemy of home, and remains a constant menace to Henry and Catherine's happiness at the hospital. Significant, too, and typical is her devotion to appearances rather than reality. She refuses to let Henry and Catherine go out together when he is able to discard his crutches, "because it was unseemly for a nurse to be seen unchaperoned with a patient who did not look as though he needed attendance" (pp. 117–18).

Other unaware characters who appear only briefly are Ettore, the hero; the first incompetent doctor at the hospital; the battle police; and toward the end of the novel, the nurses who briefly appear in the corridor while Henry is waiting for Catherine to be operated on. These two nurses and their conversation fit into a pattern that seems to occur in all Hemingway's major novels, a pattern I shall discuss in a later chapter. Here, the occasion is an extremely grim one. Catherine is at the height of her suffering, and Henry has come to suspect that she may really die. She is being taken into the operating room to have a Caesarean done when two nurses appear, hurrying toward the entrance to the gallery: "'It's a Caesarean,' one said. 'They're going to do a Caesarean.' The other one laughed, 'We're just in time. Aren't we lucky?' They went in the door that led to the gallery" (p. 324). Completely unaware of Henry and Henry's justifiable anxiety (the individual human condition) about Catherine or of Catherine's, the patient's, condition, they view the coming operation only in their own terms, as something different and exciting, as something they might enjoy. "Aren't we lucky" is the full expression of their complete self-absorption.

Even though this is a brief interlude, it comes at an extremely climactic moment and is a good example of the irony that Hemingway continually finds between the unawareness of those who are self-involved and the reality of the situation as perceived by the reader. The irony does not come against something the reader knows about Henry's condition in itself, so much as it does against the reader's consciousness of Henry's *awareness* of Catherine's condition and the full weight of his commitment to her at this time.

It should be noted that although the nurses and the carabinieri are not sentimental per se, the blindness that the unaware display is the same blindness that lies at the heart of sentimentality. Both groups are exploiting an emotion connected with their roles—the personally elevating expressions of love of country and love of profession. They both ignore the real conditions of others that are implicit in the two roles properly performed. They create a view of reality that fits their personal needs. As such, they and other characters like them can be counted as part of the general pattern of Hemingway's anti-sentimentality.

Frederic Henry begins, particularly in his relation to women and love, from a completely self-centered position. On his leave early in the novel, Henry goes to the city and immerses himself completely in self-satisfaction. Later, when he meets Catherine, he looks upon her simply as an objective in a game of chess, another avenue to self-satisfaction. As I have pointed out, initially he cares very little for her emotional well-being or the fact that she has been driven emotionally off balance by her previous misfortunes. After Henry's wounding, he still does not love. The prescription for love offered by the priest (in terms of Christian love) remains unapprehended by him. When Catherine shows up at the American hospital in Milan, he sees her differently through this demonstration of devotion to him, and feels that he loves her. But it remains for Catherine to teach Henry what love really means; the period in the hospital becomes a period of indoctrination.

Catherine begins by giving herself physically to Henry:

Catherine sat in a chair by the bed. The door was open into the hall. The wildness was gone and I felt finer than I had ever felt.
She asked, "Now do you believe I love you?"
"Oh, you're lovely," I said. "You've got to stay. They can't send you away. I'm crazy in love with you." (p. 92)

Catherine's emphasis here is on the love given in the act; Henry's emphasis is on the pleasure received and a concern for the continuation of it. For Hemingway, sex is an essential ingredient in the love between man and woman, and the continuation of Catherine and Henry's sexual relationship throughout the summer is the medium by which true regard for the other person is reached. Sex, too, is essentially an anti-sentimental ingredient of love. A full and honest giving and receiving of pleasure from the other partner contradicts those self-directed emotions of longing and self-pity which are central to love as sentimentality.

The sterility and self-absorption of love without sex are of course eminently demonstrated in the emotional trap that Jake Barnes finds himself in; the failure of love and marriage without sex is graphically illustrated in the short story, "Mr. and Mrs. Elliot." Mr. Elliot, as one would suppose, is a poet and has kept himself "straight" for Mrs. Elliot. They "try to have a baby" every now and then, but the experience is very unsatisfactory, so that Mr. Elliot turns more to his poetry and Mrs. Elliot turns to a girl friend whom she sleeps with and has many a good cry with. The last line (one of Hemingway's more moderately ironic "wows" as he calls them) becomes a statement of complete disaster and the triumph of perversion: "Elliot drank white wine and Mrs. Elliot and the girl friend made conversation and they were all quite happy" (*1st 49*, p. 262).

We can see here to some extent what it is that Hemingway means in his famous statement about morality in *Death in the Afternoon*: "what is moral is what you feel good after and what is immoral is what you feel bad after . . ." (p. 4). Mr. and Mrs. Elliot could not be more conventionally moral. Both were presumably virgins before marriage; both use sex not as a way of giving or receiving pleasure, but as in the Victorian tradition, purely for creating children. Yet their relationship could not be more immoral, as far as Hemingway is concerned.

During the summer Catherine and Henry learn to become more emotionally and mentally at one while they become physically at one with each other. The sharing of other experiences has more poignancy and meaning because of the sharing of sex. They both become more acutely aware of sights and sounds: "She came in looking fresh and lovely and sat on the bed and the sun rose while I had the thermometer in my mouth and we smelled the dew on the roofs and then the coffee of the men at the gun on the next roof" (p. 102). Henry finds himself also more able to relate to other people with affection. In the small and easily overlooked scene with the maker of silhouettes (p. 135), a genuine wave of affection passes between Henry and the artist, who refuses to take payment for the silhouettes and says to Henry's offer of money, "No. I did them for a pleasure. Give them to your girl." (Quite a bit is made of this matter of "please" or "for your pleasure" in several places in Hemingway's writing, particularly in *Across the River and into the Trees*, where these verbal forms become equivalent to the general ability to love and to consider others.)

Catherine risks a good deal in continuing to come to Henry's bed every night. At the same time, Henry's initial physical excitement passes into a more general affection for Catherine. He finds that "if we let our hands touch, just the side of my hand touching hers, we were excited" (p. 112). Henry finds himself going along the hall with her on her rounds on his crutches and carrying the basins for her. Being together and sharing experiences becomes meaningful beyond the sharing of the sexual experience itself, and yet sex remains the central core, the source of energy: "It was lovely in the nights and if we could only touch each other we were happy" (p. 114). Catherine, when Henry worries about getting married, shows him how true marriage is a sharing of identities, so that as far as she is concerned, "There isn't any me. I'm you. Don't make up a separate me" (p. 115). It is interesting to see that it is Henry, not Catherine, who wants to be "really married," not just to make a possible child legitimate, but because he is afraid that he might lose her: "But you won't ever leave me for some one else" (p. 116). And when she answers that he needn't worry about that, he replies, "I don't. But I love you so much and you did love some one else before" (p. 116).

Just before Henry must return to the front, they spend an evening in a hotel across from the railroad station, a hotel that accepts guests without luggage. The room is all red plush, mirrors, satin, and cut glass; it is enough to make Catherine feel "like a whore," but "After we had eaten we felt fine, and then after, we felt very happy and in a little time the room felt like our own home. My room at the hospital had been our own home and this room was our own home too in the same way" (p. 153). Obviously it is not just the sensations of eating and sex that have made the difference, but the communion established through their agency. "Home" becomes a metaphor for this communion established in both flesh and spirit.

Henry returns to the front and is almost immediately involved in the full-scale retreat from Caporetto. A lyric passage that runs through Henry's mind while asleep in the front of an ambulance stalled in the congestion of the retreat shows how prominent a place in his consciousness and value system Catherine and the meaning structure called "home" has achieved. Beginning with a reference to physical desire, "Stiff as a board in bed. Catherine was in bed now between two sheets, over her and under her," the passage continues by weaving in elements (as pointed out by Charles R. Anderson in an excellent analysis of the passage) from a sixteenth-century lyric, "Christ, that my love were in my arms/ And I in my bed again!" as well as a line apparently adapted from the child's prayer, "Now I lay me down to sleep," and elements from the children's lullaby, "Sweet and Low," from Tennyson.[3] Moving from the initial sexual stimulus, the passage thus continues with several fragments reminiscent of a feeling for home and then ends with a concern for the pregnant Catherine, who in the dream (it is also actually raining around the ambulance) is connected to rain in two ways: as fertility, "That my sweet love Catherine down might rain," and as danger, "Well, we were in it. Every one was caught in it" (p. 197). Up to this point, aside from being a tender and moving passage and an interesting prose experiment, the section can be seen as a lyric summary of the entire love story and its sequence, including a prefiguring in the reference to the rain of the story's end. Furthermore, in the ambiguous reference to rain there is presented in capsule form the two sides of risk (the "small rain" of Catherine, home, and life is opposed by the "big rain" of threatening nature), with special emphasis on the fatalism inherent in the human condition (the "small rain" cannot quiet the insistent storm; also note how reminiscent the phrase

[3] "Hemingway's Other Style," in Baker, ed., *Ernest Hemingway: Critiques of Four Major Novels.*

"Every one was caught in it" is of Henry's previous statement, "You always feel trapped biologically" [p. 139]).

The conclusion of the passage confirms Henry's growth to a genuine commitment. His deep concern, his wanting to do something for Catherine, marks the inception of the motive, if not yet the actions, characteristic of love:

"Good-night, Catherine," I said out loud. "I hope you sleep well. If it's too uncomfortable, darling, lie on the other side," I said. "I'll get you some cold water. In a little while it will be morning and then it won't be so bad. I'm sorry he makes you so uncomfortable. Try and go to sleep, sweet." (p. 197)

Following Henry's disengagement from the war, his first thoughts, after he has time to think, wander invariably to Catherine. There is the contrast between his miserable physical circumstances of being wet, cold, and hungry, and Catherine's promise of soft, warm love: "Hard as the floor of the car to lie not thinking only feeling, having been away too long, the clothes wet and the floor moving only a little each time and lonesome inside and alone with wet clothing and hard floor for a wife" (pp. 231–32). As he assesses the situation he is now in, it is interesting to see how "seeing coldly and clearly," which has become associated with the home of the priest and awareness, and the priest's later speech concerning the difference between lust and love, now comes to mind in combination with "emptily," a synonym for the hollowness Henry began to feel upon his separation from Catherine: "but you loved some one else whom now you knew was not even to be pretended there; you seeing now very clearly and coldly—not so coldly as clearly and emptily" (p. 232). And what Henry sees with his awareness and recently acquired commitment is that it is "not my show any more." It is time to return to Catherine.

When he finds Catherine in Stresa, where she has come to have the baby, he has the "feeling that we had come home" (p. 249). He finds that together they can feel alone against the others, and that everything he values is now concentrated in Catherine: "'My life used to be full of everything,' I said. 'Now if you aren't with me I haven't a thing in the world'" (p. 257). Actually, as we have seen, this is not true; his life up to now has been filled with practically nothing—but perhaps, in a sense, it is the same thing.

When Count Greffi, an old acquaintance of Henry's who happens to be in Stresa at this time, asks Henry, "What do you value most?" Henry replies immediately, "Some one I love" (p. 262). The count mourns that he thought when he became old he would become devout, but he has not. Henry says that his own devoutness comes only at night. But the count replies that Henry must not forget that he is in love—"Do not forget that is a religious feeling" (p. 263). Or at least it can be. Henry has come very close to fulfilling the priest's prescription of doing things for, wishing to sacrifice for, and wishing to serve. (The conversation between Henry and Count Greffi in many ways parallels the previous conversation between Henry and the priest.) As the priest predicted, Henry finds a happiness he could not have apprehended before.

As for Catherine herself, the critics may be right who insist that she needs one or two really bad qualities to set her off. She certainly is much too brave. She risks great embarrassment and ruin by devotion to Henry in the hospital. She travels to a deserted resort town to have her baby in a foreign country (having lost one man in the war and knowing that the father of her baby is at the front). She accompanies Henry across the border in the middle of the night in a storm in a small boat, without question or complaint—as a matter of fact, showing a sense of humor in response to Henry's attempt to sail with an umbrella. She endures the difficulties of pregnancy without complaint, only worrying that Henry might be bored. When she is about to die, she is concerned about Henry: "'Don't worry, darling,' Catherine said. 'I'm not a bit afraid. It's just a dirty trick'" (p. 331). But as Hemingway points out, life has a way of taking care of such imbalances in character:

If people bring so much courage to this world the world has to kill them to break them, so of course it kills them. The world breaks every one and afterward many are strong at the broken places. But those that will not break it kills. It kills the very good and the very gentle and the very brave impartially. If you are none of these you can be sure it will kill you too but there will be no special hurry. (p. 249)

Henry has learned to love from the example of someone who had a great deal of love to give. Aware at last of what is meaningful in life, fully committed at last to another's welfare, Frederic Henry now has something to lose. The tragedy and irony of life is that now that he has something to lose, he must lose it.

Simply stated, the nature of the world, for Hemingway, was to bring to man tragedy and the ironic disappointment that necessarily awaited all of man's aspirations and ideals. This sense of irony was to be the source of Hemingway's greatest strength, as well as the seed of his undoing. He appears to have had some inkling of his own overattachment to the sadness and melodrama implicit in the use of irony when, in *The Sun Also Rises*, he has Bill Gorton poke fun at the current literary fad of larding everything with "pity and irony"[4] (pp. 113–15). Attacking himself in his weakest places was a favorite Hemingway defense.

[4] A satiric thrust, also, at H. L. Mencken.

CONTROL
AND LOSS OF CONTROL THROUGH IRONY

♦ ♦ ♦ IN "CHAPTER III," from *In Our Time*, a soldier recalls ambushing German soldiers as they climb over a garden wall:

The first German I saw climbed up over the garden wall. We waited till he got one leg over and then potted him. He had so much equipment on and looked awfully surprised and fell down into the garden. Then three more came over further down the wall. We shot them. They all came just like that. (*1st 49*, p. 203)

The central irony of this paragraph is contained in its lack of overt emotion, a simple, almost childlike acceptance of horror as a perfectly natural part of life. Like some awful, yet matter-of-fact reversal of *A Child's Garden of Verses*, the surface ritual described reminds us of a children's game like hide-and-seek—the soldier who is killed "looked awfully surprised." The implicit emotion arising from this treatment of the situation is a childlike delight in the success of the surprise. The surface ritual is in turn opposed by the reality of the situation: we realize that the narrator, who in this case frames the ritual in his mind, was actually killing people; we realize that the jolly term *potted* is equivalent to a calculated, cold-blooded killing. But the point I want to make here in particular is the timelessness which is so effortlessly achieved, so that the emotional force of the passage cannot be escaped by assigning this event to the convenient pigeonhole of a particular moment or set of circumstances. The passage is like a bad dream that comes back again and again to haunt us and from which we cannot release ourselves.

There is a very profound irony in the working of this style, it seems to me, between all the mechanisms that humanity has invented to rationalize the terror of existence (including the whole area of propaganda, ritual, and mass media sentimentality) and the stark insistence, as implemented by this stylistic technique, that the dark part of human existence is not momentary or accidental, but continuing and as real as anything else in man's experience.

After looking briefly at such exaggerated examples of Hemingway's stylistic technique and reviewing in some detail Hemingway's handling of emotion in *The Sun Also Rises* and *A Farewell to Arms*, we may come to the conclusion, as most readers of Hemingway's work do sooner or later, that Hemingway is an extremely emotional writer simply because he takes such pains to avoid explicit mention of emotion. That is to say, his entire approach to emotion is related to a consistently practiced verbal irony. Feeling very deeply about man's injustices, stupidities, and brutalities, Hemingway finds it more effective to whisper rather than to shout. There is something in Hemingway's storytelling posture very similar to the posture of the satirist who recounts absurdities with a straight face. Perhaps there is a strain, too, of the straight-faced storyteller of the American frontier, with the significant difference that Hemingway shows life producing its own exaggerations and its own absurdities. Another important difference between Hemingway and such writers as Sinclair Lewis working in the satiric tradition (in the works that follow *The Sun Also Rises*) is that Hemingway seldom uses irony to achieve a comic effect, and, generally speaking, it is by remaining at least close to the comic that the satirist escapes the maudlin.

Leaving the comic uses of irony behind for the most part after writing *The Sun Also Rises*, Hemingway turns in *A Farewell to Arms* to uses of irony more closely aligned to the tragic mode. In doing so, Hemingway remains as strongly anti-sentimental as before, but takes a position that is much more likely to ensnare him inadvertently in a sentimentality of his own. This tendency of Hemingway to fall into his own trap is quite similar to the tendency of the satirist who, attacking vice and corruption, finds that most of his own subject matter is concerned with a detailed exploration into the very aspects of things he wants to eliminate.[1] Before examining Hemingway's difficulties in properly directing the emotional values he generates in his fiction (which I shall do in this chapter and the next), we should keep two propositions in mind as a basis for our examination: first, a writer may arouse deep emotions without being sentimental or employing sentimental techniques, and second, there is a great difference between endorsing a system of values that is essentially sentimental, and becoming sentimental inadvertently while endorsing a system of values which is basically antithetical to sentimentality.

Thus, Hemingway's use of irony can be said to contrast two fundamentally different world views, one that he feels is moral with one that he feels is immoral. Either the irrationality which surrounds the individual, which lies outside the circle of the light that Jake Barnes burns at night or beyond the willing hands of Frederic Henry at Catherine's deathbed, can be recognized, and on the basis of such a recognition lead to meaningful behavior, or the irrationality can be ignored or explained away, leading to behavior which is negative or destructive and making it impossible for man to love, empathize with, or become committed to his fellow man.

Just as, in Hemingway's doctrine, man does not stand in the center of the universe, so too is his morality not God-given but man-created. This man-created morality is metaphorically represented in Hemingway's works by the structure I have termed "game." This view of man's place and his moral responsibility is the reason why Christianity never becomes a very important fac-

[1] Alvin B. Kernan, "A Theory of Satire," in Kernan, ed., *Modern Satire* (New York, 1962), p. 174. Much of my general information regarding the workings of satire is drawn from Kernan's article and Northrop Frye's article in the same collection, "The Mythos of Winter: Irony and Satire."

tor in the thinking of the Hemingway protagonist. Christianity, in Hemingway's design, must be considered to be aligned with sentimentality: Christianity is both ego-centered (centered on man's welfare, conduct, and beliefs) and anthropomorphic. What is the use of praying, Frederic Henry seems to be saying in the desperation attending Catherine's death, if one cannot ask and expect to have the omnipotent Being stem the tide? If He has any relationship with man at all, it must be in terms of what is asked for in reason. But whatever is "outside," beyond the sphere of man-created order, has little regard for man's reason: Catherine dies— for no man-centered "reason." There is no higher court. There is no appeal from the necessity of courage.

Thus, in what is probably one of the best short stories ever written, "A Clean, Well-Lighted Place," the older waiter knows "it all was nada . . . Our nada who art in nada" (*1st 49*, p. 481). There is no help for man except the "clean, well-lighted places" that he carves out of the darkness for himself. The other waiter, who has "youth, confidence, and a job," is unaware of everything except his own desires. He sees no meaning in providing such a clean well-lighted place as their cafe to the old man. The young waiter does not observe the dignity of the old man who, being the last customer, delays the closing of the cafe. The younger waiter can see no difference between the *bodegas*, where one must stand at a bar, and a clean and pleasant cafe. For him, the consequences of the night do not exist. For him, the old man who from "despair" of "nothing" tried to kill himself the week before "should have killed himself" (p. 478). Although the structure of the irony is perfect, it is played at almost whisper-intensity so that many a reader has passed over the irony. The younger waiter is so real, so normal, so average, so characteristic. How then should we characterize his lack of concern, his selfishness, his lack of empathy, his shallow cynicism, his blindness?

Although the young waiter "wouldn't want to be that old," it remains a distinct possibility, just as it is possible that he, like the old man, will outlive the wife he is so impatient to go home to. It may be that he will live to be alone and be in despair over "nothing." But it is clear that he has not yet been required to face the darkness with courage or even to recognize its existence (and thus gain awareness and compassion for others faced with the same task). For now, the younger waiter lies outside the moral community; how well he will pass the tests of future disasters remains to be seen. As for the two who are joined together with "all those who need a light for the night," the very old man who is clean and maintains his dignity and the older waiter who empathizes with those who may need the cafe, the implication in the story is very strong that they have done all that it is within them to do and they are to be admired for it.

Many recent discussions of this story emphasize Hemingway's presentation of "nothingness" as a real entity, a presentation which appears to involve a strikingly profound intuitive proposal by a writer who has been thought to be so unphilosophic in his orientation to life.[2] Commented on less, but equally important to the theme of the story, is the emphasis placed on the awareness of the older waiter. In looking back over the story, the reader should note how much of the story is devoted to the older waiter's clear and accurate perceptions of himself, of the other two characters, and of what might generally be termed "the situation." The fundamental irony of the story lies in the skillfully balanced and controlled contrast between the attitude of boredom (self-absorption) displayed by the young waiter, who has "everything," and the active concern and essential "aliveness" of the older waiter, who has "nothing." The ironic paradox that results is that only through the awareness of nothing or non-meaning can meaning be created. At a certain point in one's experience with this story, paradoxes and puns begin to trip over themselves. Like Miss Van Campen in *A Farewell to Arms*, the younger waiter is in a service occupation; it is his profession to think of others, but he neither serves nor waits. Whether it was in Hemingway's mind or not, I cannot help adding that the younger waiter has not yet learned (to quote from Milton's "*blindness* sonnet," which talks of Milton's

[2] Barrett, p. 285.

relation to God's scheme and begins "When I consider how my *light* is spent"): "They also serve who only stand and wait."

Blindness versus awareness is Hemingway's most pervasive theme, and it is borne on a rippling wave of irony into almost everything he writes. Seeing oneself, others, and the situation clearly is the basic requirement for the creation of meaning—genuine concern or love for others. Illusion and self-centeredness are the enemies of meaning, just as the younger waiter is hostile to the old man and impatient with the older waiter. A wonderfully ironic metaphor for the hostility of unawareness to meaningful human relationships is the deafness of the American lady in another short story, "A Canary for One." The American lady, through selfishness and irrational prejudice against all "foreigners," has broken up her daughter's love affair with a young Swiss engineer. Ironically, she decides to substitute a caged canary for the engineer, thinking (in parallel with her own caging of her daughter) that the canary will adequately compensate the girl for her loss. It becomes clear that the woman is not only physically deaf but emotionally deaf. She participates in and becomes an enforcer of non-meaning, much like the carabinieri (who are also deaf) at the bridge in *A Farewell to Arms*. Although her physical disability is more literal, it has a distinct relation to the blindness of the younger waiter who, although standing in the light, cannot see what is in the light or even perceive that there is a difference between the light and the darkness.

Although in these two stories, "A Clean, Well-Lighted Place" and "A Canary for One," love of one kind or another is considered, and even recommended, this subject is handled without sentiment: emotion is examined without emotionalism. Compare Hemingway's handling of this theme with that of Dickens in *A Christmas Carol*. In recommending compassionate awareness of others, Dickens' technique is to squeeze all the sentimental triggers that come to hand. Scrooge, like the American lady and the younger waiter, is deaf and blind to the conditions and needs of other people, but unlike the Hemingway characters, Scrooge is caused to have a magical transformation of character. Even a villain with the hardest possible heart, the meanest man in the world, is found to have a spot of pure gold deep down inside his hardened hide. How is Scrooge reformed? Why, he is made aware of others by an appeal to his self-pity! The Ghost of Christmas Past begins Scrooge's conversion by appealing to his sentimental feelings for himself as a neglected, unhappy child. Only then is he ready to receive the scenes of other suffering victims from the past and present with the proper feeling. The Ghost of Christmas Future rounds out the picture by showing Scrooge his own death, un-mourned and unloved, appealing again to Scrooge's feelings for himself. Scrooge's magical transformation is crowned with the most poignant of all sentimental triggers, the crippled child. The reader is invited to weep for himself as unwanted and unloved, and later he is invited to weep in joyful recognition that all is right with the world: no one is really so bad that he cannot be changed by the proper appeal to his better nature, and the poor, but hard-working, will eventually be rewarded for their industry. Although admittedly an exaggerated example from the other end of the emotional scale, Dickens' handling of compassion is cer-tainly not atypical, and such a realization should lead us to some admiration for the frequency and adeptness with which Heming-way avoids the emotional cliché in his constant employment of the themes of love, compassion, and commitment.

Hemingway does arouse emotions by his use of irony, but gen-erally the emotions aroused remain unconnected with sentimen-tality. Usually the emotions aroused are those we traditionally attach to tragedy and to satire. The tragic emotions are associated with the ironies inherent in Hemingway's "world picture," whereas the satiric emotions are associated with those ironies that result from the contrast of Hemingway's view of man and his place in the world with the sentimental view of man and his place in the world. Thus, the satiric pattern of emotion is dependent on an initial establishment of the tragic pattern so that a second set of contrasts, between the tragic and the sentimental, can be set up.

The emotional values of satire are produced by Hemingway when he contrasts his value system, or game, with sentimental or ego-centered value systems. This contrast specifically opposes awareness with blindness, commitment with selfishness, courage with cowardice. The satiric pattern is really a part of the larger, over-all pattern of tragic irony except for one significant difference: the tragic emotions are evoked by necessary circumstances. Injustice, cruelty, and stupidity need not be a part of man's behavior, and when these are demonstrated in the actions of *specific* characters in opposition to the values held by the central protagonist, they arouse the reader's indignation and anger if the threat posed by them is potent, or they arouse our scornful laughter on those few occasions when the threat posed by them is impotent. So it is that we become very angry with the carabinieri at the bridge and indignant with Miss Van Campen and Lady Brett, whereas we laugh at the antics of Robert Cohn and the braggadocio of Ettore.

The irony of tragedy and the irony of satire in general are very closely allied. Both are based on a conflict of value systems, and both flow from an author who maintains a strong moral position. We can see in Hemingway's work that the tragic and the satiric frequently overlap, and we can see that the tragic and the satiric are based on the same terms—that is, of contrast: the positive individual is seen in opposition to negative forces which threaten to injure or crush him. We can see, too, that the combinations of sympathy, recognition of terror, and indignation are at work in "Chapter V" from *In Our Time* (*1st 49*, p. 225). Our sympathy is drawn to the sick minister, who appears to be in the grip of forces which, with overwhelming and relentless power, would destroy his human dignity. A sense of terror is evoked by the inevitability of misfortune suggested by the rain and the typhoid and by the timelessness created by the prose style. But we are also made indignant by specific suggestions of human blindness: the use of the hospital for the shooting, the mechanical adherence to ritual by the firing squad, and the attempt by the soldiers to force the sick minister into a ritual that he cannot participate in.

In Hemingway's fiction the forces of tragedy are necessarily impersonalized, whereas the threats posed by ego-centered individuals are usually vehicles of satire. In *For Whom the Bell Tolls* the threatened foul-up of the Republican Army of which we are made conscious from the very beginning, though representing a human rather than a natural threat of disaster, becomes necessary and unavoidable; as a threat, it plays a crucial part in the tragic irony surrounding the blowing up of the bridge, as does the Fascist gunfire which disables Jordan. On the other hand, the unnecessary egocentricity, blindness, waste, stupidity, and selfishness associated with such individuals as Comrade Marty and Pablo are vehicles for the satiric emotions of anger and indignation.

The story examined earlier in this chapter, "A Clean, Well-Lighted Place," contains both tragic and satiric irony. The tragic irony is seen in the contrasts between the power of man to create a circle of light and the vulnerability of man and the light he creates to the omnipresent power of darkness, between the courage man shows and the certain defeat the reader knows lies in wait for man. We are sympathetic with the older waiter. We see him in opposition to forces completely beyond human power to resist except temporarily and in a very small way. He maintains the light of the cafe as long as he can until the lateness of the hour and the insistence of the younger waiter force him to return to the voracious darkness. We do not identify with the older waiter's specific condition, but we can identify emotionally and intellectually with his general condition: his awareness of others, his sympathy for the old man who needs the cafe, and his ability to see the need for the cafe to provide light and dignity and protection for the old man from the forces of non-meaning. We can also experience in reading this story a very powerful recognition of the power of that non-meaning. We can feel the very fabric of the terror that awaits the old man who seeks the protection of the light for as long as possible and who does not want to go home to face the emptiness that is there, the emptiness that has led him to attempt suicide because of "nothing." We feel indignant, too. We want to shake the younger waiter who cares so little, who is so blind, who through his own selfishness contributes to the powers of the darkness that lie in wait for all of us.

Occasionally in Hemingway's writing the direction of the irony is reversed from its usual realistic course—or perhaps more accurately, turned back on itself—when a situation which of itself would normally call for the reader's sympathy is given further emphasis through the use of irony. On such occasions irony is brought into an already ironic situation. As a result, the emotional value of the situation is increased out of proportion to the dramatic context. Whenever sympathy is boosted in this way, it is made less generic and intellectual and more personal and emotional, losing its tragic context and becoming exaggerated and sentimental.

Such a jacking up of emotional values usually occurs as a result of Hemingway's inadvertent overuse of satiric irony. His tendency to overload a dramatically achieved tragic situation by the injection of satire probably stems from his own great personal hostility to human unawareness as well as from his great temptation to use irony in exposing injustice and selfishness. Add to this the great sympathy Hemingway obviously holds for the man who courageously and alone must fight a losing battle, and it becomes easy to see why Hemingway is unable at times to leave well enough alone—why he must get in that one extra blow at the enemy, that one last bitter jibe. Thus, Hemingway can be said to become sentimental when he loses his own perspective, ignores his own doctrine of restraint in the use of emotion, and overpersonalizes his discussion by becoming too intimately involved. Always a moral writer, his great weakness is moralizing. Always a dramatic writer, his weakness is overdramatization. His great sentimental lapses are really little pieces of melodrama: suddenly there is a villain hissing at the audience and a hero struggling manfully to overcome the forces that would victimize him. To put it another way, Hemingway hates sentimentality so much that he loses his balance and becomes sentimental himself in attacking it. Whereas tragedy is written in a spirit of resignation, satire is written in a spirit of impatience—the satirist cannot just sit on the sidelines and watch; he must involve himself, and his readers must become involved too.

Some of the best examples of Hemingway's overuse of irony can be found at the ends of his novels. The end of a story is the place where it is difficult for nearly any writer to maintain an emotional equilibrium in his writing, and Hemingway usually finds the temptation to overdramatize man's inevitable defeat too much for him. *A Farewell to Arms* is better balanced emotionally at the end than most of the novels that follow it, but there is one passage, the one describing the callous unawareness of the two nurses, that is unnecessarily melodramatic. Henry's suffering during Catherine's ordeal in the hospital is already sufficiently established without the episode of the nurses. Particularly effective in dramatizing this suffering is a passage pointed out by Ray B. West, Jr., as a masterpiece of indirect and restrained depiction of emotional intensity: When Catherine is in extreme danger and Henry is trying to serve her in some way by administering the anesthetic gas, Catherine cries out that it isn't doing any good, that it doesn't seem to be working. In three short sentences, Hemingway suggests Henry's anxiety and Catherine's severe danger: "I turned the dial to three and then four. I wished the doctor would come back. I was afraid of the numbers above two" (p. 323). As West points out, "Another author might have examined in great detail both Catherine's illness and the emotion which Frederic was experiencing at that time; but from the simple, quiet statement, reinforced by the dial registering the numbers above two, we get the full force of Frederic's terror in a few strokes."[3] The delicacy with which Hemingway leads his reader here to create the emotion for himself is in sharp contrast to the satiric impact of the cruel giggling and delight of the two nurses on their way to a Caesarean operation who pass Henry waiting anxiously in the corridor. Henry's pain and aloneness are brought too much into relief: our sympathy is overtaxed.

This passage in *A Farewell to Arms* is reminiscent of another, parallel passage in *The Old Man and the Sea*—a passage which concerns the ironic unawareness of the tourists who mistake the

[3] "The Biological Trap," in Weeks, ed., *Hemingway: A Collection of Critical Essays*, p. 150.

marlin which has been destroyed by sharks for a large shark. This inadvertent transposition of the marlin (which, in the terms I have established here, roughly symbolizes meaning) and the shark (non-meaning—blind, voracious ego-satisfaction) contains, through the prior dramatization of Santiago's experience, more than enough emotional dynamite of itself, yet the transposition's emotional punch is further intensified by being made by well-fed, secure tourists (a synonym in Hemingway for "unawareness") who are *eating*—blindly. The episode contrasts sharply with the condition of Santiago, who, having already suffered from the sharks of nature, is now caused to suffer lack of recognition at the hands of human sharks. As explained earlier, "lack of recognition" is a sentimental trigger. An already established sympathy has been over-reinforced.

As a matter of fact, there are really three major ironies (and several smaller touches) which contribute to what strikes me as an excessively emotional ending to a basically fine story. The emotional contrast central to *The Old Man and the Sea* consists of Santiago's courage, persistence, faith, and skill in opposition to his bad luck, his loss of the boy, and his old age (in connection with his stressed condition of being alone in a hostile element). The controlling irony of the dramatization is firmly tragic. At the end, however, Hemingway has seen fit to increase the emotional impact of the basic contrast (which, in terms of the heroic suffering and courage displayed, is emotional enough as it is) by adding several boosters. Only one of the ironic patterns that emerge at the end of the novel is dramatically justified—the pattern which emerges from the implicit comparison of the conditions of the young boy and the old man. This comparison involves the boy's youth, which of course emphasizes the old man's age and present exhaustion as well as the burden of life which he has carried so well, and the boy's devotion, which emphasizes the lonely ordeal that the old man has gone through and the hostility that he has survived without becoming bitter or hostile himself. In addition to this pattern, interjected into the ending, is the ironic unawareness of the tourists, and, in the last line of the novelette, the irony of the old, exhausted fisherman who, although deprived of his winnings by forces beyond his control, has won the battle of the human spirit—battered, he still dreams of the lions.

Before the ending of the novel, the lion has been established as a symbol of the beauty as well as the strength of youth and the lithe, regal courage that the lion traditionally represents. The old man no longer dreams of "storms, nor of women, nor of great occurrences, nor of great fish, nor fights, nor contests of strength, nor of his wife," but only of places and of "the lions on the beach" (p. 22). As with the example of Joe DiMaggio, who played to the limit of his ability despite the pain of a bone spur, the lions provide a sense of heroic perspective to the old man's struggle, as well as acting to unify a novel which deals with man's relationship with the natural world. Nevertheless, the final touch of the lions proves too much for us; it should never fail to provide a moist eye and a lump in the throat: "Up the road, in his shack, the old man was sleeping again. He was still sleeping on his face and the boy was sitting by him watching him. The old man was dreaming about the lions" (p. 127). Although I have reservations about the inclusion of the lions here, one could argue that these last lines constitute an effective summary of man's tragic condition—the heroic will to commitment in opposition to necessary defeat.[4] But in combination with the passage concerning the tourists that comes immediately before it, the emotional emphasis of the ending becomes satiric rather than tragic. The introduction of an exterior element, the tourists, changes the perspective, making Santiago more like a misunderstood, still noble, victim. The emotional underlining of the contrast of conditions, the tourists' and the old man's, boosts our sympathy for the old man out of proportion to the dramatic context itself. In effect, Hemingway forces the reader first to lose his objectivity by making him indignant and second to become personally involved by a strong demand for the reader's

[4] Hemingway's fondness for lion "gentling," a pastime strongly objected to by his wife, is recounted by Hotchner, pp. 15–16. Hemingway's rationale for risking his life in such a way is quoted by Hotchner: "It is wicked, I guess, to lay it on the line just for fun. But know [sic] no other place as good to lay it as on the line" (p. 16).

sympathy in the face of a threat to deny Santiago the sympathy he deserves. The sympathy is demanded less on the basis of man's tragic condition than on man's tragic condition unrewarded by recognition—an entirely different matter. In short, it is an emotional trick, the very thing which Hemingway had dedicated himself to fight and expose as false and a violation of "true emotion."

As we have noted, the evidence of the bulk of Hemingway's writing indicates that of all things, he is most involved emotionally with courage. Acts of courage in themselves generally arouse emotion, but are not necessarily connected with sentimentality. However, several circumstances attending courage can lead to the possibility of sentimental coloration. One, certainly, is the circumstance that the greatest acts of courage are performed by the individual, alone, and often cut off from any outside support whatsoever. If this is so, then the second condition that may lead to sentimental coloration of courage follows: the greatest acts of courage must remain unwitnessed, unrecognized, and unappreciated. When an act of courage is performed in literature, the reader often is the only witness, the only person who can accord the protagonist proper recognition and appreciation. The injustice of other characters' failing to recognize an act of courage may provoke the reader into an unwarranted emotional response by turning his sympathetic admiration into pity. This lack of recognition can be easily turned by the reader toward himself if he becomes too closely identified with the story's protagonist. On this basis, pity can be further transformed into self-pity, the cornerstone of sentimentality.

Emotion that is contained in a literary situation may be seen, perhaps, as an expanding gas looking for an outlet. When the emotion arises from a situation in what Hemingway would call a "true" way, it tends to remain suspended—the pressure of the inside and outside remain equal.(Some of Hemingway's techniques for accomplishing this will be examined in the following chapter.) But when additional pressure is added to the container in one way or another, the gas is forced out into whatever passage is available: generally, the emotion flows toward the reader. This pressure is a matter of emphasis, and if irony, an emphasis-device, is used to underline those elements I have identified as culturally defined centers of emotion, the emotion expands or even explodes.

Thus, the use of irony requires a delicate sense of balance as well as an ability to apply restraint. Hemingway's over-all use of irony to suppress the overt expression of emotion below an ostensibly bland surface and to transfer the responsibility for creating the emotion to the reader is certainly a legitimate extension of the Hemingway doctrine of letting "the facts speak for themselves." But when does the selection of facts become illegitimate manipulation? The point at which outgoing emotions such as approval, affection, or admiration for a character begin to rebound to the reader in the direction of self-love and self-pity is extremely difficult to define precisely—not because it is subjective and therefore relative to the individual reader's emotional condition and needs, but because the turning point must be determined intellectually on the basis of complex literary judgments. These judgments respond to the questions, Are the facts representative of reality as we know it? and Is any given fact dramatically justified by the realistic pattern? More difficult to discuss is the question, At what point do we sense that the author is asking or forcing us to give up our intellectual perspective and participate wholly with our emotions? It is almost tautological to point out that emotion is not antithetical to intellect, but that emotionalism cannot survive without the suspension of intellectual faculties.

Judgments about the dramatic justification of ironic contrast should be made in regard to the degree that an ironic element may force a departure from the central effect of the work. On this basis, the interjection of the tourists' conversation in *The Old Man and the Sea* would appear to be a rather obvious case of manipulation. Hemingway has attempted to weave the dreaming of the lions into the fabric of the story and has attempted to make it part of Santiago's condition. However, the use of the lions at the end of the story still remains a circumstance irrelevant to the central deed and to the emotions arising from the central deed, acting to magnify through the power of symbol and irony an emotion already dramatically established in the narrative. To put it another way, the lions have almost no dramatic relevance, only a previously established emotional relevance.

In the case of Colonel Cantwell in *Across the River and into the Trees*, an emotion-producing aspect of his condition, his heart trouble, is woven into the narrative. Although there are ironic contrasts of this condition with his occupation and with his zest for life, and although this condition, like dreaming of lions, has taken on certain symbolic overtones (namely, Cantwell's struggle to love and to leave bitterness behind), the condition of his heart is one of the terms of the dramatic conflict of the novel, so that Cantwell's death by a heart attack at the end has no sentimental overflow in and of itself. Unlike Santiago's dream of the lions, Cantwell's heart is necessary, not accessory. What is sentimental, however, is to have the sergeant (who up to this point is legitimately used as a foil of unawareness to Cantwell's awareness) violate the colonel's instructions by assigning what few valuables he has left to his loved one to the red tape of army procedure, the very machinery of insensitivity and inefficiency the colonel has been fighting all his life. The sergeant's violation of orders may be justified by his unperceptive, rule-bound character, but it is external to the terms of Colonel Cantwell's internal conflict—particularly when the colonel is dead. As a result of this final touch of satiric irony, the colonel, rather than dying in dignity, suddenly becomes an ironic victim. Again, Hemingway is carried away by his admiration for individual courage and cannot resist the final twist that brings our attention more forcibly than necessary to Cantwell's losses and alienation.

Hemingway's abuse of the power of irony is most likely in those situations in which he gets carried away in satisfying his own emotional investments. Hemingway is not a sentimental writer, but a writer who for the duration of his career was locked in a struggle between his attraction for tragic irony and his attraction for satiric irony and sentiment. Too often, when his attraction to satire overcame his general preference for tragedy, his work lost its tragic impact and became personal, bitter, and sentimental. Such a tendency is probably the eternal trap for all writers who care too much.

SUFFERING
AND LOSS WITHOUT TEARS

◆ ◆ ◆ THE "winner take nothing" philosophy is basic to Hemingway's conception of the world; the only victories in such a world are victories of the spirit, and if a man gains anything tangible, the only sure thing is that he will eventually lose it. But in such a world where the integrity of the individual is so important, victories of the spirit are enough. They re-establish one's humanity and confirm one's manhood. If a Catherine is lost in childbirth, or the significance of a bridge is lost in the confusion of war, or a great fish is lost in a sea of sharks, there is always, for the man willing to take the necessary risks, another bridge, another fish, and even another Catherine. Bringing man much closer to the terror of complete loss, nothingness, closer than the loss of something outside himself, is the possibility that man may lose himself—that he may lose his identity, his completeness, his manness. A classic statement of this fear that lies at the heart of so much that Hemingway has written is found at the beginning of the short story "Now I Lay Me":

I myself did not want to sleep because I had been living for a long time with the knowledge that if I ever shut my eyes in the dark and let myself go, my soul would go out of my body. I had been that way for a long time, ever since I had been blown up at night and felt it go out of me and go off and then come back. I tried never to think about it, but it had started to go since, in the nights, just at the moment of going off to sleep, and I could only stop it by a very great effort. (*1st 49*, p. 461)

Whereas the fear here is announced and overt, more often it is held distantly in the background, always present because, unlike this occasion, it is never thought of. When the selfhood of the Hemingway protagonist is at stake, as it often is, the emotional climate in which the protagonist exists can be loaded with terror, frequently involving a nightmarish series of events tinged with the suggestion of panic and hysteria.

The triggering mechanism for this nightmare is often a physical or psychic wound, a wound which has torn away the protagonist's sense of security or complacency. Typically alone, the Hemingway protagonist is often reduced to his selfhood as the only "place" or possession that can be secured against the erosion of time and change. A threat to selfhood is the ultimate threat, involving the ultimate horror that the irrational forces of the world can accomplish.

In addition to performing this triggering function, the wound is often a metaphor for a loss of spirit, an indication, if the wound is physical, of an interior missing part of some kind, or a gradual decay of some function. Harry's thorn scratch in "The Snows of Kilimanjaro" is a fine example, among many, of the wound that serves as both a symptom and a warning of spiritual difficulty. The gangrene that has infected his leg is perfectly suited to represent physically the spiritual rot that Harry has infected himself with. Appropriately, the scratch has become dangerous through Harry's neglect. There is no hellfire and damnation lying in wait for Harry, no searing pain as poetic punishment for his sins of omission as a writer and as a man (and Hemingway, interestingly enough, sees Harry's sins as a writer as being far more serious). There is simply the fate of lying out in the middle of nowhere and smelling his own stench.

The story is a wonderfully vivid nightmare, replete with death animals, death birds, nocturnal cries, prophecies, hallucinations, and rituals. And of course, the story contains another vehicle of horror perfectly suited to the writer who has sold out to buy luxury through a series of marriages: a platitude-spouting female ("You can't die if you don't give up," "What have we done to have that happen to us?" "I'll always love you," "You're sweet to me"). Harry's wife, with her magazine-photo good looks, her smothering compassion, her clichés, and her hot broth, serves as the perfect Mephistopheles to Harry's Faust. For like Faust, Harry has signed away his soul, and now, near the end, he is trying to preserve it. But like Faust also, Harry has become so hardened in his sins that he is not capable of identifying virtue. One rich wife after another has weaned Harry from the realities on which his talent as a writer must feed. With somewhat more self-perception than Faust, Harry realizes that the ultimate responsibility is his own (although he is continually tempted to blame others):

He had destroyed his talent himself. Why should he blame this woman because she kept him well? He had destroyed his talent by not using it, by betrayals of himself and what he believed in, by drinking so much that he blunted the edge of his perceptions, by laziness, by sloth, and by snobbery, by pride and by prejudice, by hook and by crook. . . . What was his talent anyway? It was a talent all right but instead of using it, he had traded on it. It was never what he had done, but always what he could do. (p. 158)

At first glance, Harry's ordeal may seem considerably removed from the atmosphere of panic; the passage cited above appears to be closer to a mood of languid regret, tinged with self-pity, than to a mood of desperation.

Panic, however, is usually somewhere below the surface in Hemingway's work, and sometimes it is so muted that it is easily overlooked. Harry's fear is not so much that he will die as that somewhere along the way he has irrecoverably lost himself. It is a fear that we see is perfectly justified, for Harry's cardinal sin is that he has chosen to ignore the truth for so long that he can no longer find it: "It was not so much that he lied as that there was no truth to tell" (p. 157). One of the common indicators of panic in Hemingway's fiction is ritual, and Harry's desperation is carried by means of a number of rituals all related to his last-minute search for reality and for Harry. There is the ritual of the bottle, ironically enough in terms of the confession cited above, and the ritual of the bickering and argument carried on intermittently with his wife in order to destroy pretense and discover truth. Characteristically, Harry's wife defends illusion through a metaphor from medieval romance (like Robert Cohn, she is apparently guided in part by her reading —"she read enormously"): "'If you have to go away,' she said, 'is it absolutely necessary to kill off everything you leave behind? I mean do you have to take away everything? Do you have to kill your horse, and your wife and burn your saddle and your armour?" (pp. 155–56). There are several layers of irony here, since Harry is certainly by no stretch of the imagination a shining knight; instead, he is a man who has sold out, who has betrayed "himself and what he believed in." Harry has come to Africa to "work the fat off his soul," to rid himself of the appendages that his sloth has gathered. But Harry is not capable of any really heroic break with the past. He brings his "rich bitch" with him, and his rigorous training amounts to nothing more than doing without luxuries. The results can be predicted: "he . . . felt the illusion of returning strength of will to work" (p. 158).

In addition to this ritual of self-purification by venom and spite (Harry's image of a snake biting itself is quite appropriate [p. 158]), dominating much of the story is the ritual of the before-death review of one's life which Harry conducts in a desperate attempt to find the mainstream of his selfhood. But none of the rituals work. The bottle (a petty gesture of independence) simply clouds Harry's mind and hastens his physical decay; the verbal probing intermittently peters out because of attacks of conscience and never quite finds the right targets anyway; and Harry's search through the past becomes a nostalgic review of lost loves, disappointments, and missed opportunities.

Reality remains beyond Harry's bed. Beyond his reach, circling the camp, is a ritual of death acted out by the animals of the bush. Although Harry is all too conscious of the closing circle of nature around him, he uses his "talent" to escape the implications of reality as long as he can. Behind the agile workings of Harry's mind and the rather leisurely pace of events that it creates hovers the foul smell of sheer terror. At the beginning of the story, the vultures come closer to camp than ever before. Next, there comes to Harry a "sudden evil-smelling emptiness" that tells him that he is really going to die. Then Harry sees death, as a hyena resting "its head on the foot of the cot." Finally, the hyena stops whimpering and starts to make a "strange, human, almost crying sound" which announces Harry's death to his wife. With each of these manifestations the circle of death that promises to cut off Harry's hopes of recovering himself becomes increasingly smaller, increasingly more ominous. Adding to the ominous nature of the threat is its increasingly hallucinatory quality. Harry is one who has overindulged himself, and there is something in this horror very reminiscent of the delirium tremens of the alcoholic, enough so that we should become convinced that Harry is in the process of losing, not gaining, himself. From the natural phenomenon of the vultures and hyenas, the threat turns to an "emptiness," then to a "whisper" that cannot be heard, then to something unnamed that moves in pairs "absolutely silently," and finally something, unseen by Harry's companions, that crouches on his chest. There is a suggestion of dramatic irony here (also connected with the ending), since with each appearance of death there is presented a hint of the real presence of a hyena for the reader who is tied to the reality that Harry cannot reach. Harry's end is appropriately designed to signify his death as an artist: instead of being pulled down into a trapdoor and dismembered like Faust, Harry is provided with a slick-magazine exit which comes just in time, like the cavalry, and wafts him over pink clouds and a picture landscape to his own Shangri-La. On the slopes of Harry's Shangri-La, Mount Kilimanjaro, there is a leopard which has frozen to death in an attempt to reach the summit ("the House of God") for no apparent reason; Harry has, on the contrary, seldom acted without a real or substantial reason connected with his own physical comfort. The leopard has been hard on itself; Harry has certainly not been hard enough on himself even to maintain his own manhood. (Harry's only hardness has been that erotic "hardness" that had kept him in comfortable circumstances. His real talent has been demonstrated in bed—"'Love is a dunghill,' said Harry. 'And I'm the cock that gets on it to crow'" [p. 155]). It is appropriate that Harry's climb to the summit of Kilimanjaro is made not only in wishful thinking, but in an airplane. In the meantime, signifying the reality Harry left behind a long time ago, his death actually comes from rotted flesh and poisoned blood to the mournful whimpering of a hyena, the foul king of animal scavengers. In an ironic commentary on the quality of Harry's life, the symbol of his death is an animal who lives by being a parasite.

At first glance, Hemingway's constant use of ritual elements in such stories as "The Snows of Kilimanjaro" might seem strange and contradictory. It may seem strange because it appears to be a devotion to appearances rather than reality when the ritual elements of game are emphasized more than the ethical structure which game embodies, and strange too in that ritual is one of the things that we have seen Hemingway deplore the most. We might remember that it is appearance that traps the unwary and the unaware, and it is devotion to appearances that leads one into false behavior, into using tricks. Yet it is appearance as a ritual aspect of game that Hemingway frequently seems anxiously devoted to. The constant dwelling on the right wines, the proper things to say, the right hotels and restaurants, the correct techniques, and the correct equipment is often so insistent that it has been found extremely irritating by many readers who mistakenly find this element irrelevant or reminiscent of snobbery. To be irritated by this devotion to ritual, however, is to ignore the condition of the Hemingway protagonist, whose alienation and insecurity is often revealed through his devotion to ritual patterns. Such patterns, on close reading, are prone to reveal a sense of hysteria or even at times a sense of pathos. The protagonist who is so deliberate in his activities and who must have every detail right would seem to be similar (if there could be such a thing) to a man going down for the third time who is desperately reaching out to touch as many substantial things as possible before going under for the last time. There is also a parallel to the set pattern of the racing driver before he gets into his car—who dresses in certain clothes, says only certain lucky things, kicks each tire, and touches his lucky coin—or, of course, to the ritual preparation of the bullfighter. Both face death, but what may be even more terrifying, both face the possibility that they may lose their nerve, thus losing their manhood, their identity.

It is perhaps this constant contact with substantial or sensory detail that helps Hemingway's sympathetic character maintain the treacherous borderline between "something" and nothingness. In its most extreme forms the ritual pattern becomes a constant repetition of activities, and the strain on the protagonist is obvious. Such is the case in "Now I Lay Me," where the protagonist works very hard every night to keep his sanity by repeating certain activities, such as fishing a trout stream in his mind, over and over again. Or such is the case in the story "A Way You'll Never Be," where the protagonist stubbornly insists on acting out a role, the very peculiar one of wearing an American uniform and riding around on a bicycle on the Italian front—a role that he has apparently invented for himself. More often, particularly in Hemingway's novels, the ritual is acted out with much less overt emotional strain, and the threat of disaster that hangs over the protagonist's head is much more subtly suggested, although no less ominous and complete.

The threat of disaster which abides in much of Hemingway's fiction is much less akin to the naturalistic tricks of fate of a writer like Thomas Hardy, which are very unpleasant and perhaps even threatening at times to the reader, than it is akin to the sudden clarifications one finds in Kafka or Camus that can lead one into the dark pit of complete panic. Gregor Samsa, in Kafka's "Metamorphosis," finds that upon being transformed in the night into a giant insect, all the basic anchors of life—home, family, employment—become absurdities. They no longer are relevant. But the terrifying thing, the thing that rips apart our comfortable illusions, is the gradual realization that there is really no difference between Samsa's relationships as an ugly, detestable insect and the quality of the relationships he had before. The metamorphosis has simply changed his and our perspectives so that what was true all along is now visible. Again, through the creation of Meursault, who is in a way also a kind of insect, Camus creates a sudden shift of perspective so that the reader may realize that everything that was once substantial has turned out to be nothing but a canvas backdrop. Love, justice, freedom, religion—indeed, civilization itself—are seen as parts of a gigantic hoax.

The Hemingway protagonist may transmit the same emotional shock to the reader in a number of different ways, ranging from the gradual slipping away of the sense of security as experienced by Nick Adams in a number of stories such as "The Killers," "The Battler," and "Fathers and Sons," to the gradual, heartbreaking loss of a goal gained with so much effort and courage that we see in _The Old Man and the Sea._ However, we feel the emotional shock of threatened disaster most deeply in response to the struggle of the Hemingway protagonist to save himself. It is at such times that the game structure becomes the only means by which some measure of security can be achieved, the only anchor available by which some measure of spiritual stability can be acquired. If the Hemingway protagonist seems at times overly fond of the tangible apparatus of his game, we should perhaps forgive a drowning man his need to cling to his life preserver.

The first critic to apprehend this quality of implicit terror in Hemingway's work and discuss it at length was Malcolm Cowley. Cowley probably began the modern trend of viewing Hemingway more seriously and more closely than he had been viewed during the years before World War II. In his introduction to _The Portable Hemingway_ (1944), "Nightmare and Ritual in Hemingway," Cowley suggests that Hemingway might more profitably be associated with the "haunted and nocturnal writers," such as Poe, Hawthorne, and Melville, than with the naturalistic tradition with which Hemingway is usually associated.[1]

Cowley points out that in Hemingway's fiction there "are visions as terrifying as those of 'The Pit and the Pendulum' even though most of them are copied from life" (p. 41). But Cowley makes his point largely through an emphasis on Hemingway's unusual selec-

---

[1] Reprinted in Weeks, ed., _Hemingway: A Collection of Critical Essays._ Cowley did the same thing for Faulkner criticism a year later in another _Portable_ introduction.

tion of subject matter—the corpses, the gored horses, the punch-drunk boxers, and nymphomaniacs—whereas the quality of "nightmares at noonday" is only partly dependent on the use of such subject matter. As a matter of fact, two of Hemingway's most terrifying stories, "Big Two-Hearted River"[2] and "Hills Like White Elephants," have no aberrations in them at all. It might also be added that it was Hemingway's employment of such unusual subject matter as Cowley dwells on that probably led so many readers to associate Hemingway with the naturalists in the first place and distracted them from the deeper shocks in Hemingway's fiction that have lain largely unperceived for so many years.

No, it is Hemingway's technique which makes the dream real, and reality so often like a dream. It is his ability to suggest, sometimes very subtly, that each moment of man's existence is passed on the edge of an unthinkable void, and that for no reason at all, the ground may give way at any time. Such is the precarious position of Nick in "Big Two-Hearted River," who walks the edge of chaos, testing each moment much as a tightrope walker tests his footing, step by perilous step. The very details of each sensory moment are so insisted upon, so savored, that they are the ticks of a time bomb. It is a similar technique, a variety of verbal irony, that Hemingway uses in "Hills Like White Elephants," wherein the man insists so often that "it's perfectly simple" and that "I don't want you to do it if you don't really want to" (p. 373). We know just the opposite is the case: it is not simple at all, and he does want her to get the abortion no matter how she may feel about it. The whole world is a throw rug, and with the insistent beating drum of protested good intentions, the young man is about to yank the rug out from under the young woman's feet. In "Big Two-Hearted River" the insistence on reality makes everything become paradoxically unreal; in "Hills Like White Elephants" the insistence that everything is all right makes us feel sure that everything is not all right at all.

Nick Adams in "Big Two-Hearted River," like the central char-

[2] Cowley's interpretation of "Big Two-Hearted River" in the article cited above has become the definitive reading of the story.

acter in each of Hemingway's novels, is charged with the task of saving his selfhood. For this story can be viewed not only in the context of the other Nick Adams stories, the pattern that Philip Young has so admirably re-created, but also as part of the persistent pattern of achieving self-honesty and being hard on oneself that I have already noted in *The Sun Also Rises* and *A Farewell to Arms*.[3] To lose this self-conflict is to lose everything, a possibility that haunts Hemingway's protagonists like Jake Barnes and Frederic Henry, and is detected by the recurrence of "night thoughts" and the constant determination "not to think about it." What precisely these thoughts are remains ominously unthinkable, creating a pattern of suggested terror that makes it unnecessary for Hemingway ever to resort to the Gothic materials of a Poe or the semi-Gothic materials of a Melville or a Conrad. The terror that quietly accompanies a Barnes or a Henry is the more immediate terror that accompanies every man; it does not require a monster or a trip to the Congo for us to find it. One may be reminded of the concluding stanza from one of Robert Frost's poems:

> They cannot scare me with their empty spaces
> Between stars—on stars where no human race is.
> I have it in me so much nearer home
> To scare myself with my own desert places.[4]

For Nick, in "Big Two-Hearted River," the heart of darkness that he must himself fish is the swamp, but it is also the other "heart" within his own being that he must at last face. Despite the burned-over countryside of the world in which Nick finds himself, he sees how the trout keep themselves steady even in the deep, fast-moving water, and he finds watching them "very satisfactory." But when he goes "deep," so deep that the water in the swamp is "up under his armpits," and fishes for trout "in places impossible to land them," will he be able to remain steady? (p. 329). Will Nick be able to risk himself to a commitment again now that he knows the

[3] Young, *Ernest Hemingway*. Young's interpretation of "Big Two-Hearted River" takes up the theme of terror proposed by Cowley and skillfully relates it to the entire pattern of the Nick Adams stories.

[4] "Desert Places," *Complete Poems of Robert Frost* (New York, 1959), p. 386.

experience of losing? "In the swamp the banks were bare, the big cedars came together overhead, the sun did not come through, except in patches; in the fast deep water, in the half light, the fishing would be tragic. In the swamp fishing was a tragic adventure" (p. 329).

Unperceived even by those readers who have seen the story as a story of terror barely held under control is the fact that the prime terror is held, not in the understated fabric of the story and the ritual acted out by Nick as a "spell to banish evil spirits,"[5] but in the ending and the implications that the ending casts back on the entire story. In the ending, Nick "climbed the bank and cut up into the woods, toward the high ground. He was going back to camp. He looked back. The river just showed through the trees. There were plenty of days coming when he could fish the swamp" (p. 330). Hemingway's emphasis is not on the day's fishing just completed, but on the challenge of fishing the swamp which Nick has put off to some indefinite time in the future. The evil spirits are not really banished at all by the ritual of the fishing that Nick has done so far, but only kept in abeyance. The whole purpose of Nick's fishing trip is apparently the direct confrontation with the swamp, a confrontation he cannot bring himself to.

Thus, Nick would seem, at least temporarily and possibly permanently, defeated in his attempt to risk commitment (from his shaky condition, we can add "again") and the loss that commitment inevitably involves ("tragedy"). This, then, is the picture of the unsuccessful man who is unwilling to get into "the deep water" of another Catherine, another bridge, or another marlin. There is no doubt that his mere endurance at this point involves some courage. The old forms are enough to secure for him one half of the "two-hearts"—but to be complete, to secure the other half of himself, he must press his courage to the sticking point. He must move from the heart of light, and the security of the insulation that life offers in mere procedure, to the heart of darkness. Nick's tragedy is that he cannot again face tragedy. He cannot regain himself en-

[5] Cowley, p. 48.

tire. To use Hemingway's phrase from *A Farewell to Arms*, it may be that Nick is not broken to become stronger at "the broken places"; it may be that Nick has lost his selfhood or manhood forever and can never again be complete.

Like the nightmare, which so frequently focuses on the emotional condition of the self, the loss or threat of loss in Hemingway's fiction appears always as an essentially individual proposition. There is no help available beyond the individual's own resources. Nature cannot heal Nick; Nick must heal himself. In the final analysis, man stands alone, terrifyingly alone, cut off from God and men. He is not a member of a spiritual or temporal society wherein any reciprocal benefits are bestowed; if a man contributes to society in any sense at all, he does so only by fighting and by winning his own battle. Always victimized, he need not be a victim until he stops fighting, until he allows disaster or the threat of disaster to overcome his courage. The ultimate disaster, among many kinds of loss, is that by failing in courage, one might lose one's self. This is why, when fighting victimization, the central character's emotional condition, although enveloped in the problem of loss, is more often related to terror than it is to sentimentality.

Although the central character cannot be helped, it is necessary in Hemingway's fiction that he be observed, that his condition and achievement be witnessed and recognized, if only by the reader. It is a requirement that can modify the emotional context surrounding the protagonist in many ways, sometimes leading, depending on how the emotional values of the situation are handled, to a tragic effect and sometimes to a pathetic or even sentimental effect in response to the protagonist's suffering or loss.

I have already noted how Hemingway found in the bullfight a metaphor for ethical behavior as well as a metaphor which could express the tragedy of man's condition. Of tremendous importance to Hemingway is the presence of an audience within this framework which observes and judges the behavior of the bullfighter in relation to the game context. As a metaphor, this actor-audience relationship is rather strange in its application to the fictionalization of aspects of life other than the bullfight, for the protagonist of courage becomes tied to the existence of an observer, and it often seems as important to Hemingway that the observer be qualified as it is for the protagonist to be courageous. The reader of Hemingway's work, in one way or another, is usually offered the opportunity to be observant and appreciative; however, the other part of the audience is made up of characters within the story itself who are either unobservant, learning to be observant, or already observant. When, as in the last chapter, the audience is primarily unobservant, a sense of injustice is created in the reader-audience, and sentimentality can result.

The archetypal pattern for unapprehended courage can be seen in Hemingway's presentation of the bullfight. Two such scenes are presented in *The Sun Also Rises*. The first scene concerns Belmonte, who, although he cheats by preselecting his bulls, faces a public "who wanted three times as much from Belmonte, who was sick with a fistula, as Belmonte had ever been able to give, [and as a result the public] felt defrauded and cheated" (p. 214). The audience begins to throw cushions and vegetables, and Belmonte, assuming a role of indifference and contempt for the crowd, moves to an isolated position against the barrera and leans on it, "his head on his arms, not seeing, not hearing anything, only going through his pain" (p. 215). Alone, in pain, and misunderstood, the emotions arising from Belmonte's condition have nowhere to go except to the reader.

The second example of unappreciated valor in *The Sun Also Rises* is very similar to the scene of the nurses in *A Farewell to Arms* and the commentary by the tourists in *The Old Man and the Sea*. The bullfighter Romero gets a bull that is defective in vision so that he must lure the bull with his body and then step back and finish his pass with the cape. Romero actually demonstrates great skill and courage in dealing with the bull in this way, but the tourists in the stands prefer "Belmonte's imitation of himself or Marcial's imitation of Belmonte":

"What's he afraid of the bull for? The bull's so dumb he only goes after the cloth."

"He's just a young bull-fighter. He hasn't learned it yet."
"But I thought he was fine with the cape before."
"Probably he's nervous now." (p. 218)

It is significant that the only extended scenes of bullfighting in Hemingway's fiction (the two scenes just referred to plus the story "The Undefeated") all contain unappreciated valor. Demonstrating further the lack of appreciation which Hemingway so often connects with his courageous protagonist in fiction is seen in factual contrast in one of the photographs included in *Death in the Afternoon* (p. 369). The scene shows the bullfighter Granero dead in the infirmary after being gored in the ring. He is surrounded by a crowd of men; sixteen of the faces of these men appear in the photograph. Hemingway's commentary is pointedly bitter: "Only two in the crowd are thinking about Granero. The others are all intent on how they will look in the photograph" (p. 368).

The second condition of the observer, that of the learner, can be one which balances the emotion within the story so that the burden of the reader-audience is more a cognizance of the emotion than an emotional involvement. A very effective story in which the emotional sequence of stimulus and response is well balanced *within* the story is "The Killers." Nick has witnessed the attempt to murder the former boxer, Ole Anderson, by two Chicago hoodlums who, with unemotional efficiency, have set up Henry's lunchroom for the kill in anticipation of Ole's nightly visit. But Ole doesn't show up, the killers leave temporarily, and Nick goes off to warn Ole at Hirsch's rooming house. He finds Ole in his room. When Nick tells him what has happened at the lunchroom, Ole thanks him but tells him that there isn't anything to be done about the killers. When Nick suggests getting out of town, Ole tells him, "I'm through with all that running around" (*1st 49*, p. 385). Ole, who is the protagonist of courage here, tells Nick that he hasn't been able to make up his mind to go out but that he will "after a while" (p. 386). There is the usual irony in the willing unawareness of the cook and the good-natured unawareness of the rooming-house landlady in contrast to the unavoidable doom that Ole has finally brought himself to face with a certain amount of dignity as well as resignation. But the emotional impact of the situation is placed squarely on Nick, rather than on the nonunderstanding or unwilling observers, when Nick finds the horror of Ole's position unthinkable.

Nick cannot face the fact that there are people in real life, just as there are in the movies, who force other people to do what they wish at the point of a gun and who make a kind of game (one of the killers is "like a photographer arranging for a group picture") of killing someone they don't even know. Like the steady impersonal march of some natural disaster, the killers move in for the kill without any concern for retribution or arrest and with as much passion as a plumber fixing a leaky faucet. Nick simply cannot believe what he has heard and seen is true. He becomes even more disturbed when he decides to risk playing the hero by warning Ole, only to find that his act of courage accomplishes nothing. Nick offers to tell Ole what the killers look like; he offers to go to the police; he offers to do anything that might help. But Ole replies that there is no help, that "there ain't anything to do" (p. 385). The emotions that arise from Ole's situation (as reinforced by the cynical joking of the killers in the opening scenes) are very precisely balanced by Nick's reactions throughout the story. It is Nick, not Ole, who twists and turns like a hooked trout, and because it is Nick, the emotional impact of the ending of the story is placed on the learning experience itself as well as on the lesson of general significance that Nick learns: grim, unavoidable disaster is a part of the real world and is a possibility that each man must face as he lives in that world. Despite the aloneness, the sick helplessness, and even the surrounding lack of comprehension of Ole's condition, there is no pathetic emphasis in the story on his individual suffering. There is not a shred of sentimentality in the story because there is a comprehending witness in the story to absorb the emotion and this absorption is made explicit, particularly at the crucial point of the story's ending: " 'I'm going to get out of this town,' Nick said. 'Yes,' said George. 'That's a good thing to do.' 'I can't stand to think about him waiting in the room and knowing he's going to get it. It's too damned awful.' 'Well,' said George, 'you better not think about it' " (p. 387). The structure of the story with its emphasis on Nick's reactions gives Ole's victimization intellectual distance, and by doing so, places this short story as firmly within the sphere of tragedy as any short story can be placed.

However, it is possible for the story with a learner to contain sentimentality if the reactions of the learner are suppressed. Such is the case in the story "In Another Country." Like Nick, the narrator here witnesses an extremely emotional situation, but unlike Nick's reactions, the reactions of the narrator are not indicated nearly so strongly and are insufficient to carry the emotional load. The emotional condition of the courageous protagonist of this story, the major, is much more explicitly described than that of Ole Anderson, and the major's struggle to contain his emotions multiplies the emotional values involved. The major is a patient in a hospital where he is being treated by machines (in which he has little faith) for the restoration of a hand that has been wounded and rendered almost useless. He is generally very dignified and soldierly, but one day he becomes very angry and abusive. He leaves the narrator for a moment and then comes back to apologize for his rudeness—his wife has just died unexpectedly of pneumonia. The reaction of the narrator, " 'Oh—' I said, feeling sick for him. 'I am *so* sorry,' " is hardly enough to absorb the shock of what follows:

He stood there biting his lower lip. "It is very difficult," he said. "I cannot resign myself."

He looked straight past me and out through the window. Then he began to cry. "I am utterly unable to resign myself," he said and choked. And then crying, his head up looking at nothing, carrying himself straight and soldierly, with tears on both his cheeks and biting his lips, he walked past the machines and out the door. (p. 370)

There is no further reaction by the narrator except a descriptive one in which, at the end of the story, he notes how the doctor has secured some before-and-after photographs of various wounds and placed them in front of the machines. (The wound now in question is of course neither photographable nor subject to mechanical therapy.) The understatement of the last sentence directs the emotional impact of the major's condition right toward the reader: "The photographs did not make much difference to the major because he only looked out of the window" (p. 370).

In these two stories, "The Killers" and "In Another Country," are two different kinds of emotional suppression: the implicit emotion within Ole Anderson's resignation, and the struggle to suppress and then the actual suppression of emotion by the major. The emotional condition of the major has more impact, but despite the fact that his emotions are very directly presented, they would not have the sentimental impact they have if the emotions were met in the story with an explicit reaction sufficient to balance them, such as an extreme expression of grief on the part of the observer.

In both stories the themes are implicit, and the themes in both cases relate to a discovery made by the learner based on his emotional sensitivity to the situation. In "The Killers," Nick discovers that there is evil in the world that lurks behind everyday reality and is not subject to remedy. The concentration of the emotion in him puts the emphasis of the story on his learning reaction, *not on the horror of the material itself.* In the case of the narrator in "In Another Country," the theme is probably revealed through the narrator's discovery that there is more than one kind of courage, not only the courage of the medal winners that he first admires, but also the courage of the major who "did not believe in bravery" (p. 368). Although the question, What is courage? is skillfully posed in the first half of the story, the comparison of the two kinds of courage is left to the reader, the learning experience in the story is left to the reader, and the emotional reaction in the story is left to the reader. If the narrator-observer does not react to the suffering or loss of the courageous protagonist, the reader-observer is called upon to react instead. Such a call makes the reader an emotional participant, and he is forced as a participant to leave his intellectual distance behind. In the first story we *see* and *judge* the reaction of Nick, cognizant of the emotional values of the story; in the second story, we *feel* the loss sustained by the major, and we can make his loss and suffering our own. It is not a question of one story being more emotional than the other. It is a question of to what end and in what direction the emotional pressure is applied—Are we led to emotional recognition or ego participation?

The third type of observer is the already observant character who can be characterized as the "professional." Whenever the totally competent observer is included in a Hemingway story, the emotions arising from acts of the courageous protagonist are almost always sufficiently balanced, and sentimentality is avoided. The story "A Clean, Well-Lighted Place" provides, again, a case in point. Despite his attempts at suicide, the old man who is the customer at the cafe is the protagonist of courage. His condition is ostensibly a very sentimental one—he is old, alone, and partially deaf. We may conclude from his suicide attempt that he is greatly disturbed, yet he suppresses his surface emotions with great dignity. However, the story is in no way sentimental. The emotional emphasis is not placed on the old man or on the unaware young waiter, but rather on the perceptive sympathy of the older waiter, which serves again, as such a reaction does in "The Killers," to keep the emotion within the story itself. While sharing the older waiter's sympathy and his experience of terror, we are allowed to maintain our intellectual distance.

Another case in point is the extremely successful "The Short Happy Life of Francis Macomber." Here the already observant character is Robert Wilson, and the courageous protagonist is, of course, Macomber. Unlike the arrangement in "A Clean, Well-Lighted Place," the courageous protagonist is the main character, and the observer is a supporting character. The success of this story is due to the extremely adept way in which Hemingway manipulates the emotional values at the ending. He leads up to the ending by placing a great deal of importance on the judgment of Robert Wilson, so that when Macomber chooses to hold his ground against the charging buffalo rather than run, as he did from the lion, Macomber indicates that he has accepted the value system of Wilson. Macomber at the end of his life chooses to "play the game" and by doing so indicates that Wilson's approval is more important to him than his wife's.[6]

After Macomber's wife kills Macomber, the emphasis of the story is placed on the reactions of the wife and of Wilson; the courage of Macomber and even his death itself is curiously submerged below the depiction of Wilson's and the wife's emotional conflict. Commentators on this story are still evenly divided about whether the wife kills Macomber accidentally or murders him. For my part, I think that this controversy must be settled by taking the word of the narrator, who states definitely that "Mrs. Macomber, in the car, had shot at the buffalo" (*1st 49*, p. 135). What is confusing, but quite significant, is that Wilson *thinks or chooses to think* that she has done it on purpose. This is a masterful stroke, for the dominant emotion that emerges from the story is the anger of the white hunter who had "begun to like" Macomber.

The emotional emphasis of the story cannot be placed on the "tragic" death of Macomber just as he is finding himself, for such an emphasis on the condition of the courageous protagonist, as I have explained, would probably cause a sentimental leaking of emotion to the reader. Nor can it go to the unaware observer, in this case the wife (whose role matches that of the young waiter in "A Clean, Well-Lighted Place"). If Mrs. Macomber's reaction were a cold "I'm glad he's dead—what are you going to do about it," satiric irony would turn the emotion back to the sad condition of Macomber, particularly if Mrs. Macomber's reaction were made more emphatic than Wilson's. If, on the other hand, the emotional emphasis were on the wife and her grief, and if her grief were real, the story would become sentimental by turning the reader's attention to the sad death of Macomber and the wife's consequent ironic loss. As it is, the wife's reaction is kept ambiguous and appears to involve a mixture of shock, defensiveness, and perhaps grief; but

[6] Although Mrs. Macomber's attitude toward her husband is certainly both ambivalent and ambiguous throughout the story, she is clearly bent (for whatever psychological reasons) on maintaining her dominance over Macomber. She is a monster created by circumstances at least partly beyond her own control. Considered from Mrs. Macomber's point of view, this is a very sad story, but Hemingway does not allow us to take that perspective.

more importantly, her reactions are completely overshadowed by the clear power of Wilson's rage. Wilson's angry assertion, "Why didn't you poison him?" is the only way in which Macomber's short "life" can be made a happy one, even though *Wilson's assertion may be mistaken and unjust*. The placing of emotional emphasis on Wilson and his anger (a final expression of approval for Macomber's behavior) puts the theme of the story squarely on Macomber's life, rather than on his death.

The patterns of these last two stories are fairly common in Hemingway's work: the several combinations of the unaware observer, the aware (or learning to be aware) observer, and the courageous protagonist. The main or central character may be any one of the three, even the unaware observer. This is the case in the story "A Canary for One," wherein the emotional emphasis is placed on the American lady whose ideas and behavior contrast so sharply with the perceptions and conditions of the aware observer, the narrator of the story. Seldom is the emotional emphasis placed on unawareness in Hemingway's work without a measure of sentimentality resulting, but in this story that pitfall is avoided by having the suffering condition of the courageous protagonist, the daughter, presented entirely by implication. Although not comparable to the complete blindness of the American lady, unawareness is the initial role, as we might recall, of both Jake Barnes and Frederic Henry. As each struggles to clarify his vision as a basis for emotional soundness, his role changes and he becomes a protagonist of courage, as well as a progressively more perceptive observer.

The fact that the role of the central character may shift from story to story or change in the course of a novel has caused much confusion and a great many problems for those critics of Hemingway who have attempted to codify the characteristics of a Hemingway hero. On an over-all basis, the central character in Hemingway's fiction may be either the antagonist or protagonist. If the central character is a protagonist, he may be either an observer, a courageous protagonist, or both. In regard to these possibilities, it is difficult to see what the word *hero* means. It is very misleading to talk about Romero, for example, as the "hero" of *The Sun Also Rises*.[7]

To group together all the characters in Hemingway's works who display courage—disregarding whether they are minor or major figures and what their particular functions are in relation to the central purposes of the stories or novels they appear in—is not a very useful approach. At the same time, to group together all of the central characters in order to codify their conditions or qualities is an extremely difficult and risky procedure. The fact is that although Hemingway's central themes, courage, commitment, and awareness, remain the same throughout his career, he attempts to deal with these themes from a number of different points of view, displaying more virtuosity and imagination in shifting from one point of attack to another than he is usually given credit for. It is very likely that Hemingway worked by instinct, trying first one combination of elements and then another in an effort to achieve that effect of emotional rightness which would bring to his readers the perfect moral vision, that vision by which man's ordeal could be seen in clear, and as close as possible to tragic, terms.

What does remain largely the same in Hemingway's work is the nature of the world that surrounds his characters and the ethical framework, game, by which his characters' behavior, understanding, and growth (if any) must be evaluated. The most constant demand of all in Hemingway's work is the demand for ethical judgment, a demand sometimes made of characters within the story itself, but a demand always made of the reader-observer. This demand can be met on the level of general tragic significance only on those occasions in which Hemingway has arranged the emotional values of his story in such a way that the reader can use his intellectual faculties as well as his emotional sensitivity.

[7] Mark Spilka, whose admirable article I have already referred to (p. 32, n. 4), regards Romero as "an image of integrity, against which Barnes and his generation are weighed and found wanting. In this sense, Pedro is the real hero of the parable . . ." (p. 25). Although qualified, Spilka's terminology is confusing. Romero is an image, perhaps, and a symbol of integrity, but not a hero even in the Hemingway sense. He is barely a character and certainly is not dealt with on the basis of internal conflict. The conflict may be there, but it is not the subject of this particular story.

THE ROAD FROM SELF

♦ ♦ ♦ TO MOVE to what measure of success he was able to gain in the later novels, Hemingway was required to change direction drastically, to take the risk of moving from the easier youthful postures of revolt and disillusionment, and to fight sentimentality with action rather than reaction, with a greater vision of man than the thin imagination of Victorian respectability could provide for. In this vision there is no easy affirmation of the "good things" in life or "positive values"; there are only the small but firm victories of the spirit that announce, rather than just the survival of the self, the reality of Man.

With the death of Harry Morgan in *To Have and Have Not* comes the death of the early Hemingway protagonist, the young man who is battered, but who finds enough emotional stamina to face the world alone. Harry does not have the moral depth of a Jake Barnes or a Frederic Henry, but he is the logical extension of the weakest aspects of their moral positions. He stands alone with courage against the same deluded, weak, and corrupt world. Like his eponym the pirate, he attempts to deal with the problems of his personal needs as an amoral individual agent, acting purely on the basis of an individual, pragmatic code of behavior. He defies the law when he feels the law is wrong, easily resorts to violence when he feels violence is necessary, and trampling on considerations of sentiment, clings to a role of toughness and hard efficiency.

Harry dies, not because he fails to be sufficiently hard or suspicious, but because he tries to tackle the whole world with one hand. He plays, in a very realistic way, the popular hero's role in a game from another age—damn the odds. His death does not mark the decline of the individual in Hemingway's writing, but rather the end of the romantic individual. For Harry is the victim of the self sentimentally conceived as self-sufficient.

As an object lesson, Harry's game may have some relevance, but Harry's winning or losing is not even morally significant to his own condition. If Harry's famous last words "No matter how a man alone ain't got no bloody fucking chance" (p. 225) mean that he has learned something, then they embody a lesson lost to the reader as well as to the uncomprehending witnesses to Harry's death, for the reader has been unaware up to this moment that any profound internal moral struggle had ever taken place. No, the novel does not support a change in Harry so much as it signifies the wheezy, sputtering end to an emotional position that Hemingway no longer had any stomach for. Hemingway himself felt that this novel was "in many ways the most important story he had ever written. Before it, he hadn't cared how life went as long as he could create productively. From this point on, he really gave a damn about other people's lives."[1] Hemingway does not, however, change his focus following this novel to one of "social consciousness." The individual emphasis remains, but Harry Morgan becomes the fictional transition between the individual's emotional condition as separate and the individual's emotional condition as connected.

In one sense there is an easy glamour about the early novels and stories that tends to obscure the limited, yet remarkable achievements to be found within Hemingway's later work. To look back over Hemingway's early work in a negative and simplified way, much of that work adds up to little more than a convincing denial of the conventional, a persuasive reversal of the cultural consciousness. We are compelled by the understated, the anti-dramatic, and

[1] Leicester Hemingway, p. 185. I am in debt to Robert W. Lewis, Jr.—in *Hemingway on Love*—for bringing the appropriateness of this statement to my attention (p. 113).

a position of ironic superiority to believe in a non-world. We are overcome by a superb technique; a deep sense of loss and futility enfolds us: belief becomes convincingly irrelevant, and emotions either modify or revert to the self. Love becomes a condition, rather than an act or a response—in the words of T. S. Eliot:

> Trembling with tenderness
> Lips that would kiss
> Form prayers to broken stone[2]

To overcome this paralysis and to gain positive emotional force without the possible contamination of sentimentality, Hemingway turns more and more to primitive elements that predate our present emotional constipation. Primitivism predicates an emotional relation between man and his total environment—human, animate, and inanimate—which antedates science and the debilitating effects of science on the emotional potency of nature. As seen in this light, sentimentality is partly a product of science, an attempt to attach emotions to man's environment which are no longer organically generated by that environment. Sentimentality is thus an artificial emotional response brought to bear on a situation thought to have no real emotional relevance; no actual threat exists, no real attachment is possible. Sentimentality is generated by the self and for the self in a state of isolation as a substitute for connection.

In the early novels the spring rain stirs only the dull roots of memory, but in *The Old Man and the Sea*, the gods live once again. To the extent that the gods live, so does tragedy. The tragic world is one in which emotions are possible because everything has a profound moral, and hence emotional, relevance. Connection is not only possible, it is inescapable, and even the slightest gesture of the right man at the right time may shake the world's foundations.

Whether impotent in a dead world or potent in a live one, the protagonist remains a dramatic exaggeration, but Hemingway has reversed the telescope. Jake Barnes becomes emotionally sound, but remains sterile, locked within the prison of himself; Santiago brings fertility and meaning to everything he touches, to every en-

[2] *The Complete Plays and Poems: 1909–1950*, p. 58.

vironment he enters. Appropriately, Hemingway's chronology begins with the sexually maimed Fisher King among his ruins, gathering his fragments together unto himself, and ends with the Fisherman restored whose life force spreads out across the sea, who will go out too far, catch a fish too big, and in the face of destruction, will not cease to love. The dreams of Jake Barnes reduce him: a man shivers alone and turns on the light to drive away the darkness. The dreams of Santiago extend his spirit to the very limits of man in both space and time: a young lion plays on the shore of the dark continent.

The greatness of the early novels can hardly be denied, but their greatness lies not in their vision, but in their control: they are masterpieces of refutation. As attractive as such refutations may be for the existentially oriented reader of our time, it is not until *For Whom the Bell Tolls* that Hemingway comes close to achieving that fundamental and lasting emotional relevance that he, himself, had identified as the object of his search. For it is in this novel that Hemingway is first able to re-create in modern terms the emotional climate of traditional tragedy, an emotional climate which, in the words of Joseph Wood Krutch, is the celebration of the "greatness of the human spirit. . . . an expression, not of despair, but of the triumph over despair and of confidence in the value of human life."[3]

Illustrative of one of the changes in Hemingway's thinking that apparently took place in the ten-year interval from the writing of *A Farewell to Arms* to the writing of *For Whom the Bell Tolls* is the famous, although puzzling passage wherein Jordan declares his faith. He spells out what he is fighting for in the very abstractions that made Frederic Henry sick to his stomach:

You're not a real Marxist and you know it. You believe in Liberty, Equality and Fraternity. You believe in Life, Liberty and the Pursuit of Happiness. Don't ever kid yourself with too much dialectics. . . . You have put many things in abeyance to win a war. If this war is lost all of those things are lost. (p. 305)

[3] "The Tragic Fallacy," in Richard Levin, ed., *Tragedy: Plays, Theory, and Criticism* (New York, 1960), p. 165.

To the reader of the earlier Hemingway, this declaration seems weak and incongruous. Not only has Jordan used abstractions, but he uses two slogans from previous middle-class revolutions as a basis for acting in conjunction with the Communists in Spain. It could be that Hemingway just could not decide how to have Jordan make this kind of statement without using abstractions, or it could be that Hemingway is defending himself here against charges of Communist sympathy. However, a better solution is suggested by something else Krutch says in his essay on tragedy: "We accept gladly the outward defeats which it [tragedy] describes for the sake of the inward victories which it reveals. . . . However much things in the outward world may go awry, man has, nevertheless, splendors of his own and that, in a word, Love and Honor and Glory are not words but realities" (p. 166). The most obvious answer to the puzzle of Jordan's words, perhaps too obvious to accept (or too void of sophistication), is that this is a sincere declaration of faith. Unlike the skeptic, Frederic Henry, Jordan really believes in Liberty, Equality, and Fraternity. These are not just a slogan to him but words that represent realities; they are real to Jordan, not because they exist in immediate, tangible forms, but because he has faith in their possibility. It is such a faith that makes God real to man. And by having faith in such basic social ideals, as unaristocratic as they may be, Jordan has, in a sense, made tragedy possible.

"A tragic writer does not have to believe in God," Krutch continues, "but he must believe in man" (p. 166). Above all, *For Whom the Bell Tolls* is an expression of faith in man, and even more important, an expression of belief in man's noblest possibilities with full knowledge of the worst acts of barbarism and cruelty (as well as stupidity, selfishness, and cowardice) of which man is capable. Jordan's outward defeats, represented both by his failure to accomplish anything by the blowing up of the bridge and by his death, are completely overshadowed by the glory of his power to remain true to his faith until the end. He insists at his death that his mind remain accurate and his emotions reject cynicism. Jordan's is an inward victory of some significance.

Throughout the novel, Hemingway takes great pains to show us that Jordan is not naive or gullible, so that Jordan's faith in himself and his cause is established on firm, realistic grounds. All of Hemingway's later heroes are extremely alert and aware individuals, but Jordan is perhaps the most sharply observant of them all. From the very beginning of the novel we realize that he is a man who not only sees everything, but interprets everything properly. In the opening pages we see Jordan assessing his companion ("Robert Jordan trusted the man, Anselmo, so far, in everything except judgment. He had not yet had an opportunity to test his judgment" [p. 4]) and his surroundings ("whoever was above had been very careful not to leave any trail"; "[He] noticed that the grass was cropped down in several places and signs that picket pins had been driven into the earth" [pp. 4, 12]).

In the middle of the novel, in one of the flashbacks to Jordan's early experiences in the Civil War, we learn that Jordan initially felt part of a "crusade," but after six months of fighting, his "purity of feeling" disappeared (p. 235). Jordan makes friends among the politically powerful within the Republican ranks and finds himself exposed to the cynicism and maneuvering that goes on behind the propaganda veil used to maintain the faith of the naive. At Gaylord's, the Madrid hotel taken over by the Russians, Jordan learns that "the talk that he had thought of as cynicism when he had first heard it had turned out to be much too true" (p. 228). He finds that "Gaylord's was the place where you met famous peasant and worker Spanish commanders who had sprung to arms from the people at the start of the war without any previous military training and found that many of them spoke Russian" (p. 229). Jordan is by no means a dewy-eyed idealist, and that is what makes his adherence to his ideals so convincing and important. Jordan was a man who "liked to know how it really was; not how it was supposed to be" (p. 230). The more he fought in Spain, the more he realized that "the things he had come to know in this war were not so simple" (p. 248).

This last statement by Jordan appears to announce a different direction in Hemingway's thinking. Hemingway began his search for "true emotion" by observing the "simplest things" within experi-

ence, and by the time he wrote *For Whom the Bell Tolls*, he found
that it is principle that is "simple," in the sense of being fundamental and lasting, and that it is experience, after all, which is the
complicated thing. In appending his qualification "You have put
many things in abeyance to win a war" to his abstract statement of
belief, Jordan displays a complexity of development in his ability
to deal with the world that makes the earlier protagonist, Frederic
Henry, seem like a child in comparison. Like Henry, Jordan also
is cynical about certain things, but this is not the full dimension of
his personality. Jordan, too, is suspicious of wonderful-sounding
words: "You felt that you were taking part in a crusade. That was
the only word for it although it was a word that had been so worn
and abused that it no longer gave its true meaning" (p. 235). But
like the good bullfighter, and unlike Frederic Henry, Jordan is able
to combine his cynicism with a devoutness that the most difficult
and depressing of circumstances cannot shake. No other Hemingway protagonist, except perhaps Santiago, is so strong and tough
as Robert Jordan or so truly heroic. Hemingway has made *For
Whom the Bell Tolls* a moral laboratory; he takes a strong fabric,
dips it in the strong acid of an impossibly difficult situation, and
finds that the weave has held. Jordan believes; and what is more,
we, the readers, believe that he believes. In short, he is the first protagonist of a Hemingway novel to be a "professional."

Jordan's devoutness, however, is not easily maintained, nor can
it be and still be credible. Faith, like liberty, has the price of eternal vigilance, and for this reason *For Whom the Bell Tolls* can
easily be seen as a novel of faith and the struggle to maintain it.
Hemingway's major problem in the novel is to make this struggle
both difficult and yet possible, extraordinary and yet immediate
enough to touch the moral struggle faced by every reader. Some
critics have maintained that there is too much internal dialogue in
the novel.[4] However, despite large segments of the novel that de-

[4] Among those who have indicated this are Nemi D'Agostino, "The Later
Hemingway," in Weeks, ed., *Hemingway: A Collection of Critical Essays*, p.
151; and Mark Schorer, "The Background of a Style," *Kenyon Review*, III
(Winter, 1941), 104.

part from it, Jordan's consciousness is the novel's central focus. Not to see this focus is to miss, of course, the whole point of the novel: to show *how* Jordan is able to do what he does, not just to show what he does—which, after all, would be not much more than formula heroics. Jordan's internal conflict is a highly structured one within the ethical structure which I have termed the "game context." Also, Jordan's levels of awareness and commitment are much more complex than those of previous Hemingway protagonists. Dominating Jordan's consciousness is the familiar game element in the battle to be self-honest, a battle which is a recurring motif that links together the many divergent forces, characters, and subthemes that cluster around the central external act of blowing up the bridge.

Jordan's heroic stature is in large measure achieved through his ability to transcend the many different conflicts that pull on his emotions. Under the best of conditions, Jordan's probability of success on this particular mission is extremely marginal. The reader becomes aware of the difficulty of Jordan's task at the very beginning of the novel in the flashback scene where General Golz gives him his orders. Just "how bad" the situation is becomes more and more apparent throughout the novel when we find out that Jordan is usually composed, "cold in the head," and to a certain extent gay in the face of danger. During his interview with Golz, however, he is so worried by his assignment that he is almost surly and is completely unable to respond to Golz's joking.

Through the marginal probability of the mission's success, we are made conscious of Jordan's faith as the factor which may make the difference between success and failure. In addition, a chain of being is established in the novel, starting with the large offensive at the top, moving down through the separate functions of the various units, to the function of the particular unit directed by Jordan, and resting, finally, on the accurate functioning of Jordan's mind and the soundness of his spirit. The whole weight of this pyramid-in-reverse rests on Jordan. Without his blowing up the bridge and without his blowing it up at the right time, the whole offensive (the first big Republican offensive of the war) will fail. The chain must not be broken. "Merely to blow the bridge," as Golz tells Jordan, "is a failure" (p. 4). Later in the novel, when a Fascist cavalry unit is in the mountains and there is the opportunity to "make a massacre," Jordan is careful to warn his men not to shoot unless they absolutely have to: "It would avail nothing. That would serve no purpose. The bridge is a part of a plan to win the war. This would be nothing. This would be an incident. A nothing" (p. 277).

It becomes increasingly clear that large events are crucially dependent on smaller events and that the over-all battle for Segovia is dependent on individual battles, which in turn are dependent on the internal battles fought in the minds of the key participants. General order is dependent on internal order. The importance of the individual is confirmed by glimpses given to us by the narrator of internal battles other than Jordan's, battles fought in the minds of Anselmo, Sardo, Pilar, Andres, and Maria. By employing such a structure Hemingway tries to make sure that the reader perceives that reality is an individual proposition—there is no whole except as a structure of a number of individual parts. Such a structure forces us to view the epigraph from Donne as not so much a declaration endorsing the importance of social responsibility, as a declaration endorsing the importance of the individual. "Any man's *death* diminishes *me*" because each man's battle affects every other man's welfare. The morality of the whole is the sum of the morality of the parts. There is no mankind; there are only men.

Such a view of individual responsibility is the basis of genuine Christian ethics. Although war may seem a strange setting for a demonstration of Christianity, war quite appropriately represents the inhuman forces of this world, the many pressures inherent in human existence that would seem to make it impossible for the individual to remain a responsible individual. (I have already discussed this use of war in *A Farewell to Arms.*) Caught up in the pattern of the whole, forced by "realistic" circumstances to kill and to destroy (representing all the demands for compromise that the world makes of every man, whether in war or not), man can still act with principle within such a framework. If we view *For Whom the Bell Tolls* in this way, it is possible to see the novel as a kind of "morality play." In opposition to the difficult task of maintaining principle within the worst of all circumstances are the internal emotional weaknesses, the little temptations to self-deception that would lead men astray. Principle is tested only when compromise is necessary. Human issues are never clear-cut, and from the ragged edges of experience and the complexities of emotional reactions, a "messy battle" emerges that has its larger external counterpart in the "messy" civil war which is the setting of the novel.

Hemingway is extremely careful to show that there are no real villainies in this war except those engendered by the general human frailties which make war possible. Atrocity by one side is balanced by atrocity on the other, as the tale of Pablo's massacre is balanced by the tale of Maria's rape, and the most hateful aspects of Fascism (much to the dismay of the Communist critics of the novel)[5] are seen to be implicit in the authoritarianism, pragmatic calculation, scheming, hypocrisy, and brutal blindness of the Communist elements of the Republican side. It is as difficult to pick out the principles to be endorsed on the general political scene (and Jordan spends a great deal of time in the novel trying to clarify his precise political position)[6] as it is to make the smaller, more detailed decisions involving principle in the individual's experience. Thus, not only is Jordan himself a man who prefers to see things as they really are as a basis for acting on principle, but reality is further added to the context in which principle must be demonstrated by making the war situation itself a non-oversimplified tissue of rights and wrongs. One of the most dramatic instances that Hemingway uses to achieve this careful emotional balance which prevents oversimplification is to have the Fascist lieutenant (whom we previously learn to admire for his humanity, maintained, like Jordan's, despite the barbarity of the duty he must perform) face Jordan at the end of the novel. Jordan is about to die to help save his friends by facing the troop of cavalry led by the Fascist lieutenant.

[5] This is most notably demonstrated in Ivan Kashkeen, "Alive in the Midst of Death: Ernest Hemingway" in Carlos Baker, ed., *Hemingway and His Critics* (New York, 1961).
[6] Pp. 136, 162–65, 229–30, 235, 239, 244–46, 305.

The lieutenant, who is so much like Jordan, will be the first to die from Jordan's submachine gun.

One of the major moral conflicts in the novel is that between the duty to kill under the circumstances of war and the principle which values human life. Anselmo, whom Jordan refers to as "a Christian. Something very rare in Catholic countries" (p. 287), is extremely concerned about the sin of killing another human being. Early in the novel, in a discussion with Jordan, Anselmo explains that he feels that there is a great difference between animals and men, and killing men, even Fascists, is a sin. Anselmo will kill the Fascists since it must be done, "But if I live later, I will try to live in such a way, doing no harm to any one, that it will be forgiven" (p. 41). Since God is no longer with Anselmo ("If there were God, never would He have permitted what I have seen with my eyes"), Jordan suggests that it must be Anselmo himself who will forgive Anselmo —again leading to the individual as the moral unit emphasized in the novel.

When Anselmo does his duty by killing the guard at the other end of the bridge, he comes to help Jordan place the explosives with tears "running down . . . [his] cheeks through the gray beard stubble" (p. 435). Anselmo has proved himself the most reliable man among all those available to Jordan, and for this reason, Jordan chooses him for the key job of helping with the explosive. Yet it is Anselmo (in contrast to the others' impatience when Jordan repeats his orders immediately before the battle) who is concerned that Jordan repeat his orders very explicitly so that there will be no mistake and so that Anselmo will know very clearly that it is his duty to kill the guard: " 'I will do as thou orderest,' Anselmo said. 'Yes. I order it thus,' Robert Jordan said. I'm glad I remembered to make it an order, he thought. That helps him out. That takes some of the curse off. I hope it does, anyway. Some of it" (p. 410).

Jordan, too, is deeply concerned about killing. Not only does he mourn the death of his own friends (going into near shock at the death of Anselmo), but he mourns too the death of the enemy. When the lone cavalryman rides into camp almost up to the place where Jordan and Maria are sleeping, Jordan kills him with cool precision as a matter of necessity. But later, in going over the man's papers, he recognizes that the Fascist is no longer simply an enemy figure, but an individual human being, a boy that he has probably seen "run through the streets ahead of the bulls at the Feria in Pamplona" (p. 302). Ironically, the Fascist is the son of a blacksmith, a worker, as well as a member of a very religious family. It is the medal of the Sacred Heart of Jesus that was sent to the cavalryman by his sister which Jordan aimed for when shooting him— a medal that the sister insists has proved innumerable times "to have the power of stopping bullets" (p. 303). Jordan's reaction to the sister's and fiancée's letters is a deep sense of guilt and sorrow: "I guess I've done my good deed for today, he said to himself. I guess you have all right, he repeated" (p. 303). But guilt, like other destructive emotions, must be put aside for duty. "I'm sorry, if that does any good. It doesn't. . . . All right then, drop it, he said to himself" (p. 303).

Killing, Jordan feels, can only be justified if it is a necessity and one does not believe in killing. "If you believe in it," he tells himself, "the whole thing is wrong" (p. 304). On these and other matters there is a voice within Jordan that tries to keep him straight, that insists on being heard, and insists that only if these transgressions are faced honestly and not ignored can Jordan survive as a moral agent with a clear faith:

You listen, see? Because you are doing something very serious and I have to see you understand it all the time. I have to keep you straight in your head. Because if you are not absolutely straight in your head you have no right to do the things you do for all of them are crimes and no man has a right to take another man's life unless it is to prevent something worse happening to other people. So get it straight and do not lie to yourself. (p. 304)

"Do not lie to yourself" is the motto embossed on the shield of Jordan's moral armor. It is a motto that at times is not easy to adhere to. Jordan finds, despite himself, that he is occasionally infected by blood lust. When Augustín has the "necessity" to kill like a "mare in heat," Jordan first thinks that it is the Spanish who have this lust for killing as an "extra sacrament" (p. 286), that it is part of the racial inheritance, whereas, he thinks at first, "we" do it coldly. But then once again the voice of truth interrupts him:

And you, he thought, you have never been corrupted by it? . . . Stop making dubious literature about the Berbers and the old Iberians and admit that you have liked to kill as all who are soldiers by choice have enjoyed it at some time whether they lie about it or not. . . . Don't lie to yourself. (p. 287)

Throughout the novel, Jordan is able to maintain a careful emotional balance between extremes. Not only is he able to maintain his idealism while being a realist and pragmatist, but he is able to be suspicious as well as truthful, loving as well as unfeeling and calculating, and completely loyal as well as skeptical. Jordan's suspicions in the case of Pablo are, of course, quite justified, and although he is unable to prevent Pablo's making off with the detonator and caps, Jordan is usually one step ahead of the guerrilla leader, whose only virtue is his extraordinary intelligence. Jordan knows that before "the first friendly thing he does, he will have made a decision" (p. 16), and it is when Pablo decides to go along with the plan for the bridge that Pablo steals the materials and betrays Jordan and the guerrilla band. Jordan knows too what Pablo has in mind for the guerrillas (murdering them for their horses) that he recruited during the night after changing his mind a second time. On the other hand, Jordan is able to trust others, such as Anselmo, Pilar, and Andres, completely, not because they have proved themselves entirely trustworthy (there is not time enough for that), but because Jordan is emotionally stable enough to take the necessary risks, a stability that can arise only from a strong general faith in humanity.

Just as skepticism and trust balance each other in Jordan's personality, so also do the ability to love and the ability to act with unfeeling coldness when the occasion demands it. Of course, Jordan's most direct expression of love is that given to Maria, but his attitude toward Anselmo and Pilar must certainly be said to include a measure of love. Many readers have noted the parallel between the two rabbits that are killed by the Gypsy while they are copulating and the position of Robert and Maria as they are sleeping together in the snow. (Jordan even calls Maria "little rabbit.") A Fascist cavalryman almost rides over them before Jordan pushes Maria back into the sleeping bag and shoots the Fascist. Jordan's complete switch here from tenderness to the cold posture of an efficient killer may appear to be rather cynical: Maria "had no place in his life now" (p. 267). However, Maria and Robert are not rabbits; the evidence of the immediate context (Jordan's anger at Primitivo's question, "How is she in the bed?" [p. 270] and Jordan's promise to Augustín that he will marry Maria because he cares for her seriously [pp. 290–91]), as well as the overwhelming evidence throughout the novel of Jordan's true concern, show that Maria is not just a convenient outlet for sex. If we examine the parallel with the rabbits further, we can see that one significant difference between the rabbits and the humans is that the humans are able to make a rapid transition to duty; the rabbits are dead. Principle of a sort that affects a great number of people's welfare is placed over self-satisfaction (on whatever level, sensual or romantic). Jordan's duty is primary, as we see in a fragment from a conversation that he has with Pilar:

"You are a very cold boy." [Pilar says.]
"No," he said. "I do not think so."
"No. In the head you are very cold."
"It is that I am very preoccupied with my work."
"But you do not like the things of life?"
"Yes. Very much. But not to interfere with my work." (p. 91)

When we consider that Jordan's work is no ordinary occupation, but the direct and courageous demonstration of his belief in social justice, his ability to rapidly shift gears from love to duty appears more selfless than callous.

Further moderation in Jordan is demonstrated in his healthy balance between skepticism and loyalty. Jordan knows of the behind-the-scenes machinations of the Communists. He shows a healthy suspicion of political slogans, examining their meanings carefully. He catches himself inadvertently falling into the use of "Enemies of the people." He decides that "that was a phrase he might omit.

That was a catch phrase he would skip" (pp. 163–64). He knows that the Republicans are not all pure and the Fascists not all evil: "He believed in the Republic as a form of government but the Republic would have to get rid of all of that bunch of horse thieves that brought it to the pass it was in when the rebellion started. Was there ever a people whose leaders were as truly their enemies as this one?" (p. 163). Jordan promises to give "absolute loyalty and as complete [a] performance" as possible during the war, but at the same time "nobody owned his mind, nor his faculties for seeing and hearing" (p. 136).

The "morality play" that takes place in Jordan's mind is concerned, at one time or another during the novel, with repulsing or balancing false hope, prejudice, overidealization, hatred, anger, resentment, guilt, self-righteousness, and despair. On the one side, Jordan is tempted to resent Golz's orders and what they could do to him and the people he leads; he checks himself, "That is not the way to think" (p. 43). On the other side, when he is tempted to be too optimistic and to think how it might be if everything concerned with the attack came off without a hitch, he reminds himself, "You must not get illusions about it now. . . . Keep your sense of proportion" (p. 432). On the one side, he is tempted to overgeneralize the faults he has found among the Spanish, but tells himself, "This was no way to think" (p. 135). On the other side, he greatly appreciates Sordo's gesture of bringing the whiskey to him and decides that this is one of the reasons he loves the Spanish, but quickly he reminds himself, "Don't go romanticizing them" (p. 204). When Jordan starts to think of all the things that could go wrong, he tells himself to "stop it" (p. 161). When he comes to admire Anselmo's respect for human life, Jordan finds it necessary to warn himself not to idealize Anselmo (p. 287).

Much of the structure of Jordan's internal fight is based on a paralleling of opposing ideas, values, and courses of action. Jordan spends much of his time emphasizing the extremely moral focus in the book, making distinctions, guarding against tempting inaccuracies, and weighing the evidence of his perceptions against the demands of his faith. This pattern, which on an over-all basis can be roughly referred to as comparison and contrast in nature, is closely related to another pattern wherein the individual is implicitly compared to the group. The effect of this comparison is again to emphasize the importance of the individual.

One of the major ironies of *For Whom the Bell Tolls* is that all of the things we normally tend to think of, particularly in our time, in regard to the larger order (the army, the party, the country) are successfully carried out or demonstrated only by individuals. Political belief is cynical or distorted as it is reflected in the Republican camp as a whole, but it is sincere and quite well defined in the thinking of such individuals as Jordan. Armed action fails on the larger scale of the entire offensive, but succeeds in the hands of dedicated individuals such as Jordan.

The over-all picture of the Spanish Civil War presented in Hemingway's novel is a dismal one. When Golz gives Jordan his assignment to blow the bridge, Golz fatalistically predicts that something will go wrong: "Always some one will interfere" and "I have never been given what I ask for even when they have it to give" (p. 5). So many moral cripples within the Republican ranks are described during the course of the novel that the real question, in terms of the outcome of the war, becomes whether there are enough of the "good ones" to balance and overcome the confusion and decay caused by the cripples. Infesting the Republican cause are the horse thieves, like Pablo, who have little if any real social concern and who are antisocial parasites that have been able to take power because of the confusion of the war. Pablo's concern for the welfare only of his own band contrasts strongly throughout the novel with Jordan's willingness to submit himself entirely to the welfare of the whole, a whole that can only be conceived of in abstract terms. Pablo, on the other hand, would not fight for anything that he cannot feel directly in immediate terms, such as revenge or something he can eat or drink. In addition to Pablo, another cripple on the immediate scene is Rafael, the Gypsy, who is really more of a draft dodger than a patriot. Cripples infesting the larger scene are the general, Lister, who is a "true fanatic" and executes his troops for very little reason in order to gain discipline, the "fake soldiers" of Barcelona "who like everything about war except to fight" (p. 247); and the "puffy-eyed man" who, at Karkov's party, goes into raptures over the propaganda figure, "La Pasionaria." At one point in Karkov's party, a general, disgusted at "this filthy sewing circle of gossip," declares that "one man who could keep his mouth shut could save the country if he believed he could" (p. 359). To top off the list of grotesques is the frightening Comrade Marty, whose vicious cleverness, à la Stalin, becomes so blind to reality that it approaches insanity.

In addition to such grotesque figures, the novel contains continual hints of mismanagement, intrigue, falsehood, and double standards. Karkov's explanation—"I have to go upstairs to see people. Upstairs people"—has an ominous sound as he takes his leave from Jordan in Gaylord's bar to go up to a meeting (p. 248). Indeed, the landscape is just as dismal as Jake's postwar Paris or Frederic's Italian front in World War I, if not more so. Yet the crucial difference is that whereas the earlier Hemingway protagonists form no allegiances, or else withdraw their allegiances, Jordan finds the game worth playing despite the fact that the circumstances are not perfect. Overcoming disillusionment, his determination is made even stronger:

Sure, Gaylord's was the place you needed to complete your education. It was there you learned how it was all really done instead of how it was supposed to be done. . . . Gaylord's was good and sound and what he needed. At the start when he had still believed all the nonsense it had come as a shock to him. But now he knew enough to accept the necessity for all the deception and *what he learned at Gaylord's only strengthened him in his belief in the things that he did hold to be true.* (p. 230, italics mine)

In this statement of Jordan's the difference between the early and the later Hemingway protagonists is precisely defined. The early protagonists are amateurs, the later are professionals. The early protagonists are defensive—their only advances are tentative, their commitments outside themselves are tenuous at best. Jordan does not cut off the world because it is not perfect; its imperfection only strengthens his determination to do what little he can. Similarly, Colonel Cantwell serves well in an army full of incompetents, egomaniacs, and petty politicians; the weakness he perceives around him does not weaken his pride, his dignity, his purpose, or his faith. Similarly, too, Santiago fishes for eighty-four days without catching a fish. He goes out alone, as far out as he can, and fishes on the eighty-fifth day. He catches the biggest fish he has ever seen, watches it devoured, lost, before his eyes, bit by bit. And after the incident is all over, he makes plans with the boy to fish yet again. The human spirit, Hemingway tells us in his last story, is like the dream of a lion: A lion in itself is powerful, beautiful, sensual, dignified, as well as gay and playful. But the dream of a lion is even better. It can never be destroyed and lives in the hearts of certain men forever. The individual does count.

The individual man can become a significant moral agent even in our time, and the manner of Robert Jordan's death illustrates this as well as anything that Hemingway has written. At the end of *For Whom the Bell Tolls*, as Robert Jordan lies wounded, ready to die as he knows he must, forcing himself not to pass out or take the easy way by shooting himself, one is reminded of his earlier statement that "he would much prefer not to die" and that he "would abandon a hero's or a martyr's end gladly" (p. 164). Just as Jordan's ideals are made more meaningful by his insistence on viewing life realistically, so his death is made more meaningful by his genuine desire to live. One is also reminded of the thoughts of Sordo as he faces death on a hilltop surrounded by Fascist cavalry on the ground and aircraft overhead (thoughts that are so similar to the statement by Catherine Barkley at her death): "If one must die, he thought, and clearly one must, I can die. But I hate it" (p. 312). Like Sardo, who is able to face death with a certain gaiety, telling himself little jokes (earlier Jordan points out to himself that "all the best ones, when you thought it over, were gay" [p. 17]),[7]

---

[7] Compare these lines from Yeats's "Lapis Lazuli": "[They] Do not break up their lines to weep./They know that Hamlet and Lear are gay;/Gaiety transfiguring all that dread./All men have aimed at, found and lost." *The Collected Poems of W. B. Yeats* (New York, 1951), p. 292.

Jordan through his pain is able to get off a small joke to himself before the end:

We ought to have portable short wave transmitters. *Yes, there's a lot of things we ought to have.* I ought to carry a spare leg, too.

He grinned at that sweatily because the leg, where the big nerve had been bruised by the fall, was hurting badly now. (p. 469)

Typically of Jordan, the battle within his spirit is fought to the very end, not just to maintain consciousness and courage, but to keep his thinking straight. One of his last injunctions to himself during the final moments is "Keep it accurate . . . Quite accurate" (p. 466). Having kept himself straight inside, he is ready to perform his last external, social act (an act that is symbolic in a way of the moral dilemma posed by the entire novel, since it is a necessary killing) with a dignity and skill befitting a professional: *"And if you wait and hold them up even a little while or just get the officer that may make all the difference. One thing well done can make —"* (p. 470).

"One thing well done," like Golz's statement on the telephone when he learns, after all, that the attack will probably fail (*"Nous ferons notre petit possible"*), is our modest hope. It is not much, but neither is it a whimper. Jordan dies with one of the most believable heroic flourishes of the mind and spirit in modern literature. Because he wins the game, is stern with himself to the end, he is able to do in truth all that is possible for him to do, and what he has done somehow makes faith seem possible, even in our time. Hemingway's search for "true emotion" turns out to be the search for the truth about man. Within *For Whom the Bell Tolls* the results of this search are presented with the deepest honesty and faith a skillful professional could employ.

THE MASK
OF HUMBLE PERFECTION

◆ ◆ ◆ IN AN AGE that demands complexity in its literature as a mark of excellence, *The Old Man and the Sea* first appeared to be a consciously contrived anachronism. In the years that have followed publication, however, the novel has been subjected to possibly as much scrutiny as any work of modern fiction has ever received, and the result, cumulatively considered, has produced a superstructure of such technical complexity as to suggest that *The Old Man and the Sea* could rival, word for word, the intricacies of James Joyce's *Ulysses*.

In an opposite direction to this reception, many have tried to make the novel a worthy successor to *Little Women*, a return to the good old days when books were good and clean, and told a real story with a real lesson. The shortness of *The Old Man and the Sea*, its simplified diction, its religious-allegorical aspects have combined with the absence of controversial subject matter to produce a modern high school classic that has pleased school boards and conservative politicians, and has almost convinced those women's book clubs that never read books that Hemingway might have at last reformed.

Further complicating the emotional climate that surrounds the novel is the temptation to see it as a poetic, happy ending to the Hemingway publication story, coming, after the disaster *Across the River*, like the cavalry over the hill to the rescue, with the Pulitzer Prize on the one flank, and the Nobel Prize on the other.

The original reaction to *The Old Man and the Sea* was enthusiastically favorable from almost all quarters. Not only the public and the general press, but distinguished scholars were applying terms like *epic, allegory,* and *parable*—terms that in retrospect seem suspiciously grandiose, as if all were carried away by a dramatic moment and are now embarrassed to deal with the subject at all. Partly as an embarrassed counterreaction and partly as a natural response to any work of such tremendous popularity, scholars and critics have become increasingly hostile to the book. Disparagement of the book has become an intellectual shibboleth, making any dispassionate evaluation of the novel extremely difficult.

Defenders of the novel have often been led to increasingly more elaborate and ingenious readings, apparently to justify the novel's intellectual respectability. Many of the attackers, on the other hand, have stopped looking at the novel at all and have gone back, as in the old days, to whipping the poor old "dumb ox." The novel has become a cause, a test case: those who see Hemingway's career as a gradual decline in power have gone out of their way to load the novel with pejorative generalizations; those who see the novel as a final triumph in a steady growth of achievement have gone out of their way to find in the novel that "fifth dimension" and that use of "calculus" aimed for by the author. That so many different fifth dimensions have been discovered in recent years in connection with the book is at least a tribute to its suggestiveness.

As he grew older, Hemingway obviously invested more and more emotion in what he wrote. A more intense application to the writing process accompanied a growing lack of self-confidence. The tremendous emotional involvement of the author in *The Old Man and the Sea* can be perceived primarily in the tightly controlled style (he does not "imitate himself" so much as he is simply very, very careful) and in the extreme precision with which the form is shaped and balanced. This control is not immediately apparent, however, without careful analysis; on the contrary, the surface impression of the narrative given to the casual reader is typically flat. The story's emotional posture is much like that of a professional athlete who has trained himself to relax physically, with an iron will, at moments of great stress.

In other words (and I think this holds true throughout Hemingway's career), the more placid and deliberate the surface, the more turbulent and intense are the forces behind the story. Nothing Hemingway has written, certainly nothing of such length, shows more careful and deliberate execution than *The Old Man and the Sea*. I suspect that there never was a problem in writing that Hemingway felt he could not solve by greater and greater applications of self-discipline, and certainly the period following the publication of *Across the River* presented the greatest "problem" of his career. In a figurative sense, *The Old Man and the Sea* may have been Hemingway's own "Big Two-Hearted River," and instead of carefully laying out his camping gear as Nick does in the story, Hemingway appears to be carefully mapping out a cosmos, with each element, heavenly body, and animal species in its place, precisely balanced, counterbalanced, and diagramed in regard to its influence on the human archetype that stands at the center.

Such artfulness, although admirable in some respects, can also be a bit dreary and arouse suspicion about the honesty of the artist in an age that is still largely Romantic in its taste. Santiago becomes a figure too removed, almost precious in his highly stylized role, and his tragedy, with every carefully contrived suggestive detail in its proper orbit, lacks the spontaneity of moving passion. The bullfight, which is the primary model for both the tragedy and the allegory of the novel, is able to maintain a high level of intense excitement because of the accelerated action, the moment-to-moment unpredictability of the bull, and most important, the real danger to the matador in the shape of an immediate physical confrontation of an animal whose power within the same element is obviously superior. In the bullfight the spontaneous and the formal can join together in perfect harmony, but despite the many efforts by Hemingway to make the confrontation between man and fish parallel, the emotional effect is not the same, and the formal dominates.

Partly, the failure is due to the weakness of the basic situation: fishing is not really a confrontation but is seen, regardless of the effort and pain and the size of the fish, as a passive activity, a test of strength and fortitude rather than courage. Partly the failure is due to the characterization of the fish. Hemingway is caught in the "Miltonic dilemma": Moby Dick is believable as a totally negative entity, but Santiago's marlin lacks force and conviction as totally good. Cold and dumb, and, regardless of its motion and force, essentially passive also, the fish is a victim of the poetic terms of the allegory.

Santiago, too, falls victim to the allegory. The few details presented about Santiago's background suggest a man of heroic stature, but very little heroic energy radiates outward to warm or inspire the reader. The total impression of his character is one of almost impassive piety, even though Hemingway tries to invest him with that combination of pride and devoutness which to Hemingway characterized the best bullfighters. Neither the momentary doubts which cross his consciousness nor the experience of intense pain can come to life and disturb the reader because of the smothering weight of the unreal language. Everything negative in Santiago's experience fades into the lacquered design as simply an interesting variation in texture. In other words, the internal conflict is really a series of rhetorical questions.

Such sentiments as "I wish I could feed the fish, he thought. He is my brother" lack warmth and real breath, and appear to have mental quotation marks around them. They are neither self-imitative nor overdone; on the contrary, they are so carefully proportioned and phrased that we feel as if they are an animism measured out like a flavoring in cubic centimeters and injected with precision by hypodermic. Even the slightest emotion expressed by a character becomes suspect when appropriated with such calculated precision. Thus, art is brought to the edge of the ridiculous by its very artfulness, and we are constantly uncomfortable; we tremble lest crude humanity intrude and someone start to jeer in the rear of the audience. The mood is even more precarious because the author obviously wants so much to succeed. As Hemingway himself has said, the audience comes to watch the tragedy of the bull, not the tragedy of the bullfighter.

Sadly, Hemingway himself becomes the protagonist of his last novel, not because there is any sense of "self" in the work in the overt way the self is mourned or exalted in *Across the River*— that is precisely what he is doing everything in his power to avoid—but because the author really perceives himself in the game situation. The more we read and think about *The Old Man and the Sea*, the more we worry and think about Hemingway rather than Santiago. Like the aging bullfighter, he must depend on technique and courage alone "to stay alive," and whereas this is enough to save Santiago, it is not enough in real life where the Santiagos of the world are simply lost at sea. Even sadder is the fact that Hemingway himself must have realized this. Suggestive of this realization is his comparison in "The Dangerous Summer" of the bullfighter Dominguin, who is admired for his skill and intelligence, and Ordoñez, who is treated with a mystical reverence because of his great natural ability. Although the comparison is not directly one of youth and age, throughout his work Hemingway usually attaches skill and intelligence to age and natural ability to youth, and in comparing the assets of the two bullfighters, his preference is made quite clear.[1]

Throughout his career, Hemingway had an ambivalent attitude toward youth and toward age. From the beginning, even when he himself was relatively young, he satirized the inexperience and the frequent insensitivity of youth, yet was awed by the natural talent displayed by such young performers as Romero, who is treated with religious reverence in *The Sun Also Rises*. Older performers, like Garcia in "The Undefeated," are both admirable, for sticking it out with what tricks their experience has taught them (Santiago, too, brags of his "tricks"), and despicable, for no one

[1] "The Dangerous Summer," *Life*, XLIX (September 5, 1960), 77–109. The difference in Hemingway's attitude toward these two bullfighters was brought to my attention by Bickford Sylvester in his article "Hemingway's Extended Vision: *The Old Man and the Sea*," *PMLA*, LXXXI (March, 1966), 131.

likes watching "nerved-up bullfighting."[2] This ambivalence is clearly demonstrated in both *Across the River and into the Trees* and *The Old Man and the Sea*. Cantwell, as we have seen, is meant to be both admirable and contemptible—admirable for his skill and experience, and contemptible for his lack of youthful confidence and real talent for life. So, too, Santiago is made the source of so much admiration it can be embarrassing, and yet the old man who is so admired for his skill and wisdom calls out repeatedly for the boy, a ritual of restoration certainly, but also a plaintive cry for the lost ease and natural talents of youth, and a protest against the injustice of being old and alone.[3]

The Old Man was written as a demonstration of the double *dicho* "Man can be destroyed but not defeated."[4] But hidden behind this "winner take nothing" philosophy where loss turns out to be really a victory, behind the surface pessimism, is a sentimentality as glittering as the gold deep within Scrooge's heart. It is pretty to think that old men can salvage their dignity, and it is pretty to think that the Manuel Garcias of the world can ever win anything but anonymity and contempt, that anyone would ever let them go down in a blaze of glory (glory at least to one qualified observer) in the first place. And it is pretty to think that somehow there would be an observer around like Zurito to make the final act of courage worth while.

The fact is, as Frost has so aptly put it in "Home Burial," "From the time when one is sick to death,/One is alone, and he dies more alone."[5] Critics have pointed to Auden's statement about the Old Masters' understanding of suffering, which so often takes place while "someone else is eating or opening a window or just walking dully along," as something Hemingway also understood. But al-

[2] *D.I.A.*, p. 167.

[3] Carlos Baker notes that the repeated call for the boy becomes an "invocation" which "is nearly magical as if, by means of it, some of the strength of youth flowed in to sustain the limited powers of age." *Hemingway: The Writer as Artist*, pp. 306–7.

[4] Hotchner, p. 73.

[5] *Complete Poems of Robert Frost*, p. 72. The quotation that follows is from Auden's "Musée des Beaux Arts," *Selected Poetry of W. H. Auden* (New York, 1959), p. 49.

though Hemingway may have understood this, in the final analysis he is not able to accept it, and that is the source of most of his difficulties as a writer. In a way, Hemingway's audience becomes "sort of what we have instead of God." What happens when a man, alone, has a moral decision to make that may or may not affect other men, but which will never be apprehended by anyone else? His suffering will never be appreciated, his decision never approved, and his courage never applauded—worst of all, his very existence may not even be acknowledged. What then? Does he roll his stone up the hill anyway, or wait, since he doesn't have the means to hang himself, for Godot? And what if Godot comes and says, "Who are you? What is all this foolishness? Don't waste my time"?

Although Hemingway writes about a naturalistic world, a world where ants fall into the fire and where people are caught off base, he only partly believes it. As long as there is an older waiter around, as in "A Clean, Well-Lighted Place," to observe the old man and have compassion for him, all is certainly not *nada*. Hemingway hedges his nihilistic bet not religiously, but emotionally. When he gets to the sticking-place, he just can't stand the implications of his own position, for "it's too damned awful."

A strange paradox of *The Old Man and the Sea* is that it is filled with one person, and yet there is no overt sensation of self or unhealthy ego. The whole world echoes the estrangement of the young protagonists of Hemingway; the whole world echoes the connection of this old protagonist. In the achievement of this absence of self and the establishment of a disciplined connection, one may be reminded of the emotion-laden refrain from one of Ezra Pound's *Pisan Cantos*, written also during a period of sore personal and artistic trial: "Pull down thy vanity,/I say pull down . . . 'Master thyself, then others shall thee beare' . . . How mean thy hates/Fostered in falsity, . . . Pull down thy vanity,/ I say pull down."[6] Ironically, one of the traits that weakens San-

[6] "Canto LXXXXI," *The Cantos of Ezra Pound* (New York, 1948), p. 99 (*Pisan Cantos*).

tiago's heroic force is his completeness. Santiago is perfectly male, and he gains that perfection by the very fact that the question is never raised. He doesn't so much prove his masculinity as he demonstrates it. For the first time in any sustained way, the Hemingway protagonist is able to combine, without any self-consciousness in the matter, the male virtues and the female virtues.

In this, Santiago is the end product of the search for completeness which is begun by Nick, most dramatically exemplified in Jake, still bothers Cantwell, and is somewhat foreshadowed in the character of Robert Jordan in his physical and spiritual union with Maria: "As long as there is one of us there is both of us" (p. 463). Softness and hardness combine in such a way in Santiago's character that the entire story is filled with the beauty of their balance. This combination of pride and humility, courage and love, strength and pity is, of course, also an attribute of the Christ figure (foreshadowed again in the conscious attempts to achieve a balance between these same elements by Jordan). Such a wholeness and such an identification with Christ, even on a very limited basis, avoids the artificial separation of male-female traits as fostered by both the masculine epic tradition and the feminine courtly love tradition. Thus, the sense of self with its accompanying sexual anxieties is lost; man again, in Santiago, becomes whole, and as he becomes whole, he is able to function. The Hemingway story is shifted so that it is not a question of the success or failure of the male, but the success or failure of man.

However, the devoutness of Santiago is more akin to the courage and confidence moderated with humility that is the mark of Hemingway's true professional (as Christ, in "Today Is Friday," is seen to be) than of the Christian. On Santiago's own terms, by his own preference, the sea is perceived as a woman, and Santiago's fishing is presented as a sexual act. The story matches in detail the Hercules myth of the dead man, or castrated man, who is brought back to life after a journey across water, bringing fertility back to his community. As Melvin Backman has said (in this case referring to *For Whom the Bell Tolls*, although equally applicable here), Hemingway defines "Christianity's condemnation of killing and its concept of sex as a sort of necessary sin" and instead presents "love as a mystic ceremonial experience and killing (killing cleanly with honor, pride, and humility) as a spiritual experience."[7] The game structure thus becomes or is elevated to what Joseph Waldmeir calls "Hemingway's religion of man,"[8] and the complete professional, Santiago (who is also the complete father), becomes the perfect exemplification of the game code in action: commitment to an ideal of behavior more important than the goal to be achieved; honest self-judgment; awareness of oneself, the rules, and the game situation; skill and game knowledge; and courage enough to take genuine risks.

The complete professional is able to unite in harmony, for the first time in Hemingway's fiction, father, mother (sea), and son (boy). Hemingway's own emotional conflict regarding the roles of father and mother and their relationship to each other and to the son reaches a fictive resolution. The solution can be seen as predictable: The mother is destroyed as a figure and made primarily passive and receptive (although she is potentially dangerous, the professional can deal with her), and the son is made literally into a student who is able to give, without reservation, devotion and admiration to the father. The father is "sound" (to quote from "Fathers and Sons") in every way—not just in fishing, but because of his fishing. Through male assertion, through producing from the reluctant mother with heroic masculine effort and authority the ultimate, gigantic fertility, the father is made worthy of the boy ("I wish the boy were here") and "produces" the son (that is, the boy is reunited to Santiago and his faith in the powers of the old man has been confirmed). In return, the boy loves as defined by the priest in A Farewell to Arms: "When you love you wish to do things for. You wish to sacrifice for. You wish to serve" (p. 72). Upon Santiago's return, the boy cannot stop crying because the effort paid for him, to "produce" him, has been so overwhelming in its devotional dimensions, and the father has been so

---

[7] "Hemingway: The Matador and the Crucified," in Baker, *Ernest Hemingway: Critiques of Four Major Novels.*

[8] "*Confiteor Hominem:* Ernest Hemingway's Religion of Man," in Baker, *Ernest Hemingway: Critiques of Four Major Novels.*

completely insistent and has so completely mastered the "mother." The domestic dilemma has been solved by switching the context from the feminine-Victorian to the masculine-primitive, and then moderating the primitive with elements from the Christian ethic. As manhood and true fatherhood are possible and even central, so is love possible.

In *The Old Man and the Sea* Hemingway has contrived a set of circumstances perfectly attuned to his own emotional needs and his view of the world which has evolved out of those needs. Although connected to and in harmony with his world, Santiago is paradoxically nearly self-sufficient. He depends only on the boy, who is at once his audience, student, heir, and wife, and this dependence is primarily emotional. Everything is done to create persuasively a world where man and boy can successfully interact without interference. Santiago catches his fish to prove, in part, that he is a more worthy father-mother than the boy's real parents, who have no faith ("But we have. Haven't we?" p. 7) and are shortsighted (having chosen a new mentor for the boy who is "almost blind" physically and spiritually). The reader is thus brought into a never-never land where the masculine will toward life is enshrined in amber—isolated, perfected, and magnified. The male occupation becomes central not only to physical and emotional well-being, but becomes equivalent to the essential spirit of life itself. Using all the literary techniques at his command with great care and skill, Hemingway tries his utmost to convince us that this private vision of life is also a universally valid one.

In this world the sea, which Santiago perceives as female, simply exists, waiting for the complete man to exercise his powers to challenge her great potential. In a way she is an adversary, "something that gave or withheld great favors" (p. 27), but never a personal rival. She is the reservoir of possibility; whereas the life force itself, the key, is masculine—both procreation and survival are pictured in the novel as functions of masculine effort, both internal and external. The sexual image pattern of the porpoises emphasizes these distinctions. In a dream Santiago sees a vast school of them at the time of mating: "they would leap high into the air and return into the same hole they had made in the water when they leaped" (p. 80). During the night Santiago can hear the difference between the active male porpoise and the passive female, "between the blowing noise the male made and the sighing blow of the female" (p. 46).

All the animals that surround the old man are pictured as living in desperate circumstances where they must either exercise will and effort or succumb; even the little bird that rests for a time on Santiago's fishing line must take its chance "like any man or bird or fish" (p. 53). Santiago lives in a world where the coming of the sharks is "no accident," and each animal must by necessity pursue a role defined by its own nature. By his nature, however, man has a choice whether he will live up to his potential or not— or, as the novel defines it, whether man will choose to remain in shallow water or go out into the deep water and exercise his abilities to the fullest.[9] Only man must fight the internal as well as the external battle; only man is really conscious of the risk and the consequences of accepting the responsibilities of his role—he can hold on to the line or let go. When Santiago comments to himself that "pain does not matter to a man" (p. 84), he is talking about some men, defining the difference between those who "know how to suffer like a man" (p. 92) and those who do not.

Although the dramatic forces of the novel are in position, they are never really set free and used. Hemingway's admiration for the hero is brought in this novel to the pitch of religious fervor. Jordan, because he conquers true human weakness in a truly human, ragged world, is a true hero. Santiago, because he is not convincingly weak at any point (the weakness of his left hand is an example of the stylized human frailty that he must overcome), is more an exemplum or an endorsement than a dramatized protagonist. He is the first Hemingway protagonist who doesn't really change or progress, in the ordinary sense. What development

[9] Santiago's role is determined: "Perhaps I should not have been a fisherman, he thought. But that was the thing that I was born for" (p. 48). But the extent of his risk and effort within that role is a matter of choice: "My choice was to go there to find him beyond all people" (p. 48).

in Santiago's character that does occur might be best compared to the spiritual progress a saint might achieve as a result of an ordeal that tests character traits already acquired. The story does not use ritual; it is a ritual—almost a text for "worship."

As a saint should, Santiago lives and moves within a medieval world of sorts, with a clearly defined chain of being. The continuous allegorical use of animals may even remind us of a bestiary.[10] Santiago's world is to a large extent Aristotelian, in that it is one of order and degree, of careful assigned natures and proper spheres, of balance and counterbalance. Everything is sharpened, properly placed, and polished. There are none of the ragged edges of the true moral dilemmas faced by a Robert Jordan in a world where courage must be maintained regardless of the fact that neither men nor circumstances can be uncompromisingly categorized. Santiago lives in a deductive world; Jordan, in an inductive. Jordan must act in a context of war where the right side is sometimes wrong and the wrong side is sometimes right, where your friends may also be your worst enemies, and your enemy may be someone much more like you than your friend.

By contrast, *The Old Man and the Sea* presents a diagram of unity and interaction, where motion seems static, as in a Japanese painting, and the force of conflict is balanced and held in eternal apposition. Time and space, the weather and the elements, land, sea, and air, bird, beast and fish, sun, moon, and stars converge; and the basic question is not, Will Santiago succeed?—for he succeeds as he must and fails as he must—but, Who will believe?

Hemingway appears to have risked what has been derogatorily termed a "fake biblical prose" because he was writing, in effect, his own "Bible."[11] His idea of "calculus" in prose fiction appears

[10] Hemingway is a master of suggestive stylistic flavorings which are more reminiscent of a particular age or literary period than they are directly allusive. Various flavorings in *The Old Man and the Sea* may remind us of the primitive, the classical, the biblical, the medieval, and the modern. Perhaps the introduction of such a wide span of temporal suggestion is Hemingway's way of attempting to transcend the limitations of historical time.

[11] Most people in reading *The Old Man and the Sea* are probably reminded of biblical prose because they are directed to such a connection by the parallels between Santiago and Christ and by the general compatibility of the sub-

to have involved the attempt to copy the effect of the Bible in reproducing the center of Western man's cultural consciousness, creating a document available to continuous reinterpretation. Hemingway's method in his last novel is, at any rate, certainly suggestiveness, with perhaps some slight motivation of malice in making sure that the "symbol-searching machines" of the scholars never run out of material. Basic cultural symbols form the terms of Hemingway's mathematics, and their functions and operations are classical structure, allusive context, ambiguity, and paradox. Richard Cantwell's question, as pursued through Renata, is, How can man be reborn? Hemingway's answer as presented in the story of Santiago is posed in the terms of those paradoxes central to religious faith: one is reborn through death, just as one finds love in violence and joy in tragedy.[12]

Appropriately for the story's classical and medieval materials, the novel's execution is classical in many ways, in its proportions and balance, and in its restraint and over-all grace. (One might say that the form was mathematical in its precision, particularly

ject matter with the simplicity that surrounds Christians and Christianity throughout most of the New Testament. In a more detailed way, our memory of the Bible (which may be rather dim) is engaged by the restrained inclusion of a few elements in the style of the novel which go back to the parts of the Bible most of us remember most vividly—the narrative sections, for example, or "Bible Stories," which include the parables of Christ, the stories of events in Christ's life, and the less complicated and moralistic Old Testament tales. These are brought to mind by the simple diction and the direct sentences; by the impersonal sentence beginnings, "There are," "It was," and the simple pronoun-verb beginnings, "He was"; and by the linkings with simple adverbs of time, "then," "after," and "when." These narratives as well as what might be called the semi-imperative sections of Ecclesiastes or Psalms are recalled in the novel's use of impersonal references or commands to the body: "What kind of hand is that? . . . How does it go, hand? . . . Come on hand." We are also reminded of the lyricism of certain parts of the Bible, such as the Psalms, in the use of the personal pronoun *he* in reference to the marlin, and such simple statements of kinship with nature as "He is my brother."

[12] Sylvester rightfully points to "a fundamental natural principle of harmonious opposition" in the novel. From this principle flow "oxymorons: compassionate violence, comfortable pain, life in death, aged strength, and victorious defeat" (p. 132). The possible list of paradox derived from the novel is almost endless: the most beautiful of sea life is also the most untrustworthy; the weakest of sea life is most subject to the sea's violence; the oldest man has the best eyesight and takes the most risks; the unluckiest fisherman is the luckiest (in several ways).

in such matters as the sequence of major events in catching the fish, the allotment of time, and the recurrence of major images.) Many of the best American romances have provided a unique combination of convincing particulars with an emotional magnitude of almost timeless and spaceless validity,[13] but *The Old Man and the Sea* accomplishes this combination and more. It also contains those palpable dimensions of unity—time, place, and action —and formal magnitude—beginning, middle, and end—which usually characterize only the finest tragic dramas. Such dimensions, which connect the novel with the emotional climate of other forms more ancient and traditional than the modern novel or romance, by their very existence perform the function of extending the particular and providing a wealth of association. However, such associations serve artfully to contrive an aura of sanctity and importance around the novel that transcends the importance earned by the merits of the work itself and as such constitutes an emotional trick which the reader has every right to resent.

[13] Part of the reason that the novels written at the beginning and at the end of Hemingway's career display the firmest control and the most unity of effect might be explained by the possibility that each really represents an achievement within a different genre. *The Sun Also Rises* is the only long work of fiction among Hemingway's works which (to use a distinction developed by Richard Chase) is properly speaking a *novel*—a work of fiction that deals with manners, morals, and social distinctions (*The American Novel and Its Tradition* [Garden City, 1957], pp. 2, 12–13). In his other long fiction, Hemingway turns to another genre, *romance*, which veers "toward mythic, allegorical, and symbolic forms" (p. 13). Only at the end of his career does Hemingway totally master this second form.

The greatest works of American fiction, with few exceptions, have been romances, occasionally borrowing the realism of detail associated by Chase more with the novel tradition, but more often dealing with human beings in ideal relationships and frequently moving toward moral allegory. Not all the greatest works of American fiction within the romance category can be related, even in the broadest sense, to tragedy, but these romances seem to share a common requirement with tragedy, the achievement of emotional dimensions beyond the particular.

Both emotional magnitude and distance have been achieved in romance within the narrative itself and through the special treatment of narrative or the establishment of certain frameworks exterior to the narrative. Whether in or out of the narrative, it is the use of myth or myth-like materials which extends the significance of the particular in the dimensions of time, and the employment of symbol (which may approach or become allegory) which extends the significance of the particular in the dimension of space.

As a prior condition to the classical dimensions discussed above, brevity, one of the most obvious features of *The Old Man and the Sea*, becomes one of its most important. Many have said, to the point of cliché, that Hemingway has worked best as a short story writer and that he loses impact and dissipates his power in longer efforts. There is much truth to this, primarily because Hemingway's major achievement is as a stylist. He triumphs with the application of self-discipline to narrowly limited and carefully defined materials. Rather than working toward the center of meaning with successive verbal formulations or tentative definition, as Faulkner and James might be said to work in their own separate ways, really suggesting the definite with the indefinite, Hemingway works from a finely wrought definite center to suggest dimensions operating in all directions to the "outside." Faulkner works as an anthropologist, searching the ruins, collecting pieces, looking for a common denominator; Hemingway works as an architect, carefully constructing a classic arch.

Hemingway is an artist after Pound's Mauberley (although Hemingway never loses his passion nor discards his discipline in defeat), whose fundamental passion was "To present the series/ Of curious heads in medallion."[14] Although not Flaubertian in his reasons for "the right word," Hemingway nevertheless was a meticulous craftsman, who revised and revised, polished and refined, and who never gave in to what "the age demanded." At his best he etched medallions when he wrote—Attic, not kinematic. In this sense, his first published work of literary importance, the sketches of the Paris edition of *in our time*, were prophetic of his greatest talents as well as of his greatest limitations.

Hemingway's method has always been to load the simple and direct by the use of image, allusion, metaphor, and symbol, but such loading often has an emotional backlash which must be carefully directed. When Hemingway is operating within the ironic mode, this backlash is carefully directed. The British speaker of "Chapter IV" (*1st 49*, p. 211), for example, condemns himself and exposes the callousness of war in such expressions

[14] "Hugh Selwyn Mauberley," *Selected Poems* (New York, 1957), p. 73.

as a "simply priceless" barricade and "we were frightfully put out" when the barricade was lost. The imagery of the "wet dead leaves" and the minister "sitting down in the water" in "Chapter V" (p. 225) reflects ironically on the quality of justice and the military pageantry of the firing squad scene described. On a larger scale, Jake Barnes, Frederic Henry, and Richard Cantwell are ironically treated by means of similar techniques. Hemingway uses the same loading techniques in *The Old Man and the Sea*, but this time we are, apparently, required to view the protagonist with a complete seriousness, a seriousness so complete that it approaches reverence. Unfortunately, this is impossible, and the complex mechanism set in motion by the author behind the simplified diction tends to mock the simplicity and the humility of the central character. The situation is very similar to that of the comedian who tries to become a serious actor, but no one can take him seriously. Worse, not only his sentiments, but his very effort toward seriousness becomes ludicrous.

The style of *The Old Man and the Sea* is appropriate to the plot and characters, if these could be considered alone, but not to the entire burden of the allegory and allusion placed on the plot and characters.[15] Since this burden is so heavy, the primitive simplicity of Santiago must be felt as a kind of hypocrisy expressed

[15] The short sentences (average 13.7 words, as versus 35.3 for Henry James in *The Ambassadors*, and 51.4 for Samuel Johnson in the early *Ramblers* [the counts for James and Johnson are from R. W. Short, "The Sentence Structure of Henry James," *American Literature*, XVIII (1946), p. 72]) are filled with concrete nouns, nouns that selectively and repeatedly name certain immediate objects—parts of Santiago's body, fishing equipment, and things in, around, and over the water—and that name immediate sensations—hand cramps, eye glare, nausea, thirst, fatigue, and pain. These have the paradoxical effect of extending meaning rather than overparticularizing it. A very few fundamental impressions are constantly reinforced, creating on the one hand a sense of reality, and on the other connecting, if not in fact, at least on the impressionistic level of memory, to generalized conceptions of man's struggle against the elements, his search for food, his battle with enemies, and his battle to sustain himself.

Striking a primitive note also are the unsophisticated Hemingway modifiers—*good, bad, fine,* and *beautiful*—which are in this story particularly effective in reinforcing the cultivated tone of masculine directness and verbal naiveté. Hemingway's modifiers, however, are "heavily loaded," as Harry Levin has said, and ripe with possibility ("Observations on the Style of Ernest Hemby an author who seems to be trying to manipulate his audience. The very intensity of Hemingway's drive toward perfection, which is reflected in both the unmarred perfection of his central character and in the precise structuring of the narrative itself, contradicts the humility of the protagonist and the humility assumed by the tone of the language.

Unfortunately, the old man's tricks and the old man's strength are not enough. Although Santiago perfectly expresses grace under pressure, Hemingway himself cannot. For all too obviously, *The Old Man and the Sea* behind its surface ease betrays an iron hand and a consequent rigidity which is not graceful at all. In many ways *The Old Man and the Sea* represents both the typically best and the typically worst in the Hemingway canon, and the best and the worst are tied together as manifestations of the same force, Hemingway's driving emotionalism.

ingway," in Weeks, ed., *Hemingway: A Collection of Critical Essays*, p. 77). But the possibilities extend inward when used by Santiago, providing the reader with broad areas of possible identification with human states of being, rather than extending outward toward the thing or situation described.

As Levin points out also, contrary to our general impression of Hemingway's style, it does not contain many active verbs (p. 81). Instead, Hemingway displays a "fondness for all kinds of participial constructions," which in conjunction with his use of continuous verb forms presents, in a very elliptical and compressed way, a continuous sense of timelessness to the reader's consciousness, thus heightening through style the emotional dimensions of the narrative.

The implications of the style, both in time and space, are further extended by certain "formalisms" which bring to the American reader connotations not just of the Spanish-speaking background of Santiago, but of foreign cultures in general (which tend to be thought of en masse as having more formal characteristics in speech than our own). For Santiago to be "foreign," no matter what the nationality, provides a touch of distance, but it is even more helpful in providing distance that he is Spanish-speaking. For it is in the Spanish people (recalling the discussion of *Death in the Afternoon* above), that Hemingway found so many traits that contradict our emotions and attitudes as Anglo-Americans, particularly in regard to the "simplest things," such as death, love, and violence. We think of the Spanish and the Spanish-American as closely connected to the earth and the elements, to the basic functions of life, and to ritual and primitive thought processes (animism and superstition). Hemingway found in the Spanish the ability to regard nature with affection without sentimentality (see, for example, the story "Old Man at the Bridge"). He also found in the Spanish the ability, demonstrated by Santiago and also by Anselmo in *For Whom the Bell Tolls*, to have pride and dignity, and at the same time have humility.

"LET BE BE FINALE OF SEEM"

♦ ♦ ♦ BOTH ERNEST HEMINGWAY and his writing have had the curious quality of seeming to be one thing and turning out, time after time, to be something else entirely. At first he appeared to be a cocky young journalist who wrote stories about tough people on the fringes of society, and yet in the collected stories, the stories concerned with relatively normal people in domestic situations far outnumber those concerned with gangsters, boxers, and prostitutes. He was then branded the recorder of the lost generation and seen as the prime example of the American expatriate in Europe, but neither he nor his writing could be so narrowly categorized for very long. He was thought of as an aficionado, a self-proclaimed authority on the bullfight, but only one work of fiction, a short story, was primarily concerned with bullfighting and his major work on the bullfight, *Death in the Afternoon*, was as much about aesthetics, art, and writing as it was about killing bulls. He was thought of as a professional tough guy, big game hunter, and sport fisherman, but in those works that deal with hunting and fishing, his themes are more concerned with the mental and moral conditions of the participants than with the physical aspects of the sports themselves. He was thought of as a simple,

NOTE: This chapter title is from Wallace Stevens, "The Emperor of Ice-Cream," *Poems by Wallace Stevens*, selected and with an introduction by Samuel French Morse (New York, 1959), p. 28.

blustering soul who brought unsophisticated vigor to the manner of his storytelling and unsophisticated thought to his stories' content. Yet, at least one story waited twenty years for disclosure of its major ideas; other stories, such as "The Killers," "A Clean, Well-lighted Place," and "The Short Happy Life of Francis Macomber," were found to be as sophisticated in their technique and thought as any stories written by any contemporary author; and two novels, *The Sun Also Rises* and *The Old Man and the Sea*, have been discovered to be as complex in their uses of literary materials as nearly anything written in this century.

Hemingway's work, because of its apparent simplicity, seems destined to attract simplistic labels. The root cause for much of the confusion and misjudgment is Hemingway's use of irony, which has been much more extensive and complex than most readers at first recognized—and more than some, filled with personal antagonism, were willing to recognize. Connected to this use of irony (and often a part of the ironic structure itself) is a loading process similar to the employment of metaphor in contemporary poetry, wherein levels of meaning are achieved through the use of image, symbol, and allusion. This loading is usually accompanied by a simplified diction and sentence structure that both ironically denies the possibility of complexity and contrasts sharply with the other levels of meaning. The hard, direct style often possesses a surface tension that, like good poetry, resists immediate penetration even after the loading has been discovered.

Hemingway's "narrowness" is another part of the simplistic fallacy. It has never, to my knowledge, been noted how very diverse much of Hemingway's art is. No two of his novels really have much in common; certainly his book-length nonfiction is very different in subject matter and technique; and the range of subject and technique in his stories is also amazingly broad, particularly if one stops to think how many single stories explore a manner that is never repeated or a context that is never used again. Very few prominent writers of fiction have achieved such a variety, even though their over-all scope may not have been so limited as Hemingway's was by his own intense emotional preoccupations.

The fact that Hemingway has seldom been given credit for continuous experimentation and change has severely inhibited our apprehension of his work.

As many of the more recent critics of Hemingway have indignantly pointed out, many major misjudgments have become enshrined in Hemingway criticism because of the early failure to perceive him as an intelligent, knowledgeable, and clever craftsman. Faulkner once slightingly commented on Hemingway's apparent lack of vocabulary, and Hemingway, in return, replied that he knew all the big words but just didn't choose to use them. The information we have about the respective reading habits and libraries of the two men would seem to suggest that Hemingway, in his own haphazard way, was at least a more serious and perhaps even a wider-ranging student of literature and art in general than not only Faulkner but at least a few of the critic-writers who have held Hemingway's intellect in such contempt. The myth of Hemingway's simplemindedness has led us into the wrong path of constantly taking him too seriously when he is joking, too literally when he is being ironic, and too pompously when we think that he is taking himself far more seriously than he really is. We have also been led to identify, in an oversimplified way, Hemingway's protagonists too closely with their creator, failing to perceive the ironic detachment which is the primary ingredient of so many Hemingway stories and novels. Too often, realizing that his work generates emotion, we have been led to brand his work in general as "sentimental," failing to distinguish between those occasions when emotion is honestly generated by the dramatic terms of the stories, and those occasions when Hemingway becomes victimized by his own emotional attachments and unknowingly or dishonestly magnifies the emotional values of his material. The myth of simplemindedness has helped to obscure the deliberate concern shown by Hemingway for the emotional patterning of his art, a concern revealed directly in the nonfiction but even more convincingly discovered in a study of the cleverly varied emotional terms of the stories themselves.

This is not to say that Hemingway's weaknesses do not exist.

His juvenile humor, his petty attacks on other authors, his inability to resist, on occasion, the "wow" ending or the excessively pointed barb, his need to overload his satire of unaware or unappreciative characters, his need to have an audience for heroism, his tendency to overmoralize and overdramatize, and his excessively emotional identification with the lonely and unappreciated hero are just some of the major weaknesses that grew out of his supercharged emotional capacity. But Hemingway's weaknesses, limitations, and failures—as serious as they may be—can be fairly assessed only when they are put into the entire context of the variety of materials and techniques which he employed, the constant spirit of inquiry and experiment that marked much of his work, and the many risks he took in pursuing the extremely ambitious goals that he set for himself.

Ernest Hemingway's journey may have started as an escape from Aunt Sally, but it ended as a journey into the heart of man; for Hemingway, like all the very great novelists of our century, Joyce, Mann, Kafka, Camus, and Faulkner, was essentially a philosophical writer who searched for the bedrock of man's experience and who tied that search to the parallel quest of finding newer, more immediate, and more vigorous ways of expressing the living experience in words. Hemingway certainly has a valid claim to being one of the authors who has contributed most to identifying and combating the most pressing literary problems of our age: the bankruptcy of our language, and the growing superficiality of our literature—a fiction weighed down with romantic historical novels and nostalgic stories of childhood on the one hand, and with a naturalistic devotion to the "times" on the other.

The writer of our time, be he novelist, poet, or playwright, seems to have found the problems of art and the problems of living to be more crucially joined together as aspects of the same problem than did most of his predecessors. Certain unique aspects of this age with which we are all familiar—science, mass media, and weakening religious faith—have made the old fundamental questions about life and its purposes more imperative and immediate to our civilization than they have been very possibly since

189 •

the birth of Christ. The questions for writers of our time have not been Should we love? Should we act?—but, Can we love? Can we act? and Can these things be expressed with honesty and conviction in words at all? The ultimate question for the literature of our time may very well be, Can literature have meaning? Which is to ask the question that Hemingway asked, Can literature express emotion truly?

It may be that the answer to Hemingway's question is no. It may be that the emotions of man which have characterized his greatest triumphs and greatest tragedies have been lost to us, and that fear of the bomb and repetition of cheap emotional formulas in mass media have made anything but the literature of disgust, disorganization, and alienation impossible; any emotional conditions but either fear or apathy unnatural. It may be that the story, as Faulkner so aptly phrased it, "of the human heart in conflict with itself" is not only irretrievably soiled, but totally irrelevant. If so, a literature of courage must be viewed as either eccentric, egotistical, or ludicrous.

Then too, it may be that we are still Victoria's children, torn between a covert Romanticism on one side and a pressing need to rebel, escape, and refute on the other. If so, at least part of Hemingway's work must continue to be considered irrelevant, and we shall continue to identify much more closely with his literary adolescence than with his literary maturity. In any case, whether we find more admiration for Hemingway's refutations or his affirmations, we may be able to grant that if he was led into certain excesses, some of which he was later to regret, these excesses of reaction may be partly excused by the enormity of the provocation. If Hemingway was to admire courage a bit too much, and find a bit too much sympathy for the isolated individual, these emotional excesses, even when communicated by the very tricks he had abjured, must be judged within a context of an over-all devotion to realism and honesty unexceeded in modern literature. If a sense of self creeps out from behind some of his narratives, these lapses of emotional distance must be balanced against a lifelong fight against egocentricity and self-pity.

In an age when most people have abandoned the concept that what an individual does can have any importance, Hemingway's message is that what each man does is important, if not to anyone else, at least to himself. If a man is courageous enough, he can win himself; man's selfhood is sacred and must not be abandoned to self-pity or lost in the morass of those forces in modern life which seek to castrate man—rendering him sexless, faceless, and fearful. Although Hemingway's direction in literature followed a path largely dictated by his own emotional need to achieve a masculine independence from a cultural atmosphere dominated by feminine respectability and by a smug, middle-class parochialism, it was a direction that fitted the needs of our literary and emotional condition more often than not.

What carried Hemingway along his path was a total dedication to art and an unrelenting will to make his writing true. Perhaps his range of vision can be seen in some respects as limited, but his aim was penetration, not comprehensiveness. Hemingway, unlike many of his contemporaries, was *there* during the wars, the evacuations, the social convulsions. Despite the attempt by many to minimize the importance of such direct experience with most of the major events of his time, and despite the exhibitionism that often colored Hemingway's attempts to expose himself to danger, this effort to sense the actual event and to reproduce its emotional effect artistically as precisely as possible is exactly what we need in an age when even war itself has become a spectator sport and our sensitivity to the suffering of others has dimmed.

The emotional intensity which led Hemingway into his excesses also led him to his victories and fostered those qualities of character that made his victories possible: self-discipline, self-honesty, and a very real courage. He was locked in mortal combat all his life with an opponent, art, which grants no quarter and never allows total victory. The artist can be, will be, and must be destroyed by such a conflict, but he need not be defeated. In this sense, destruction is the function of man's material and temporal limitations, the words and paper of the artist, whereas defeat is a function of the spirit, the essence of art. Art can be a true transcendence from the limitations of form, yet form—and this is the pity and irony of it—will always destroy, in one way or another, the hand of the artist. If the artist brings too much courage to this world, the world has to kill him to break him, so of course it kills him.

INDEX

Halliday, E. M., 25n
Hardy, Thomas, 135
Hawthorne, Nathaniel, 136
Hemingway, Dr. Clarence (H's father), 4, 5, 9, 10, 15, 20
Hemingway, Ernest: as reader, 18; reading material of, as youth, 19; central theme of, 21; doctrine of emotion, 21; philosophy of composition of, 21; writing process of, 22; as anti-Marxist, 44; as humorist, 47, 50, 61 (see also Humor); emotional control by, 49 (see also Emotion); as wary of emotionalism, 51; as high school wit, 54; sexual anxiety of, 57; dual personality of, 71; as moralist, 71–72; the tragic vision of, 101 (see also Tragedy); as an emotional writer, 114; sentimental lapses of, 122 (see also Sentimentality); attitude toward youth and age of, 173–74; as a stylist, 183; as classicist, 183 (see also Classicism); weaknesses of, 188–89; emotional intensity of, 191

—FICTIONAL CHARACTERS:
Adams, Dorothy (Nick's sister), 111
Adams, Dr. Henry (Nick's father), 6–16 passim
Adams, Mrs. Henry (Nick's mother), 6, 7, 8, 18, 60, 67
Adams, Nick: 5–12 passim, 15–19 passim, 57–59 passim, 67, 73, 82, 91, 136, 137–40 passim, 142–45 passim, 176; the son of, 13
Alice (in "The Light of the World"), 58, 59
American lady (in "A Canary for One"), 118, 148
Anderson, Ole (in "The Killers"), 142–44 passim
Andres (in F.W.B.T.), 158, 162
Anselmo (in F.W.B.T.), 155, 158, 162, 164, 185n
Ashley, Lady Brett (in S.A.R.): 20, 31–42 passim; as a central character, 36–37; egocentricity of, 40; sense of martyrdom of, 41; mentioned, 64, 73, 120
Augustín (in F.W.B.T.), 161, 163
Aymo (in F.T.A.), 97n
Barkley, Catherine (in F.T.A.), 45, 46, 55, 82, 85, 86, 90, 92, 95, 99,
101–11 passim, 115, 116, 123, 129, 167
Barnes, Jake (in S.A.R.): 31–44 passim; growing self-awareness of, 40; outward awareness of, 41; clarity of vision of, 42; internal battle of, 43; mentioned, 53, 54, 57, 61, 64, 65, 73, 81, 107, 115, 138, 148, 150, 152, 153, 176, 184
Bell, Mrs. (in "The Killers"), 142
Belmonte (in S.A.R.), 141
Bill (in "The Three-Day Blow"), 19, 67
Bolton, Dick (in "The Doctor and the Doctor's Wife"), 8
Bonello (in F.T.A.), 97n
Boy (Manolin in O.M.), 124, 125, 174n, 177, 178
Campbell, Mike (in S.A.R.), 31, 35–36, 37, 64, 65
Cantwell, Colonel Richard (in A.R.I.T.): 44, 48–53 passim; as comic figure, 50; as Richard the Lion-Hearted, 51; as Don Quixote figure, 51–52; as adolescent, 52–53; mentioned, 73, 80, 82, 90, 128, 167, 174, 176, 181, 184
Carabinieri (in F.T.A.), 97, 98, 118
Cavalryman (in F.W.B.T.), 160–61, 163
Clyne, Francis (in S.A.R.), 31–32
Cohn, Robert (in S.A.R.): 20; 31–37 passim; as humorous character, 35; mentioned, 46, 51, 64, 65, 120, 132
Cook (in "The Light of the World"), 58–60 passim
Elliot, Cornelia (in "Mr. and Mrs. Elliot"), 66, 107
Elliot, Hubert (in "Mr. and Mrs. Elliot"), 66, 107
Ettore (in F.T.A.), 68n, 69n, 105, 120
Fascist lieutenant (in F.W.B.T.), 159–60
Ferguson (in F.T.A.), 68n, 85
Garcia, Manuel (in "The Undefeated"), 75, 173, 174
Garner, Mrs. Joe (in "Ten Indians"), 12
George (in "The Killers"), 73, 143
Georgette (in S.A.R.), 65n, 73

topics of, 57; gross, applied to fellow writers, 61–62

Hunting: as escape for male, 8

Hunting and fishing: as male role, 5; as symbol, 9; as escape from feminine environment, 9; as natural experience, 11

Huxley, Aldous: *Brave New World*, 88

Idaho, 21

Indian artifacts, 7

Individual, the: as ultimate moral unit, 43; as value focus, 44; importance of, in H's fiction, 165, 167, 191

In-group in S.A.R., 31. *See also* "Code"

Irony: importance of, in H's work, 25; as vehicle, 26; as contrast of world views, 115; as contrast of awareness, 117; as leading to sentimentality, 122; mentioned, 105, 113–128 *passim*, 184, 187

—satiric, 120–124 *passim*, 128

—verbal, 114, 137

James, Henry, 15, 184*n*

John Halifax, Gentleman (Dinah Maria Mulock), 19

Jourard, Sidney M., 24*n*

Joyce, James: 66; *Portrait of the Artist as a Young Man*, 53; *Ulysses*, 53, 169

Kafka, Franz: *The Castle*, 88; "Metamorphosis," 135

Kashkeen, Ivan, 159*n*

Kernan, Alvin B., 115*n*

Key West, 21

Killing, 160–62

Killinger, John, 79*n*

Krutch, Joseph Wood: 153*n*; quoted, 153, 154

Lardner, Ring, 33*n*

Laughter: as an expression of emotion, 56

Learner, the: as a figure, 142–46 *passim*

Legend, the Hemingway, 47

Lehan, Richard, 79*n*

Levin, Harry, 184*n*

Lewis, C. S., 29*n*

Lewis, Robert W., Jr., 26*n*, 40*n*, 64, 151*n*

Lewis, Sinclair, 34, 114

Light, James F., 95*n*

Literary allusion: in H's fiction, 63–68

Little Women (Louisa May Alcott), 169

Loss of self, 129–30, 138, 140

Love: Nick Adams', for father, 17; as a theme in H's work, 28; in S.A.R., 39; Frederic Henry's, 84–85; seen as game, 85; in *F.T.A.*, 106, 111; as a condition, 152

Male: reduced by Victorian feminism, 9

Man's will: in H's philosophy, 14–15

Marriage: Frederic Henry's concern for, 108

Martyr-victim: as female role, 29

Marxist critics of H, 44

Masculine tradition: view of role, 29; mentioned, 30, 30*n*, 176

Masculinity: versus H family gentility, 5; as issue in Adams stories, 12; H's concern for, 15, 16; mentioned, 176, 178

Matador, the: as archetypal hero, 76; as combination of roles, 76

Medievalism, 180

Melville, Herman, 136, 138

Michigan woods, 5, 21

Milton, John, 117–18

Moby Dick (Herman Melville), 172

Montgomery, Constance Cappel, 55, 57*n*, 58

Moral imperatives: for game hero, 75

Morality, 107

Morality play: *F.W.B.T.* as, 159, 164

Morris, Wright: 21*n*; quoted, 21

Multiple point of view, 43

Myth: 182*n*; of H's simple-mindedness, 188

Napoleon I, 88

Non-meaning, 102, 104, 121

Nothingness, 117

Novel tradition, 182*n*

Oak Park, Illinois, 3, 4, 5, 19, 20, 21

O'Faolain, Sean: 80*n*; quoted, 80

Oral reading: of H's fiction, 69*n*

Ordeal of Richard Feverel, The (George Meredith), 67
Ordoñez (the bullfighter), 173
Orwell, George: *1984*, 88
Oxymorons, 181*n*

Pamplona (in *S.A.R.*), 39, 42, 42*n*
Panic, 129–30, 131, 135. *See also* Terror
"Papa" role, 13
Paradox (in *O.M.*), 181, 181*n*
Parents, Hemingway's, 6. *See also* Hemingway, Dr. Clarence; Hemingway, Grace Hall
Pastoral (in *S.A.R.*), 38
Penrod (by Booth Tarkington), 20
Perception: the problem of, 22
Physical violence: in H's fiction, 15
Picaresque narrative, 30*n*
Poe, Edgar Allan, 136, 138
Political slogans: Robert Jordan's suspicion of, 163–64
Pollyanna (Eleanor H. Porter), 20
Poore, Charles, 56*n*
Pound, Ezra: factive reproduction theory of, 24; "Hugh Selwyn Mauberley," 53, 183, 183*n*; *The Cantos*, 24, 53; "Canto LXXXXI" (quoted), 175, 175*n*
Preacher, the (Ecclesiastes), 64
Primitivism, 152, 178, 184, 185*n*
Professional, the: 12; role in H's fiction, 45; figure, 176–77; complete, 177–78
Protagonist, the: 43, 46; as actor, 72–73; as developing character, 82; as figure of courage, 142, 144, 146, 148
Puritanism, 18
Purple Land, The (W. H. Hudson), 20

Querschnitt, Der, 68

Rain: as symbol in *F.T.A.*, 103, 109–10
Richardson, Samuel, 18
Ritual: masculine, 18; mentioned, 131–32, 134–35
Romance (form, as opposed to novel), 182, 182*n*
Romantic: H seduced by, 19

Romantic attitude: of Nick Adams, 11, 12, 15
Romantic-sentimental: tradition in literature, 18
Rovit, Earl, 32, 40*n*, 68
Rules: in male sports, 9; of the game, 74

San Sebastian (in *S.A.R.*), 40, 42
Sanford, Marcelline Hemingway, 6
Satire: in *S.A.R.*, 31; use of, in H's apprenticeship, 33, 33*n*; emotional values of, 119–20
Satiric irony: 120, 121; overuse of, 122, 123, 124, 128
Schorer, Mark, 156*n*
Scott, Arthur L., 35*n*
Scrooge, Ebenezer (in Charles Dickens' *A Christmas Carol*), 118–19, 174
Self, the: reliability of, 16; dual, 71
Self-discipline: as a central theme, 43
Self-honesty: as a central character trait, 76; mentioned, 138
Self-parody: in *A.R.I.T.*, 48
Self-pity: attacked by H, 28; in *S.A.R.*, 34, 35
Sensory detail: protagonist's contact with, 135
Sentimental courtship, 34
Sentimental novel, 18
Sentimentality: 18, 23; defined, 23*n*; as inadvertent trap, 115; aligned with Christianity, 116; mentioned, 105–6, 119, 122, 124, 126, 128, 140, 143, 144, 146, 147, 148, 151, 152, 188
Seventeen (Booth Tarkington), 19
Sex: in *F.T.A.*, 106–7, 108, 109
Sexual anxiety: in Nick Adams stories, 12
Sexual chaos: in *S.A.R.*, 32
Sexual role: traditional, 18
Short, R. W., 184*n*
Simplistic labels: applied to H's work, 187
Spanish Civil War, 165–66
Specimen collection: of Dr. Adams, 7
Spilka, Mark, 32*n*, 149*n*
Sports, 186
Stein, Gertrude, 42, 62, 66